LOST
CIVILIZATIONS

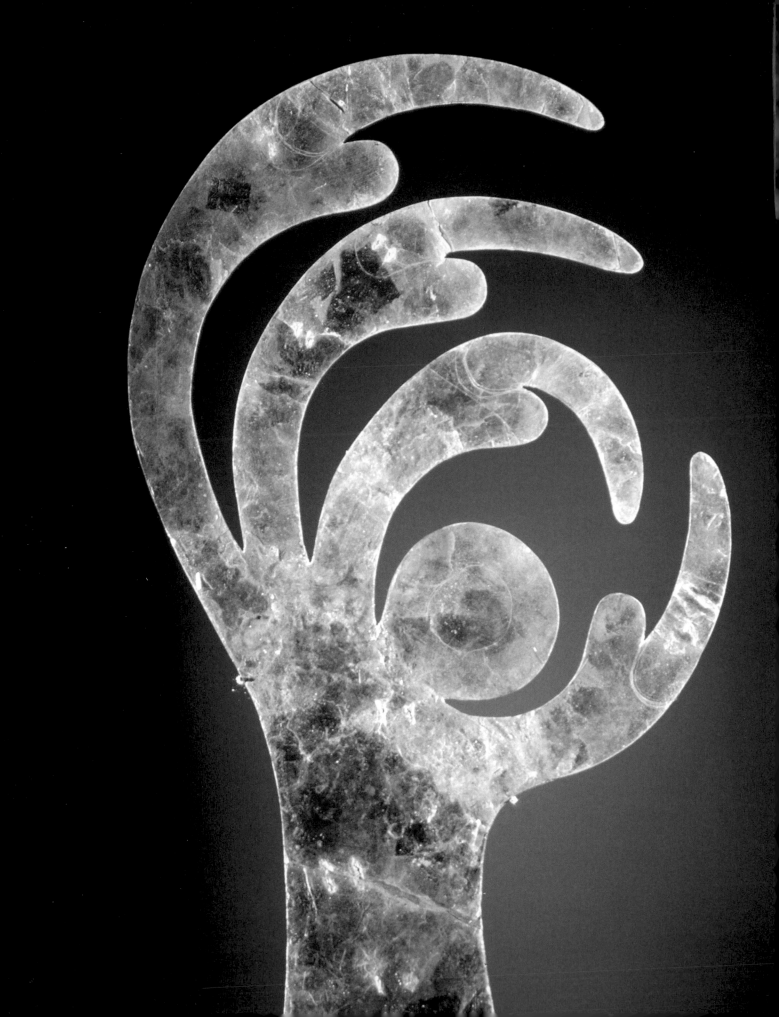

LOST
CIVILIZATIONS

MYSTERIOUS CULTURES AND PEOPLES

MARKUS HATTSTEIN

Bath · New York · Singapore · Hong Kong · Cologne · Delhi · Melbourne

Contents

INTRODUCTION

This book provides a comprehensive insight into the lost civilization of early human history and describes the cultures, as rich as they are varied, of the earliest societies on every continent. Some of these early peoples and civilizations are still familiar to us today, whereas others we know of only by name. Some of them were living nomadic or sedentary lives organized in clans, tribes, or cultural groups while others, even at an early stage in history, were already creating highly organized empires or emerging as global powers.

The book examines all the continents and the cultures and civilizations that shaped their history, but cannot claim to be exhaustive, even though the events depicted here occurred over a period of more than 10,000 years, from initial human settlement during the Neolithic Revolution through ancient times and classical antiquity until well into the early Middle Ages. In the case of civilizations that have continued into modern times, for example, those of India, China, and Japan, ancient line is drawn at the end of an era.

The early Anatolian and the Mesopotamian and Persian cultural areas, with their large numbers of population groups, mark the beginning of the development of modern civilization. This book begins by examining these, and then turns its attention to Egypt and the Mediterranean, followed by the various regions of Europe. Next, it looks at the Asiatic horse-riding peoples and their extensive migratory movements, as well as the other peoples and empires of the Asian continent. It continues with a description of the Indian tribes of North, Central, and South America, followed by the significant early cultures of the African continent, and concludes with a look at the early peoples of Australia and Oceania.

Equal weight is given to the distinctive features of the individual peoples and civilizations; their cultures, ways of life, and political organization—and the diversity of their relationships; their alliances, their wars, their migratory movements and influences upon one another, their conquests, and their trading links. Numerous quotations from historical sources also allow these lost civilizations to speak for themselves.

Vivid and varied photographs provide glimpses into the cultural achievements, buildings, and artifacts of these peoples as well as their living conditions. Outlines and detailed maps identify the most important cultural centers, capital cities, and centers of the civilizations and trace historical changes in the form of expansions and migratory movements. Furthermore, timelines highlight significant periods in the history of individual peoples to illustrate the point at which each of these appeared in the course of human history.

In this way, lost worlds are brought to life and the reader is invited to delve into the early periods of human history, searching for the traces left behind by early peoples, whether their legacy is still remembered by the global society of the twenty-first century or whether they have long since vanished from view.

**The mysterious stone ancestral statues on Easter Island,
the *moai*, are one of the biggest puzzles of
ancient civilizations.**

The Neolithic Revolution

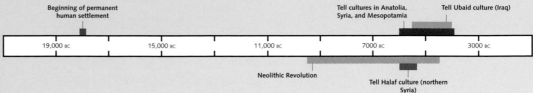

Above: A painted ceramic vessel from China, dating from the Neolithic era (circa 5000–1700 BC).

The development of human societies from communities of hunter-gatherers to crop and livestock farmers living in permanent dwellings began in around 9500 or 9000 BC; the Neolithic Revolution, which set this change in motion, marks a key turning point in the emergence of cultures and civilizations and represents one of the greatest upheavals in human history.

were Anatolia, Mesopotamia, southern China, and Central America. We assume today that the reasons for permanent settlement were above all the climate change between the end of the Ice Age and the beginning of a period of warming, and changes in the available food supplies, as well as increased migratory movement. The beginning of a farming culture went hand-in-hand with the building of permanent houses and settlements, knowledge of animal and crop husbandry and

Above: The megalithic temple of Hagar Qim ("Standing Stone") in Malta consists of a single oval structure of interconnecting stones, many of them standing upright, on a rocky hilltop. It was erected by the temple-building culture during the Tarxien period (3200–2500 BC), used continuously, and rebuilt many times. Discoveries of statuettes and animal bones around the temple point to the existence of a mother-goddess cult involving animal sacrifice.

CHARACTERISTICS OF THE CHANGE TO A SEDENTARY LIFESTYLE

As far back as 20,000 years ago, people in the Middle East were establishing settlements for the first time. However, it was not until approximately 8,000 years later that sedentarism began to spread out from isolated centers to entire regions; first and foremost among these

harvest and irrigation cycles, the domestication of farm animals (especially cattle), and a storage economy in which animal and plant products could be preserved (dried). Production of ceramics is also found in all early civilizations. Overall, the process of settlement, with its various stages and organizational structures, lasted for a period of around 4,000 years.

At over 328 ft. (100 m) in length, Long Barrow burial mound (circa 3600 BC) at West Kennet near Avebury (in the county of Wiltshire, east of Bath, England) is one of the largest Neolithic burial chambers in England. Forty-six skeletons of persons of various ages and of both sexes were excavated here.

THE NEW SOCIETY

Hordes of hunters and clans of gatherers generally consisted of groups of between 20 and 30 individuals, all related to one another. Settlement led to the emergence of so-called segmentary societies (this term was coined by the French sociologist Emile Durkheim, 1858–1917), which were more complex than had previously been the case and were distinguished by the fact that different hordes and clans, not necessarily related to one another, worked together in settlements or villages. Initially, there was no centralized authority or state power and cooperation and disputes were decided by means of communal discussion; as groups were now settled, disputes could no longer be resolved as they had been previously, that is, by forcing others to move on or doing so oneself. In addition, the appropriation and settlement of land and territory gave rise to a new area of conflict for communities, involving issues of ownership of land and its exclusive or communal use and cultivation, the sharing of water and of the grazing areas, raw materials, and resources. The appropriation and ownership of land, as well as the fact that the composition of the population began to extend beyond family and clan groups, led for the first time to the establishment of universally applicable laws that were not based purely on power and which had the potential to put in place sound structures enabling the peaceful coexistence of all the inhabitants of a settlement. Cooperation between the inhabitants of a settlement, as well as with the inhabitants of other settlements, was regulated principally through bartering.

The Tell cultures: Sedentary populations and nomads

The earliest large settlements, particularly in Anatolia and the region of Syria and Mesopotamia, were established near rivers on hills (Arabic *tell*) and it was usually not long before these were defensively fortified with town walls. One particularly significant settlement, whose ceramics gave the name to an entire cultural epoch (6000–5300 BC), was Tell Halaf, in northeast Syria, near the source of the Khabur River. The stores kept there and the increase in the amount of material possessions in the settlements meant that these became the target of repeated raids by warlike nomadic tribes. However, the nomads did not simply overrun the settlements, but gradually encroached on their cultivated lands from the surrounding deserts, steppes, or mountainous regions. The resulting antagonism between defensive farmers and warlike nomadic tribes, of whom the horse-riding peoples proved particularly successful, shaped the history of the Middle East in particular for a long time. In later centuries, too, nomads continued to be a source of trouble for the sedentary civilizations.

The "hydraulic societies"

The first states and civilizations with urban centers (Egypt, Mesopotamia, China, and India, as well as in Central and South America) formed predominantly in areas where there was already intensive water regulation and where use was made of the rivers and the fertile floodplains. The German sociologist and Sinologist Karl August Wittfogel (1896–1988) coined the term "hydraulic societies" to describe them: water regulation necessitated a centrally planned economy in which an army of laborers could be coordinated for large technical construction

The civilizations of the ancient Orient were all characterized by a high degree of state organization of labor. This image (based on an Assyrian stone carving) shows laborers—possibly deportees—pulling carts within the confines of Nineveh (near the city of Mosul in present-day Iraq).

projects (dams, dykes, sluices, canals, and projects for draining swamps and irrigating desert areas as well as cities and palaces) and required the central storage of supplies for times of need. Such societies generally took the form of temple economies, with large public buildings that simultaneously fulfilled political, economic, and ritual functions. Wittfogel used the term "oriental despotism" to describe this type of state, which was generally ruled along absolute lines by priest-kings or political leaders with cult/religious leadership functions. This included the rational administration of goods, the increasing division of labor (encouraged by the state), the formation of a state bureaucracy and civil service (including scribes, overseers, and provincial governors), the development of a written script for administrative and ritual purposes, a legal system for settling disputes and ownership relations, and the formation of barracked troops for protecting not only the state territory, but also its cities, markets, and trade routes; these troops were also deployed in wars and territorial expansion. Control of nomadic tribes—for example, their subjugation and forced settlement—was seldom successfully achieved.

Below: The remains of the city walls of the ancient royal city of Qatna (now Tell el-Mishrife in Syria), which was destroyed by the Hittites in 1340 BC; the clay tablet archive of King Idanda (circa 1400 BC) was discovered in the ruins of the city.

Right: A vase in what is known as "Style 1" from Susa (Iran), later the capital of the Elamite Kingdom (circa 5000–4000 BC, now in the Louvre Museum, Paris, France).

Ancient Anatolia: Çatal Hüyük

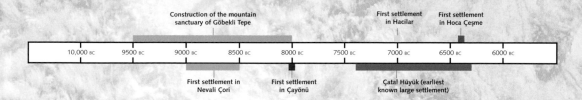

| | Construction of the mountain
sanctuary of Göbekli Tepe | | | | | First settlement
in Hacilar | First settlement
in Hoca Çeşme | |

| 10,000 BC | 9500 BC | 9000 BC | 8500 BC | 8000 BC | 7500 BC | 7000 BC | 6500 BC | 6000 BC |

| | First settlement in
Nevali Çori | | First settlement
in Çayönü | | | Çatal Hüyük (earliest
known large settlement) | |

The numerous archaeological digs in the Anatolian region since the second half of the twentieth century have caused people to qualify the assumption that the "cradle of urban civilization" lies in Mesopotamia, as it is in Anatolia that the earliest large settlements known to date have been excavated. Since excavations there are still ongoing, the results of research provide only provisional information.

THE BEGINNING OF URBANIZATION

The enormous scale of the settlement of Çatal Hüyük ("Hill at a Fork in the Road") on the Anatolian Plateau (near Konya), of which 14 layers have so far been excavated since

1961, has only gradually become apparent. It was first built on two hills between the first half of the eighth millennium and the first half of the seventh millennium BC; the eastern hill was settled earlier, in the Neolithic era, the western hill in the later Chalcolithic. A honeycomb of densely packed houses without streets has been

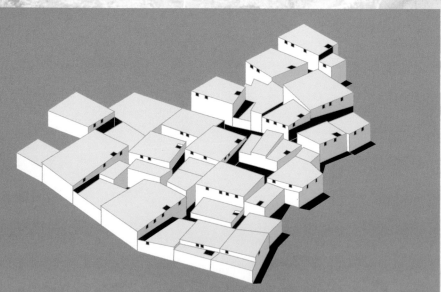

HOUSES IN ÇATAL HÜYÜK
The drawing shows the interlocking houses of the settlement, with no roads or paths between them; they were entered via ladders and openings in the roofs.

unearthed, accessed by means of ladders and openings in the roofs, the latter also serving as chimneys. The alluvial land of the Çarşamba River provided the settlement with an abundant range of food; it is now thought that the number of inhabitants once exceeded 2,500. The floors of the houses (160 have so far been excavated) were on different levels. Platforms in front of the walls were probably used as sleeping areas; in most houses there were separate smaller storage rooms.

THE SOCIAL ORDER IN ANCIENT ANATOLIA

Çatal Hüyük bears the characteristic features of the transition from a village to a large settlement, in which it is possible to see the beginnings of an urban way of life, albeit still without any element of central government. The inhabitants lived by hunting and gathering, but also by growing crops (e.g. wheat, wild emmer, barley, bread wheat, peas, and

Stone statuette of a double-headed deity from Çatal Hüyük; such finds have led some researchers to conclude that there was perfect equality of the sexes in this large settlement.

of public buildings such as can be found in a temple economy.

Although numerous female figurines with voluptuously curved figures led to speculation about a matriarchal society, it has not yet been possible to prove this conclusively. Yet more

vetch) and keeping animals; social change is particularly evident in the way in which they kept cattle: in the early excavation layers (on the eastern hill) signs were found that wild cattle had been kept, but it was then shown on the western hill, which was not settled until later, that domesticated cattle had been reared. Storage of supplies and the production of food and tools seem to have been undertaken independently by the individual households, as until now no evidence has been unearthed

figures show no gender features, and the murals make an obvious distinction between female portrayals in connection with agriculture and depictions of males in the hunting field. This has led some researchers to conclude that perfect equality of the sexes reigned. Furthermore, in the preparation of human skulls, probably in connection with a cult of the dead, no gender-specific differences were found. The preparation of cattle skulls and horns with clay suggests a possible cattle cult.

An aerial photograph of the excavation work at Çatal Hüyük (Anatolia, Turkey, circa 1990); the structure of this early settlement and finds made there have given rise to far-reaching theories about the organization of early forms of human communities.

Murals in Çatal Hüyük

The interiors of some houses exhibit murals in red, black, and white, which in places have been overpainted several times and which show mainly hunting scenes and abstract shapes, as well as reliefs of headless human forms. Leopards are frequently depicted, as are humans clad in leopard skins. These depictions have led some researchers to conclude that there was a definite hunting cult.

The cult sanctuary of Göbekli Tepe

The excavation of the mountain sanctuary of Göbekli Tepe, in the foothills of the Taurus Mountains, has turned out to be an archaeological sensation. Systematic digging has been taking place since 1995, although only a small part has thus far been excavated. The layers here indicate a time of origin prior to the Neolithic Revolution, that is, between 9500 and 8000 BC; it is assumed that it was constructed by hunter-gatherers before settlement began. Of particular interest are the four preserved constructions encompassing stone monoliths weighing several tons, with connecting layered stone walls, fashioned into circular or oval-shaped rings; in the center of each stands a pair of pillars that tower above the other stone pillars. The pillars are decorated with carefully carved reliefs of wild animals and with pictographs, which have been interpreted as cult symbols. Some pillars were erected in a T shape with a stone lintel resting on top.

The building of such constructions, which may have involved up to 500 people, would have demanded considerable logistical and

Many of the murals on the walls of houses in Çatal Hüyük represent hunting scenes, but there are also indications that an earlier cattle cult existed (circa 6000 BC).

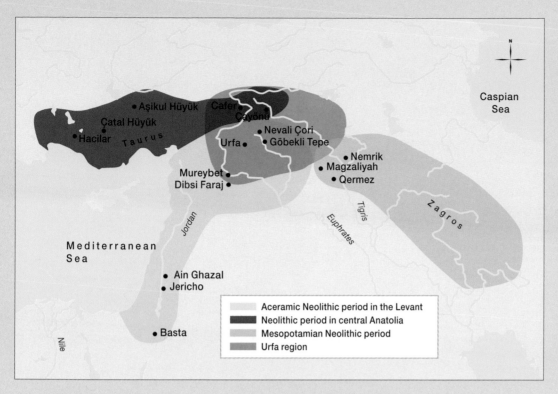

Caspian
Sea

• Aşikul Hüyük
Çatal Hüyük
• Hacilar
Taurus
Cafer
Çayönü
• Nevali Çori
Urfa •
• Göbekli Tepe
• Nemrik
• Magzaliyah
• Qermez
Mureybet •
Dibsi Faraj •
Zagros
Tigris
Euphrates
Mediterranean
Sea
Jordan

• Ain Ghazal
• Jericho
Nile
• Basta

Aceramic Neolithic period in the Levant
Neolithic period in central Anatolia
Mesopotamian Neolithic period
Urfa region

NEOLITHIC SETTLEMENTS IN ANATOLIA AND THE MIDDLE EAST
The map shows the various cultural spheres of the early colonization of Anatolia, northern Mesopotamia as far as Persia, and the Mediterranean coastal region. The settlement centers formed part of the Tell cultures—large fortified settlements on hills.

organizational skills. Researchers see it as a site of a cult of the dead, with wild animals as guardians of the dead. The fact that large settlements were not established in the vicinity of the site until later led to far-reaching theories about the beginnings of human civilization, which were summarized by the German chief archaeologist in Göbekli Tepe, Klaus Schmidt, as follows: "First came temples, and then came towns."

FURTHER CENTERS

Of the numerous other sites discovered in Turkey, Nevali Çori is particularly worthy of mention. It lies in the foothills of the Taurus Mountains and was settled in five stages from the second half of the ninth millennium BC. The foundations of the rectangular houses were laid on several levels, seemingly to facilitate floor ventilation and drainage. A cult site with monolithic pillars has been uncovered at Nevali Çori. Further significant settlements have been discovered at Çayönü also in the Taurus Mountains, where samples of seeds were found, and at Hacilar in

southwest Turkey, near the present-day town of Burdur, where there was evidence of arable and livestock farming. A further outstanding site is that at Hoca Çeşme, in Edirne province, which consists of at least four layers, the earliest dating from 6400 BC, with roundhouses measuring 9 to 12 ft. (3 to 4 m) in diameter and sophisticated black polished ceramics in the oldest layer; this settlement was later surrounded with a wall.

Painted clay vessel in the form of a human figure from the Anatolian settlement of Hacilar (Turkey, circa 5500 BC; Ashmolean Museum, Oxford, England); in Hacilar, nine settlement layers have been uncovered from the sixth millennium BC alone, through which the constant refinement of ceramics, with numerous representations of animals and humans, can be traced.

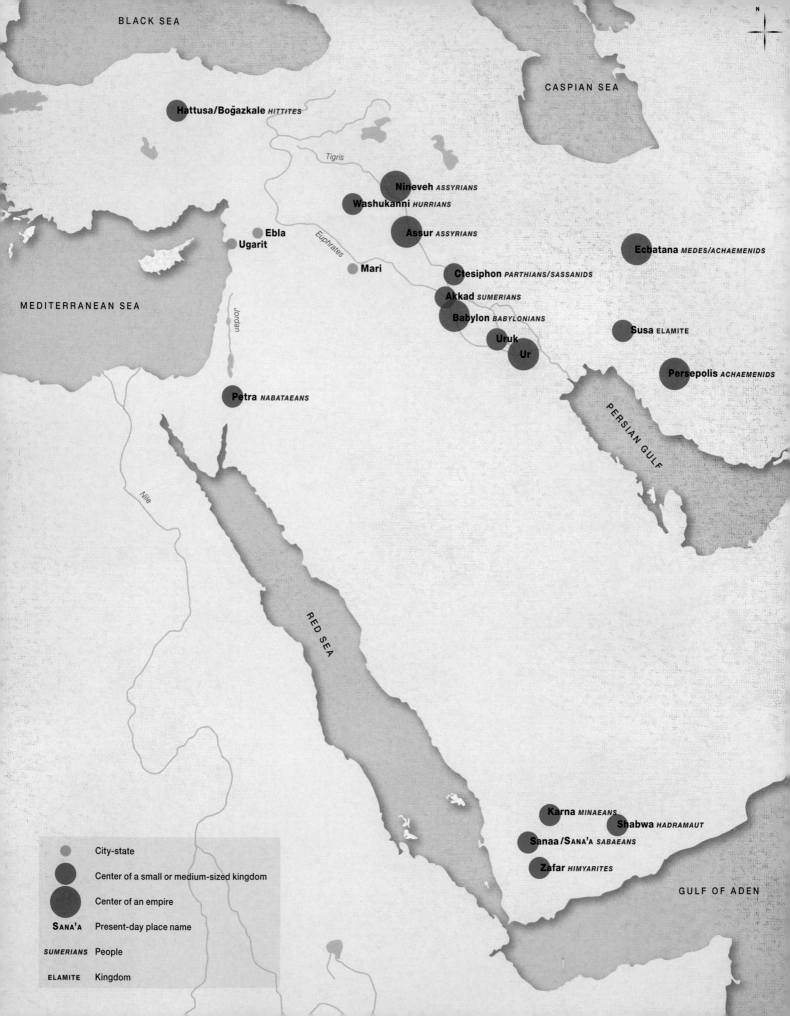

BLACK SEA

CASPIAN SEA

Hattusa/Boğazkale *HITTITES*

Tigris

Nineveh *ASSYRIANS*

Washukanni *HURRIANS*

Assur *ASSYRIANS*

Ecbatana *MEDES/ACHAEMENIDS*

Ebla

Ugarit

Euphrates

Mari

Ctesiphon *PARTHIANS/SASSANIDS*

Akkad *SUMERIANS*

MEDITERRANEAN SEA

Babylon *BABYLONIANS*

Susa *ELAMITE*

Jordan

Uruk

Ur

Persepolis *ACHAEMENIDS*

PERSIAN GULF

Petra *NABATAEANS*

Nile

RED SEA

Karna *MINAEANS*

Shabwa *HADRAMAUT*

Sanaa/Sanaʾa *SABAEANS*

Zafar *HIMYARITES*

GULF OF ADEN

City-state

Center of a small or medium-sized kingdom

Center of an empire

Sanaʾa   Present-day place name

SUMERIANS   People

ELAMITE   Kingdom

Babylonians   Persians   Assyrians   Akkadians   Nabataeans

MESOPOTAMIA, ANCIENT ARABIA, AND PERSIA

It was in the fertile river valleys of the Euphrates and the Tigris that the first major city-states and empires of the Middle East developed. This "fertile crescent" of Mesopotamia has long been considered the "cradle of civilization."

The independent city-states in the third millennium BC that were shaped in terms of culture, religion, and politics by the Sumerian civilization and the first Akkadian Empire developed rudimentary forms of state administration; this can be deduced from cuneiform texts on trading and legal relations.

From about 1500 BC, the Babylonian and Assyrian Empires were dominant. They repeatedly came to blows, but also formed strategic alliances and installed rulers who were acceptable to them in weaker neighboring states. Farther north, as far as the Black Sea, the Hittites held sway. Babylon initially fell behind in the face of the expanding military might of the Assyrians, but experienced a final golden age under the Chaldeans in the middle of the first millennium BC.

On the Arabian Peninsula, the kingdoms in the south especially profited from the trade along the Frankincense Road and established efficient forms of communal organization. In the north, in the gorge of Petra (Jordan), the Nabataean Kingdom emerged.

With the conquest of the Chaldean Kingdom in the sixth century BC, the Persian Empire became the leading power. It united a wide variety of peoples under modern administrative structures and its Zoroastrian religion shaped the history of ideas at that time. Its incursions into the Greek cultural region were the first lasting encounters between East and West.

MESOPOTAMIA, ANCIENT ARABIA, AND PERSIA
The map shows centers and city-states of the kingdoms in Mesopotamia, Syria, and Persia—from the Elamites to the Sassanids—as well as those of the Hittites and of Ancient Arabia.

Sumer and Akkad

				Rise of Ur	Akkadian Empire	Gudea period (Lagash)	Third Dynasty of Ur (Ur III)		
	Uruk period								
4000 BC	3600 BC	3200 BC	2800 BC	2400 BC	2000 BC	1600 BC	1200 BC		
		Jemdet Nasr period	First Dynasty of Lagash	Sargon of Akkad	First (city-) states of the Hurrians	"Sumerian Renaissance"	Hurrian Kingdom of Mitanni		

The land of Mesopotamia covered the present-day region of southeast Anatolia, Syria, and Iraq. The culture of this "fertile crescent" between the Euphrates and the Tigris was shaped by the first large city-states, who were continually fighting among themselves for dominance, the Sumerians (a non-Semitic people with their own language and script), and the Semitic Akkadians, who established the earliest empire in history.

THE SUMERIAN-AKKADIAN CULTURE

The population was chiefly engaged in agriculture, using rain-fed farming methods in the north and the artificial irrigation of fields by means of canals and hydraulic engineering technology in the drier south; they were already familiar with numerous cultivated crops (e.g. barley) and livestock. They used the plow and the wheel and harnessed oxen as draft and pack animals. The towns, mostly in elevated positions, were fortified, and their buildings varied according to their function; the people here also carried out a variety of occupations as craftsmen and traders. At the head of the community was the city's ruler (*en* or *lugal*) who performed both political and

Background image: Stone relief of King Ur-Nanshe of Lagash (circa 2480 BC), who founded the First Dynasty of Lagash, which ruled until approximately 2350 BC.

Above: Babylonian cuneiform tablet containing a text on the conquests of Sargon of Akkad (circa 2334–2279 BC) and an early world map (Babylon, circa 600 BC).

military as well as ritual and religious leadership functions. Most cities had a large central building that probably served as a temple and a public assembly hall and which was likely also the place from which foodstuffs were centrally distributed (temple economy).

THE INVENTION OF WRITING

The development of the cuneiform script in Mesopotamia's late Uruk period (from circa 3400 BC, *see p. 20*) was akin to a revolution. It had its origins in tokens and count stones as well as pictographs and cylinder seals later used in connection with the administration of goods; these were gradually replaced by more abstract symbols that could be imprinted on soft clay tablets using styluses, the tablets then being fired. The earliest texts are administrative documents dealing with accounts and distribution, but also lists of animals, plants, places, and gods; they were probably also used as teaching materials for training scribes. The lists of gods and kings that appeared later, as well as dedicatory inscriptions on buildings and statuettes, document ritual and religious ideas and a general desire to order, classify, and organize, and in so doing, assigned names to the things in their world. What had previously been subject to the volatility of the oral tradition could now be protected against the passage of time and preserved for subsequent generations.

The ruins of the ziggurat of Ur (present-day Iraq), one of the earliest centers of the Sumerian culture; the topmost part of the structure formed a temple.

Uruk—City of monumental buildings

The city of Uruk was the first to leave its mark on Mesopotamia; like almost all urban centers, it was overbuilt many times (circa 3900–3100 BC). The cult center of Jemdet Nasr (circa 3100–2900 BC) was the next major center of influence. In Uruk, where up to 50,000 people lived, numerous monumental buildings such as palaces and temples were erected, as well as large-scale sculptures. The labor force and the distribution of goods were organized on a rigidly hierarchical basis; ritual life based around the priest-kings (*en*) must have played a central role, as the city believed itself to have been founded by the gods.

The subsequent Early Dynastic Period (circa 2900–2340 BC) was characterized by the rivalry, which often manifested itself in wars, between various centers such as Uruk, Ur, Lagash-Girsu, Umma, Adab, and Kish; during these centuries the region was dominated by Uruk and Kish.

Ur and Lagash

In approximately 2700 BC, a new center, that of Ur, came to the fore; the royal tombs of Ur, which were uncovered in the twentieth century, magnificently furnished with gold, jewelry, and items of furniture, date from circa 2550 BC. Skeletons discovered there show that the family and entourage of a ruler followed him to the grave, taking their own lives by swallowing poison. Cuneiform texts from that time tell of the extensive trading relations of these cities.

The center of Lagash blossomed under the royal dynasty founded by Ur-Nanshe (circa 2480 BC). Ur-Nanshe constructed numerous temples and canals, known to us through administrative and dedicatory inscriptions that have been preserved. His grandson Eannatum (circa 2450 BC) undertook,

The ruins of Uruk (present-day Iraq), one of humankind's earliest cities; it also marks the beginning of the Sumerian culture.

through several successful wars in the name of his city god Ningirsu, the first attempts at a political unification of Mesopotamia. Eannatum proclaimed in his inscriptions, such as the famous Stele of the Vultures, that Ningirsu had bestowed upon him the kingship over several cities, including Lagash and Kish. Lagash's kings and their wives presided over a rigidly organized temple economy that had some of the features of a state planned economy.

SOCIAL REFORMS AND ATTEMPTS AT UNIFICATION

The last ruler of Lagash, Urukagina (also known as Urunimgina, circa 2350 BC), came to power during a crisis situation brought about by the emerging private economy and responded by introducing comprehensive social reforms: he reclaimed numerous privileges of the ruler (vis-à-vis the temples), granted tax concessions, and freed the majority of the poor population from bonded labor. As the "protector of widows and orphans" (as he styled himself) he forbade the exploitation of the poor by the rich.

Lagash's downfall was sealed by the warlike city ruler (*ensi*) of Umma, Lugalzagesi (circa 2375–2340 BC), who conquered Lagash and Uruk and claimed sovereignty over the whole of Sumer. He caused himself to be worshiped under numerous names as the governor of the various Sumerian state gods and was the first to designate himself the "good shepherd of his people"—a title for a ruler that is also found in the Old Testament.

Scenes from everyday Sumerian life on a textile find from Ur. Society in the city already exhibited a high degree of organization and division of labor.

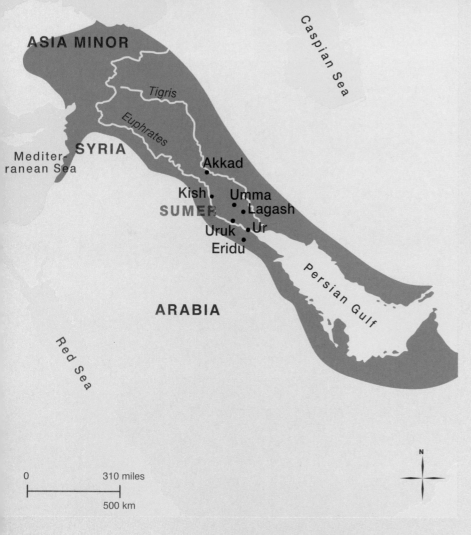

ASIA MINOR

Caspian Sea

Tigris

Euphrates

SYRIA

Mediter-
ranean Sea

Akkad

Kish

Umma

SUMER

Lagash

Uruk

Ur

Eridu

Persian Gulf

ARABIA

Red Sea

0   310 miles

500 km

N

THE AKKADIAN EMPIRE
The map shows the formation of the First Empire under Sargon of Akkad (circa 2334–2279 BC) and his grandson Naram-Sin (circa 2273–2219 BC); they brought numerous city-states under their control.

of Mesopotamia; his military expeditions made advances as far as Ebla and Mari in Syria (*see pp. 26–7*).

The "King of the Universe" and "Chosen of the War Goddess Ishtar," at whose court 5,400 men were fed every day, spared no expense when it came to having his life and deeds extolled in inscriptions and epic poems. Indeed, Sargon was seen as the epitome of an ideal and just ruler far beyond the borders of his cultural sphere.

Naram-Sin, the "God of Akkad"

Sargon succeeded in establishing a dynasty: his two sons were followed as ruler by his grandson Naram-Sin (circa 2273–2219 BC), who managed to crush a series of rebellions by the city-states of south Mesopotamia and Syria. He strengthened trade links with all his neighbors, concluded treaties with Elam (*see p. 54*), and also installed his daughters as priestesses. To consolidate his sovereignty, the "King of the Four Quarters of the World" caused himself to be elevated to "God of Akkad" and "Husband of Ishtar" and had a temple erected. Subsequent rulers worshiped him with the

Sargon of Akkad and his empire

The founding of the state of Sargon of Akkad (circa 2334–2279 BC) marked the entrance of the First Empire onto the stage of history. After Sargon had vanquished Lugalzagesi of Umma, allegedly "in 34 wars," he subjugated the numerous city-states and established Akkad as the royal capital of a new kingdom. He instituted Akkadian, a Semitic language, as the official language of administration, standardized weights and measures, centralized long-distance trade (especially with the Arabian Peninsula) and water resources management, and appointed loyal followers and family members to high office, for example, his daughter Enhedu'ana as high priestess of the moon god in Ur. He controlled the kingdom through a network of loyal military garrisons and relocated large contingents of Akkadians from the north, who formed his power base, to the southern cities

> ▶ **THE LEGEND OF SARGON**
> A clay tablet in the palace library of Nineveh (*see p. 41*) contains the legend of Sargon's childhood. As the illegitimate son of a high priestess and an unknown father, he was placed by his mother in a reed basket caulked with pitch and committed to the river Euphrates. He was found by Akki, a drawer of water, who brought him up as his son and trained him as a gardener: "While I was a gardener, [the goddess] Ishtar grew very fond of me". She enabled his rise to power. Researchers were not slow to notice the clear parallels with the childhood story of the Israelite prophet and lawgiver, Moses.

same reverence as they had his grandfather. However, the reign of his son ushered in the rapid decline and fall of the Akkadian Empire from around 2200 BC.

"I am Sargon, the mighty lord, the king of Akkad. My mother was a high priestess; I did not know my father, nor my father's brothers, who roam the mountains there. Azupiranu [saffron city] was the name of my city on the banks of the Euphrates . . . . So I became king for fifty-four years, ruling over the people with a powerful hand."

From the Sargon legend, probably circa 2200 BC

Left: The so-called Mask of Sargon (circa 2250 BC), a bronze mask that may represent Sargon of Akkad or his grandson Naram-Sin.

Below: The reconstructed Ziggurat of Ur; the photograph gives an idea of the monumental scale and the impact of the edifice built in honor of the gods.

THE PIOUS KING GUDEA OF LAGASH

Following the decline of the Empire of Akkad, the Sumerian city-states enjoyed a "renaissance." In Lagash, Gudea (circa 2122–2102 BC) founded a new dynasty; his numerous inscriptions and statuettes show a pious ruler, who saw himself as the son of the state goddess Gatumdu, as a peaceful priest-king and as a "good shepherd," who let his people "rest in peace like sheep on the meadow." He made it the ritual duty of the ruler to construct temples and import numerous plants, minerals, and metals.

THE ADMINISTRATIVE STATE OF UR III

At the same time, Ur-Namma (2112–2095 BC) founded the Dynasty of Ur (Ur III), which continued in existence until 2004 BC. The state of Ur, with its administrative, trade, and legal records comprising tens of thousands of tablets, exhibited features of a modern, centralized administrative state. Ur-Namma, who styled himself "King of Sumer and Akkad," provided trading routes with comfortable inns and wayside stopping points, coordinating numerous public works and feats of labor. He gained particular significance as a legislator through his law code, the Ur-Namma codex (*see p. 32*). He and his successors saw temple building and law enforcement as the preeminent tasks of a ruler. Under his son Shulgi (2094–2046 BC), a great builder, the empire, divided into provinces and administered by means of the detailed distribution of tasks, became one of the most significant and magnificent political entities of the ancient world. Under the last ruler of the Third Dynasty of Ur, Ibbi-Sin (2028–2004 BC), however, the state suffered a series of food supply crises and was then invaded by the Elamites. Later, control of the region was taken over by other city-states and finally fell into the hands of the Babylonians (*see pp. 30–35*).

Votive statue of the pious King Gudea of Lagash (circa 2122–2102 BC); he saw himself as the "good shepherd" of his people.

" The kalû priest did not play the lyre, nor did he allow any complaints to be heard . . . .
In the territory of Lagash, no one who had a legal dispute went to the place of the oaths,
no one's house was visited by creditors . . . . For seven days no corn was ground,
the slave woman was equal to her mistress, the slave man walked next to his master,
high-born and low-born slept side by side in my city. **"**

From a temple-building hymn of Gudea of Lagash, circa 2110 BC

The Hurrian Kingdom of Mitanni

In the second millennium BC, while Babylon ruled in the south, the Hurrians, who were originally from the area south of Lake Van (eastern Anatolia) and had an independent culture, probably with Indo-Aryan roots, were expanding into the region of northern Mesopotamia and northern Syria. In around 1500 BC they established the Kingdom of Mitanni, in which cattle- and horse-breeding were important, war chariots were used, and there was a centrally organized palace economy in the capital, Washukanni. After 1450 BC they became involved in lasting conflicts in Mesopotamia with the expanding Egyptian Kingdom, but were able to hold on to Syria and until their downfall, in the middle of the thirteenth century BC, they were successful in maneuvering between Egypt, the Hittites, and Assyria, which was then gaining in strength. King Tushratta (circa 1380–1350 BC) entered into an alliance with Egypt through marriage and called Pharaoh Amenhotep III his "brother"; his son Shattiwaza (circa 1350–1320 BC), on the other hand, acceded to the throne only with the aid of the Hittites and thereby became their vassal. The complex Hurrian pantheon of the "thousand gods" influenced the religion of the Hittites and even the Greeks' families of gods.

Statuette of King Gudea of Lagash holding a vessel overflowing with water as a symbol of fertility (green calcite, Louvre Museum, Paris, France); organized irrigation of the land laid the basis for material prosperity.

The kingdoms of Syria

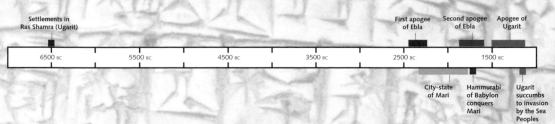

Settlements in Ras Shamra (Ugarit)

First apogee of Ebla | Second apogee of Ebla | Apogee of Ugarit

| 6500 BC | 5500 BC | 4500 BC | 3500 BC | 2500 BC | 1500 BC |

City-state of Mari | Hammurabi of Babylon conquers Mari | Ugarit succumbs to invasion by the Sea Peoples

The Syrian city-states of Ebla, Mari, and Ugarit were for a long time seen as being on the fringes of advanced Mesopotamian civilization, until excavations in the twentieth century brought to light their autonomy and significance.

EBLA

The city-state of Ebla in northern Syria (present-day Tell Mardikh, where excavations began in 1964) experienced its first apogee in around 2400–2240 BC. This major trading center (for timber, particularly Lebanese cedar) between Egypt and the city-states of Mesopotamia rose to great economic power and political influence and was probably dominated by a confident trading aristocracy; the precise status of the city's leaders and kings is to date still uncertain. Eblaite was a distinct Semitic language, related to Akkadian; the religion and rituals of the inhabitants had Semitic and Hurrian features. Under the huge palace of the rulers was discovered the palace archive, containing over 20,000 clay tablets that provide remarkable insights into the economics and everyday life as well as the laws and diplomatic contacts of the trading metropolis. Ebla's increasing economic and political power was a thorn in the side of Sargon of Akkad (see p. 22): he undertook military expeditions against the city, and it was destroyed by his grandson Naram-Sin in circa 2240 BC. Under the Amorites, a Semitic nomadic people, Ebla experienced

Background image: Cuneiform text from the palace archive excavated at Ebla (Syria).

Above: A finely worked necklace from Ebla with disk-shaped pendants; sumptuous items of jewelry demonstrate the wealth of the Syrian city-states.

The remains of the city of Ebla in northern Syria, the center of an independent and confident urban culture, discovered in 1964 and identified in 1968.

a second golden age from around 1800 to 1650 BC, but was then definitively destroyed by the Hittites.

MARI

The Syrian city of Mari (present-day Tell Hariri) also enjoyed considerable prosperity as a trading metropolis from circa 2350 BC; however, it was soon conquered by Sargon of Akkad and subsequently flourished under the protection of Akkadian sovereignty. Here, too, a central palace was uncovered, which had 300 rooms, murals, and a library of around 25,000 clay tablets, whose texts show that alongside the trade in metal, timber, agricultural products, and wine, water engineering and regulation also played an important role. Several temples were also excavated, including a significant one dedicated to the Sumerian goddess Ishtar. Besides large vases and clay vessels, one of the striking things about the finds at Mari are the numerous votive statues with folded

> " In the whole of time, [since] the creation of Man, no king has laid waste the land of Armanum and Ebla. The god Nergal, having prepared the way for the valiant Naram-Sin, has now delivered Armanum and Ebla into his hands . . . . "
>
> From an inscription of Naram-Sin of Akkad, circa 2275–2250 BC

hands, which are up to 20 in. (50 cm) tall and made of limestone or white alabaster, each having distinct individual features and possibly representing a portrait of the person who donated it.

The kings of Mari are known by name, even though dating them precisely in the early period is still a problem today. The diplomatic and military activities of the last king, Zimri-Lim (circa 1773–1759 BC), an Amorite—he built the palace complex—are well documented by the archive of Mari; he extended the kingdom far into the desert areas of Syria, thus risking conflict with the Babylonians and Assyrians. In around 1759 BC, Mari was captured and destroyed by King Hammurabi of Babylon (*see p. 32*).

Ugarit: City of maritime trade

The north Syrian coastal city of Ugarit (present-day Ras Shamra) reached the pinnacle of its power later than Ebla and Mari, in the time of the Phoenicians (*see p. 90*), although traces of settlement dating back to the seventh millennium BC have been found. As a trading partner and trans-shipment point for the maritime trade with Egypt and Mesopotamia, Ugarit rose rapidly after 1600 BC and experienced its golden age between 1400 and 1200 BC (despite tribute payments to Egypt), only to be vanquished in around 1194 BC by the invading Sea Peoples. The merchants' spokesmen had a special role to play in the hierarchically organized administration of the city-state, which boasted fortifications, rows of houses, and an extensive sewage system; in the west of the city, archaeologists have uncovered the royal palace that had over 100 rooms and was built in several stages. The considerable wealth of the city is attested to by fragments of beautifully designed furniture found in the royal palace, as well as gold and silver jewelry, bronze statuettes, and ornate bowls made of precious metals.

The Ugaritic alphabet

The discovery in Ugarit of the earliest alphabet in human history, by the French archaeologist Claude Schaeffer in 1929, caused a huge sensation. While excavating the city's extensive clay tablet archive, he discovered a previously unknown cuneiform consonant script, which had been in use since around 1400 BC. Unlike the Sumerian-Akkadian symbols, it did not represent syllables, but rather 29 or 30 letters; in that the symbols could be combined almost at will, the structure of this script can be compared to that of a modern alphabet. It influenced the Greek script and thus also the development of modern written language.

The excavated remains of a castle built in circa 1400 BC in the middle of the ruins of Ugarit (Syria); it was from Ugarit that the alphabet began its triumphal march around the world.

"The staff in the hand of Baal swoops like a vulture in his fingers.
It strikes Prince Sea on the shoulder and Lord River between the arms.
The well experienced takes a staff and reads out what is written on it:
'Your name, yes your name is: he-who-expels, oh, he-who-expels!'
Let it expel the sea!
Let it force Sea from his throne and River from the seat of his power.
You shall swoop in the hand of Baal, like a vulture in his fingers!
It shall strike Prince Sea on the head, and Lord River between the eyes!
Then shall Sea collapse and fall to the ground . . . ."

From an Ugaritic hymn to the power of Baal

Statuette of Baal, chief god of the Phoenicians (fourteenth century BC); as the Old Testament testifies, the cult of Baal also spread to neighboring peoples.

THE RELIGION OF THE UGARITES

The clay tablet archive of Ugarit was significant in a further respect, in that it contained records of the myths and religious concepts of the entire region, prayers, lists of sacrifices, and burial rituals, as well as oracles and the Ugarites' notions of their gods. The influences that this world and that of the Old Testament had on one another soon became apparent. The chief Ugarite god El, first worshiped as the creator of the world and humankind, who was represented as a bull but also in human form as the ruler of the world, was incorporated in the biblical name of God, Elohim, and the story in Genesis of the Creation by Yahweh/Elohim exhibits parallels with the Ugarite myths. The dance around the Golden Calf (Ex 32:1) also reveals connections with Ugarite religious practices. In the Old Testament, the prophets of Israel often come into conflict with the priests of the later chief god of the Phoenicians and Ugarites, the fertility-giver Baal (Baal-Haddad), who also became the protector god of the Canaanites (as in 1 Kgs 17).

A cuneiform cylinder from the state archive of Ugarit (circa 1400 BC); the texts mainly relate to economic/political and ritual topics.

The Babylonian Empire

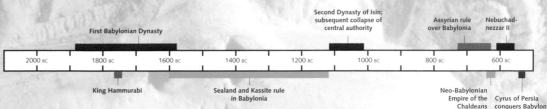

								Second Dynasty of Isin; subsequent collapse of central authority		Assyrian rule over Babylonia	Nebuchad-nezzar II
2000 BC		1800 BC		1600 BC		1400 BC		1200 BC	1000 BC	800 BC	600 BC
	First Babylonian Dynasty										
	King Hammurabi		Sealand and Kassite rule in Babylonia							Neo-Babylonian Empire of the Chaldeans	Cyrus of Persia conquers Babylon

The Babylonian culture in the south of the Mesopotamian region represents in many respects a high point of Sumerian-Akkadian civilization. The economy, which generally flourished despite political crises, was based on agriculture, long-distance trade, and irrigation works. It included both centralized temple economies and organizations of merchants who leased temple land as private entrepreneurs and conducted business on behalf of the temples and the city rulers. The majority of the records found are concerned with economics and commercial law; slavery, based chiefly on bonded labor, was common. There was as wide a range of artisan trades as of temple-related functions.

EPIC OF GILGAMESH AND CULT OF MARDUK

The literature of the Babylonians encompasses both prayers and hymns and also mythical stories. The most famous of these, the *Epic of Gilgamesh*, was inscribed on 12 tablets, and dates from circa 1200 BC. The hero, two-thirds god and one-third human (historically a king of Uruk in circa 2500 BC), lives through numerous adventures. Much of the poem focuses on Gilgamesh mourning his friend Enkidu's death, and Gilgamesh's quest for immortality. One interesting aspect here is

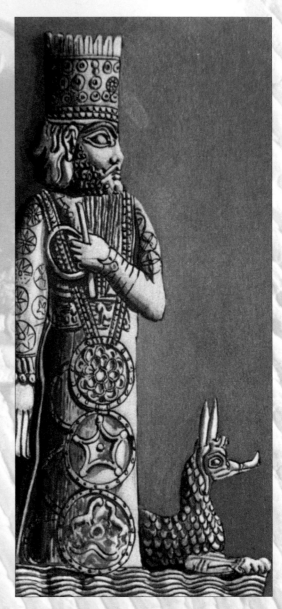

Background image: Stone sculpture of a lion's head from Babylon, symbol of the development of sovereign power (circa 1600–1400 BC).

Above: Marduk, the chief god in the Babylonian pantheon, with the dragon that is the animal associated with him (illustration from a Kassite relief).

the story-within-a-story of Utnapishtim, the "Babylonian Noah," who builds an ark and in this way rescues himself and his family from the Flood.

The principal god of the Babylonians was Marduk, whose story illustrates a kind of political theology; originally merely the city god of Babylon, in parallel with the rise of the capital he becomes the "son" of the chief gods and finally the savior of the cosmic order, before whom the Old Sumerian gods, who had originally ruled, retreat.

CHECKERED HISTORY

Following the downfall of the Third Dynasty of Ur (*see p. 24*) after 2000 BC the fortunes of the city-states rose again, with Isin and Larsa the first to assert themselves in the southern region (Babylonia). Under Hammurabi (*see p. 32*), the sixth king of the Babylonian Dynasty, Larsa seized power for itself and established a larger kingdom; however, this soon disintegrated into a number of small states once more. In 1595 BC, the Hittites destroyed Babylon on a military expedition, but the city subsequently recovered, especially economically, under the rule of the Sealand Dynasty and the indigenous Kassites. The Kassites held their ground courageously against raids by the Elamites and the aggressive power politics of the Kingdoms of Mitanni (*see p. 25*) and Assyria (*see p. 36*). Following a devastating invasion by the Elamites in 1157 BC, a powerful dynasty was established in Isin that once again unified Babylonia. Their most important king, Nebuchadnezzar I (1125–1104 BC), conquered Susa, carrying home in triumph the Marduk statue that the Elamites had pillaged.

The reconstructed walls (near Al Hillah, in present-day Iraq) of Babylon, once the world's major city, simultaneously admired and feared.

> " Fear not
> For Marduk has spoken
> Marduk will hear your prayer
> He will enlarge your dominions
> He will exalt your kingship "

From the penitential prayer of the king in the Marduk temple

King Hammurabi and his Law Code

The most significant ruler of ancient Babylon was King Hammurabi (1792–1750 BC); he not only waged wars successfully, but was also a brilliant diplomat who succeeded in playing his enemies against one another and extending his kingdom as far as Mari (see p. 27). However, his most important legacy is his legislation, into which he assimilated and incorporated several of the Mesopotamian legal systems, such as that of Ur-Namma (see p. 24).

The "Codex Hammurabi," passed down on clay tablets as well as on a diorite stele discovered in 1902, was divided into 282 paragraphs covering all areas of law. The stele shows King Hammurabi standing before the enthroned sun god Shamash and receiving the laws from him. In the preface Hammurabi glorifies himself as a just and benevolent ruler. Only a few of the paragraphs deal with criminal law, and in some of these, harsh physical punishments are laid down. Bodily injuries are generally dealt with according to the law of retaliation (cf. the Roman ius talionis: an eye for an eye . . .), but there was also the possibility of paying compensation if the aggrieved party consented. Most of the paragraphs are concerned with legal transactions in everyday life: property and ownership, rent, leases, and profit margins; the duties and rights of merchants and farmers. It is notable that doctors and builders are responsible for injuries to patients or for buildings that collapse, respectively. Paragraphs on family and marital law regulate adoption and inheritance, dowry and the rights of a wife; she too can institute a divorce, and a marriage is legal only with a marriage contract.

Bronze statuette of the king and legislator Hammurabi of Babylon (circa 1792–1750 BC), one of the most famous rulers of antiquity, kneeling submissively before the gods.

Justice under Hammurabi

Hammurabi's law code takes a tough stance on bearing false witness and making false accusations: even judges can be brought to account for this. The archives that have been found show that Hammurabi took his role as the good shepherd of his "black-headed people" seriously. Even simple date-growers, musicians, and farmers could take complaints (e.g. about dispossession) directly to the king, who on many occasions instructed his governors and ministers to attend to such cases personally and not to belittle the private property of small farmers. It is striking that Hammurabi as a ruler did not seek to deify himself, but instead emphasized the ethical mandate of the god Marduk and his requirement for justice.

> "The gods have called me, Hammurabi, the vigilant, god-fearing king, by name, to make justice visible in the land, to destroy the blasphemers and the evil-doers, so that the strong shall not remove the rights of the weak; so that I should rise like the sun over the black-headed people and brighten the land, for the well-being of the people."
>
> From the preface of the stele of Hammurabi, 1792–1750 BC

▶ SCIENCES IN BABYLON

The sciences flourished, particularly in the later periods of Babylon; they were originally closely associated with the education of the temple priests and scribes in their own schools. As well as mathematics—often within the framework of economic calculations—a complex form of astronomy developed, albeit (still) closely linked to astrology and magic in the sense of predicting the future using "omens." Numerous texts pass down information about their medical knowledge as well as incantations for warding off diseases in humans and animals and for assisting with childbirth.

Facing page: Illustration of the Hanging Gardens of Babylon, one of the Seven Wonders of the Ancient World (from *Histoire Ancienne* by Charles Rollin, 1829).

The beginnings of Chaldean rule

After 1026 BC, central power in Babylonia once more fragmented into small rival dynasties. The people who chiefly profited from this were the tightly organized Assyrians, who expanded farther and farther toward the south and eventually after 729 BC ruled directly over Babylon, having annihilated Babylon's arch-enemy, Elam. From around 650 BC, the Semitic Chaldeans organized opposition to Assyria; in 626 BC their king, Nabopolassar (626–605 BC), not only conquered Babylon and founded the Neo-Babylonian Empire, but also played a leading role in the destruction of the Assyrian Kingdom in 614–609 BC, which led to Babylon becoming the major power. The devout Nabopolassar described himself as a "weakling" and "son of a nobody," who owed his rise solely to his being chosen by Marduk.

The Tower of Babel (Ziggurat of Babylon), biblical symbol of humankind's sinful arrogance (painting by Pieter Brueghel the Elder, circa 1563).

Nebuchadnezzar II, the Builder

His son, Nebuchadnezzar II (605–562 BC), initially had to combat rebellions across the entire region. In 598 BC he put down revolts in the Kingdom of Judea and brought its elite to Babylon; following a series of uprisings he occupied and destroyed Jerusalem in 587 BC and once again sent the elite into "Babylonian exile." This measure led to his being seen in the Judeo-Christian tradition as a megalomaniac power-seeker; however, this hardly does justice to his achievements. The old tale of the "Babylonian confusion of tongues" (Gn 11:1–9) has always been associated with his tower.

Nebuchadnezzar's goal was to establish a peaceful rule so that he could devote his vigilance and energies to his monumental building projects. He had a 100-ft. (30-m) -high defensive wall built around Babylon and

The reconstructed Ishtar Gate of Babylon, magnificent entry point to the center of the city (near Al Hillah, present-day Iraq).

commissioned the artificially irrigated Hanging Gardens, one of the Seven Wonders of the Ancient World. He then erected the Tower of Babel (ziggurat), which measured approximately 300 ft. (91.5 m) in height, length, and breadth, as well as a temple to Marduk at the top of the tower, and the Ishtar Gate, together with the Processional Way. Both the temple and the gate were decorated with striding lions, bulls, and unicorns. Vast New Year processions in honor of Marduk took place here; Babylon had become a "world city," whose praises were sung but which was also vilified.

THE END OF THE NEO-BABYLONIAN EMPIRE

The last king to rule the empire was Nabonidus (555–539 BC). He worshiped the moon god Sin and spent several years in the Arabian oasis of Tema, while his son Belsharussur (the Belshazzar of the Book of Daniel in the Bible, to whom the writing on the wall appeared) acted as regent in Babylon. Whether Nabonidus actually planned to carry out a major religious reform is still a matter of debate today. In any case, the priests of Marduk in Babylon rose up against him and voluntarily opened the city gates to the approaching Persian King Cyrus II (*see p. 56*), who moved in and reinstated the

Marduk cult. Babylon's time as a world power was at an end.

The king and builder Nebuchadnezzar II of Babylon (604–562 BC), condemned in the Christian tradition, delivering a speech to his followers (illustration for the Bible's Book of Daniel).

The Assyrian Empire

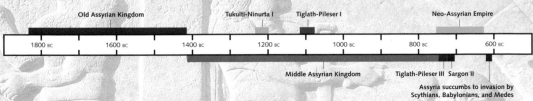

The Assyrian Empire is considered to be the first military power in history; its dominance was seen by neighboring countries as oppressive and cruel, and this led to its being portrayed in a uniformly negative way in the Bible—for example, in 2 Kgs and in Is 37:11, "Surely you have heard what the kings of Assyria have done to all the countries, destroying them completely . . . ." This image contributed to the fact that the Assyrians were for a long time seen purely as conquerors and tyrants. However, their kingdom did have a highly developed system of government, and its strict economic policy ensured a considerable degree of prosperity. The palace buildings in particular are testament to this.

EARLY DAYS AND ASCENDANCY

The heartland of the Assyrians in Mesopotamia corresponded to the north of present-day Iraq. The population comprised Semites and the Indo-Aryans of the Hurrian Kingdom of Mitanni (see p. 25). The culture had distinct Sumerian-Akkadian traits and took on numerous elements of the predominant Babylonian culture.

The capital, Assur, had its origins in a local settlement in the third millennium BC and subsequently rose to become one of the most important staging points on major trade routes. Under Assur-Uballit I (1353–1318 BC), who threw off the Hurrian yoke and strengthened

▶ KING TUKULTI-NINURTA I

The rule of King Tukulti-Ninurta I (1234–1197 BC) represented the first high point of Assyrian power. He won a major victory against the Hittites at the Battle of Nihriya in the first half of his reign thus ensuring total power over Mesopotamia, occupied Babylon, and took the title "King of the Universe"; this made him a protagonist of the Assyrian imperial ideology. He had his deeds immortalized in the *Tukulti-Ninurta Epic*. He built a new royal residence, Kar-Tukulti-Ninurta, near Assur. When he moved the main shrine of the state god of Assur (see p. 38) to his new capital, the priests and nobles conspired against him, and he was murdered by his sons.

Left: The "Mona Lisa of Nimrod" (circa 720 BC) also displays an enigmatic smile.

Background image: Stone relief containing scenes from an Assyrian military camp; a powerful army provided the backbone of Assyrian supremacy.

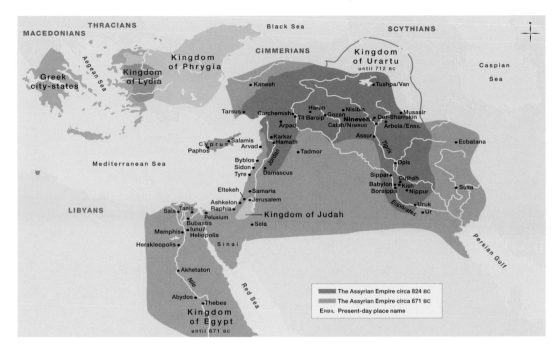

THE ASSYRIAN EMPIRE

The various phases of expansion of the empire illustrate the dominant role of the Assyrians in the Middle East: they made the whole of the Syrian-Phoenician and Babylonian regions tributary and ultimately advanced far into Egypt.

Map legend:
- The Assyrian Empire circa 824 BC
- The Assyrian Empire circa 671 BC
- ERBIL Present-day place name

trade links with Egypt, Assur became the independent center of a territorial empire.

Old Assyrian and Middle Assyrian Kingdoms

Assyria had a checkered history with political and cultural downs followed by periods of strength. Its relationship with its neighbor to the south, Babylon, fluctuated between alliance, open hostility, and mutual political interference.

The Assyrians steadily enlarged their territory, annexing their neighbors or turning them into vassals rendering tribute; they used the spoils of war to expand their cities. As early as the time of Adad-Nirari I (1295–1264 BC) and Salmanassar I (1263–1234 BC), they annihilated the remains of the Kingdom of Mitanni and deported the conquered population to their heartland in order to prevent unrest on the periphery. After the death of Tukulti-Ninurta (see box), the Old Assyrian Kingdom perished when the Sea Peoples and nomadic Arameans threatened the states of Mesopotamia. The Middle Assyrian Kingdom, under the rule of the warlike Tiglath-Pileser I (1114–1076 BC), managed to regain and even extend its former supremacy; the king forced the nomadic peoples to settle permanently.

Stone relief of a muscular Assyrian guard or soldier; the Assyrian warriors were feared throughout the Orient.

"They are impetuous, full of rage, transformed like the storm god,
They charge into the fray with no outer garments,
They check their belts, they rip their clothes from their bodies,
They bind their hair and let their swords dance around in circles.
These wild fighters, these valiant men
They leap, they hold their sharp weapons in their hands,
Their charge is like lions wrestling . . . ."

From the *Tukulti-Ninurta Epic*, on the Assyrian way of fighting, circa 1200 BC

ASSYRIA'S ADMINISTRATION AND ARMY

The Assyrian Empire had a hierarchical administrative system. At the top was the king with his numerous court officials and palace eunuchs. Under the "Grand Vizier" of Assur (Sukallu Dannu) came the empire's governors and provincial governors, who also controlled the army and trade. Well-constructed and carefully monitored roads connected the cities, and a network of riders and runners, catered for by relay stations en route, provided a functional postal service.

The battle-tested army was rigorously drilled and tightly led. Elite troops performed special tasks; the infantry consisted of lance carriers, archers, and slingers, and in addition there were special units for besieging cities and for fighting in the mountains. Contingents of soldiers from subject peoples were incorporated. The Assyrian war chariots that were used in pitched battles were particularly terrifying.

THE RELIGIOUS CULT

The Assyrians worshiped the Sumerian/Babylonian pantheon, especially Assur, who rose from being the city god of the royal city of the same name to become the chief god of the empire. The kings, who were simultaneously heads of the cult, saw themselves as being accountable to him. The Assyrians did not force their religion on their subject peoples.

VASSALS, TRIBUTES, AND PUNISHMENTS

Assyria was both a military and a trading power, and most of its campaigns served not only to expand its territory, but also to control trade routes. Under Salmanassar III (858–824 BC), they reached the Mediterranean for the first time and forced not only Syrian but also Phoenician trading cities to pay them tribute. The vassal states, bound by oath, generally enjoyed partial autonomy. A portion of the population from conquered regions was systematically deported to provide labor in Assyria.

The Assyrians viewed rebellions among subject peoples, as well as breaches of the oath, as sacrilege against the "order of peace" of the god Assur and punished them with

The most-feared weapon of the Assyrians: the war chariot, with a driver, archers, and sword fighters or spear throwers, all trained to work in perfect unison.

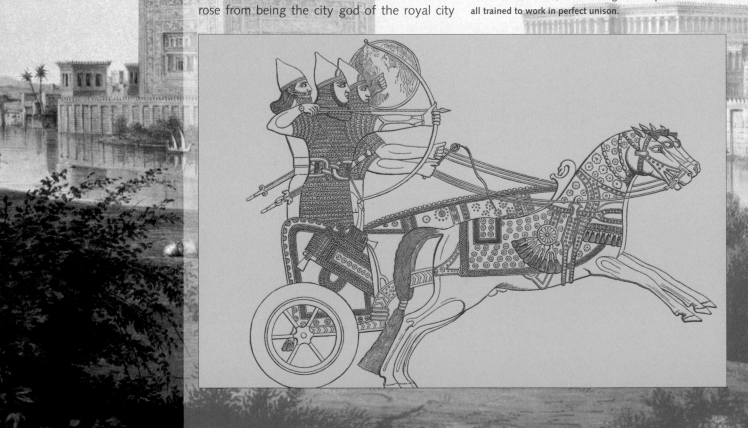

barbaric penalties. Several kings provide on their steles detailed accounts of burning, flaying, and dismembering their enemies, and of "slaughtering them like sheep." Legal and property relationships, as well as sales contracts, played an important role in the life of Assyria, as numerous cuneiform tablets testify.

King Assur-Nasirpal II (883–859 BC) built an immense palace in Nimrud (Calah) (print dated 1853).

THE NEW ROYAL CAPITAL

Assur-Nasirpal II (883–859 BC), famed for the ferocity of his military campaigns, had a magnificent new royal city built at Calah (Nimrud). An inscription leads us to believe that the king entertained a total of 69,574 invited guests at its consecration in 879 BC, feasting them on "2,200 cattle, 17,000 sheep, 1,000 gazelles, 34,000 fowls, 150,000 ducks, 10,000 fish, 10,000 eggs, 10,000 skins of wine, and 10,000 pitchers of beer."

The Neo-Assyrian Empire: Tiglath-Pileser III and Sargon II

Following another period of decline, Tiglath-Pileser III (745–727 BC) was the true founder of the Assyrian Empire. He devoted a considerable amount of energy and effort to modernizing the army and the administration, and instituted a new settlement policy: he transported hundreds of thousands of people from the heartland to the peripheries and simultaneously from the provinces on the edge of the empire to the center, in order to achieve extensive cultural unification of the population. In the north, the Assyrians faced a powerful opponent in the Kingdom of Urartu, which controlled large sections of the trade routes and threatened to cut off supplies to Assyria. Tiglath-Pileser defeated the Urartuans conclusively; in the fight against the Aramaic tribes of Babylon he made advances in the south and in 729 BC he himself ascended the Babylonian throne under the name of Pulu.

Sargon II (722–705 BC) successfully continued the expansion of the empire; in 721 BC he annexed Israel and reoccupied large areas of Babylon. In 717 BC he began construction of the royal city Dur-Sharrukin—"Sargon's city"—with a magnificently furnished palace complex. As in Calah, the walls were clad with large-scale stone reliefs.

The Sargonids

Sargon's son Sanherib (704–681 BC) made his mark with technical innovations and the building of huge irrigation systems. In 701 BC, he chose Nineveh as the last royal residence. He frequently fought against the rebellious cities of Judah and the Babylonians; in 689 BC he destroyed Babylon completely. His successor, King Esarhaddon (680–669 BC), had Babylon

A reconstruction of a well-fortified and imposing gateway to the palace city of Nineveh (Iraq), the last of the Assyrian royal capitals.

rebuilt and in 671 BC advanced far into Egypt. Meanwhile, the peoples of the Cimmerians and the Scythians (*see p. 172*) were encroaching from the north, although it initially proved possible to appease them by means of alliances.

Tradition says that during two eclipses of the moon (which were supposed to bring bad luck) Esarhaddon placed a substitute on the throne, so that the substitute would have the bad luck, while he himself went undercover as a farmer.

FINAL FLOURISH AND VIOLENT END

The last significant king, Ashurbanipal (668–631/627 BC), did wage wars, but his prime objective was economic prosperity. "I am skilled at the occupation of all scholars," says one of his inscriptions; and indeed, he instigated a cultural refinement of the Assyrian Empire and created a cuneiform library in Nineveh containing tens of thousands of texts. After 626 BC, his weak successors were invaded by the Scythians from the north, and also by the Babylonian

King Esarhaddon (680–669 BC) destroyed the rebellious city of Sidon in 677 BC: the Phoenician port city had attempted to shake off Assyrian rule and refused to pay tribute. Assyrian punitive expeditions cracked down mercilessly on those vassals who broke their oaths (painting by the Victorian artist G.D. Rowlandson).

Chaldeans (*see p. 34*) and the Medes from the south. Assur fell in 614 BC, and Nineveh in 612 BC. The oppressed neighboring countries vented their hatred by destroying the royal city, including the cuneiform library.

The excavations at Nimrud (Calah) in 1957; the British archaeologist Max Edgar Mallowan (1904–78, at the bottom of the picture, wearing a hat) led the excavations from 1947 onward, discovering a significant cuneiform archive in 1955.

The Hittites

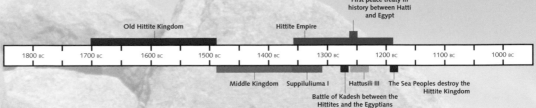

1800 BC	1700 BC	1600 BC	1500 BC	1400 BC	1300 BC	1200 BC	1100 BC	1000 BC

Old Hittite Kingdom

Hittite Empire

First peace treaty in history between Hatti and Egypt

Middle Kingdom · Suppiluliuma I · Hattusili III · The Sea Peoples destroy the Hittite Kingdom

Battle of Kadesh between the Hittites and the Egyptians

The significance of the Hittites was long overlooked and their culture totally forgotten; they were seen as an adjunct of the advanced Mesopotamian civilizations. The first meager finds were collected together in the nineteenth century, but it was not until the systematic excavation of the capital Hattusa (present-day Boğazkale, Turkey) after 1906 that found over 30,000 writing tablets bearing witness to the way of life, rituals, and laws of the Hittites, and thus the significance of this civilization began to be understood. Today it is known that the Hittite Empire in its heyday could bear comparison with those of Egypt, Babylonia, and Assyria.

Origins and beginnings

The Hittites, an Indo-European people with the oldest known Indo-Germanic language, used various systems of writing. At some point between 2500 and 1700 BC they are thought to have moved from the Caucasus to Anatolia and mingled with the indigenous Hattians, and they referred to their kingdom as "Hatti" right to the end. At first they established city-states that rose to become trading hubs; numerous conflicts with their neighbors over control of trade routes led in 1700 BC to the destruction of the center of Hattusa, which, however, subsequently flourished again as the capital of the kingdom. The capture of Aleppo by Hattusili I (circa 1565–1540 BC) marked the first expansion of the kingdom into the north Syrian region, but it repeatedly had to fend off marauding mountain peoples.

Telepinu's constitution

Following a series of crises and revolts, King Telepinu (circa 1500–1475 BC) was the first to issue a constitution, which shows us the political structure of the kingdom. The king-emperor (*labarna*) was the leader in times of war and peace, as well as being the chief justice and the religious leader; the queen, as the high priestess,

Background image: Ruins of the Hittite royal capital Hattusa (present-day Boğazkale, Turkey).

Below: Stone relief of a two-headed eagle on the walls of Hattusa (fourteenth century BC).

> **"**Sun God of Heaven, my Lord,
> shepherd of mankind.
> You rise out of the sea,
> Sun God of Heaven,
> and ascend into the sky.
> Sun God of Heaven, my Lord,
> each day you decide
> the legal disputes of mankind,
> dogs, pigs, and
> all the beasts of the field
> O Sun God.**"**

Hittite prayer to the sun god, circa 1300 BC

enjoyed a high degree of independence, even in political matters. At the king's side was a senate (*panku*) composed of representatives of the nobility that had great powers and could even depose the king. The *panku* also controlled the king's clan and its approval of the king's choice of successor from among his sons was required (there was no right of primogeniture).

Telepinu's constitution not only regulated the distribution of land (e.g. the leasing of royal and temple land) and supplies for the cities, but also set out a remarkably humane legal system that placed the emphasis on fines and compensation payments rather than on the ancient oriental system of retribution; blood feuds, kin liability, and death sentences were largely abolished.

▶ **THE PEOPLE OF "1,000 GODS"**
The pantheon of the Hittites, headed by the weather god Teshup and the sun goddess Arinna, was extremely complex. Moreover, new gods, dedicated in particular to mountains, good fortune, and protection, were continually being added, as the Hittites integrated the gods of the vassals they annexed and of their neighbors into their array of gods. When state treaties were signed, special oath-gods were called upon.

The chief Hittite god, the weather god Teshup, depicted striding forward, flanked by two stone lions (part of a monument at Eflatun Pinar/Fasillar, Turkey).

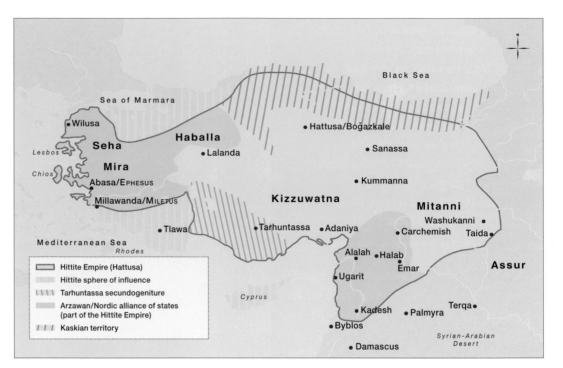

THE HITTITE KINGDOM IN THE THIRTEENTH CENTURY BC
The Hittite heartlands and the annexed vassal states differed in terms of their constitutional status: the seminomadic Kaskians in the north were under Hittite control, whereas a younger branch of the Hittite Dynasty ruled the Tarhuntassa region.

THE RULE OF SUPPILULIUMA I

Suppiluliuma I (circa 1355–1320 BC) was to become the creator of the Hittite Empire. He made the Syrian city-states, particularly Ugarit (*see p. 28*), vassals of the Hittites; the constitution, with its strict legal orientation, now differentiated between the centrally governed "inner lands" and the "outer lands" of the vassal states. In addition, the king extended the capital, Hattusa, to three times its former size. He also succeeded in conquering the Kingdom of Mitanni (*see p. 25*) and by appointing vassal kings, he neutralized them as rivals. Suppiluliuma came very close to making his dream of a world empire a reality when the widow of the Egyptian pharaoh Tutankhamen asked the king for one of his sons to be her husband and the new pharaoh; when the Hittite prince arrived in Egypt, however, the balance of power had shifted. The prince was killed and relations with Egypt deteriorated rapidly.

EMPEROR VERSUS PHARAOH

The battle between Egypt and Hatti for supremacy over the rich trading and port cities in Syria and Phoenicia was only a matter of time. In 1274 BC, Pharaoh Ramses II, certain of victory, marched against the Hittites and almost lost his life in the Battle of Kadesh against Muwatalli II (circa 1290–1272 BC); nevertheless, this did not prevent him portraying the battle as a great victory for Egypt. However, the Hittites held onto Kadesh, and were now negotiating from a position of strength. In 1259 BC, Ramses II and Emperor Hattusili III (II) (circa 1265–1236 BC) concluded the first known peace treaty in history as a pact of nonaggression and mutual assistance; this has survived in two languages, in hieroglyphics and in cuneiform script. Subsequently, there were extensive trade links and marriages of alliance between the two kingdoms.

FINAL FLOWERING AND LINGERING DECLINE

The rule of Tudhaliya IV (circa 1236–1215 BC), who conquered Cyprus, expanded the capital Hattusa, and erected numerous shrines, as well as having the sanctuary at Yazilikaya clad with rock reliefs, represented a last high point of Hittite supremacy. At the end of his regency the kingdom was already beset by the emerging Assyrians; economic crises and famines descended upon Hatti. The last king, Suppiluliuma II (circa 1215–1190 BC), sent desperate appeals to his Egyptian allies and the vassal state Ugarit imploring them to send grain.

Meanwhile, however, the mysterious Sea Peoples, who probably came from the Aegean and Asia Minor, had appeared on the scene, conquering Cyprus and occupying the coast of Syria. Ugarit fell in 1194 BC, and in circa 1190 BC they overran the Hittite Kingdom, which by now was utterly weakened internally. The capital, Hattusa, was abandoned and forgotten for over 3,000 years.

"On the river Halys I fell at the feet of the sun Suppiluliuma, emperor and hero, beloved of the weather god. The emperor took me by the hand and was pleased with me, and he asked me all about the land of Mitanni, and when he . . . had listened to everything, the emperor, the hero, spoke thus, 'I will make you my son . . . . I will set you on your father's throne.'"

From the account of King Shattiwaza of Mitanni, circa 1340 BC

The relief carved in rock at Yazilikaya shows a procession of Hittite gods. The Hittites worshiped entire legions of gods, who were responsible for every conceivable area of life.

The Arabian kingdoms

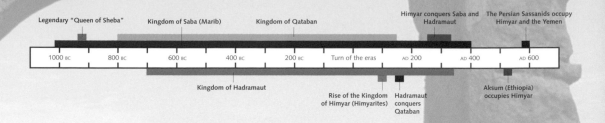

Legendary "Queen of Sheba" | Kingdom of Saba (Marib) | Kingdom of Qataban | Himyar conquers Saba and Hadramaut | The Persian Sassanids occupy Himyar and the Yemen

1000 BC | 800 BC | 600 BC | 400 BC | 200 BC | Turn of the eras | AD 200 | AD 400 | AD 600

Kingdom of Hadramaut | Rise of the Kingdom of Himyar (Himyarites) | Hadramaut conquers Qataban | Aksum (Ethiopia) occupies Himyar

The ruins of the city of Marib in the Yemen; as the capital of the Sabaean Kingdom, Marib was for centuries an important center of southern Arabian culture.

The advanced ancient Arabian civilizations evolved from the tenth century BC onward in the climatically favorable south of the Arabian Peninsula in a region extending from present-day Yemen and Oman to the south of Saudi Arabia. City-states developed into kingdoms with constantly changing alliances and power relationships.

KINGDOMS ALONG THE FRANKINCENSE ROAD

These kingdoms owed their rise and economic success above all to their control of the Frankincense Road, which began in Dhofar (Oman) and made its way through the Yemen, the Hejaz, and Petra, up as far as Syria and the coastal cities on the Mediterranean. Myrrh and the resin from the frankincense tree, which also

grew in the Yemen, were both used in incense, particularly for ritual purposes, and in medicine; the domestication of the dromedary (desert camel) made the grueling transportation of these desirable goods possible. The kingdoms in the southwest of the Arabian Peninsula provided hospitality and relay stations for caravans, levied tolls, and for a fee, provided protection along the way for the traders.

ORGANIZATION OF THE KINGDOMS

In southern Arabia, a key role was played by the tribes (sha'ab) or clans and the villages (bayt), which were constantly switching alliances and business relationships. The clan leaders controlled territories, oases, and caravans; in the cities, particularly the kingdoms' centers, which were rapidly becoming cultural and ethnic melting pots thanks to long-distance trade, an aristocracy of merchants and large landowners evolved, forming a sort of council of state around the king. The ruler bore the title "king" (*malik* or *mukarrib*). The generally senior title of *mukarrib* was given to the head of a federation of tribes; he was also the cult leader and had access to the wealth of the temple. They worshiped the ancient Arabian pantheon of sky gods (Sun, Moon, Venus).

Besides the caravan trade, sea trade with Africa and Asia (from India to China) was also vitally important for coastal cities, as was livestock breeding and agriculture (cultivation of millet, wheat, dates, and corn). To distribute the precious resource of water, the kingdoms built impressive dams and canal systems. The most important construction was the dam at Marib that was 2,231 ft. (680 m) long and 66 ft. (20 m) high with two sluice systems. The urban south Arabian peoples disassociated themselves from the nomadic tribes of inner Arabia with their austere way of life and were constantly having to ward off attacks by the tribes from the north.

The trade in the resin of the frankincense tree, which flourishes even in stony deserts, was a source of prosperity throughout southern Arabia.

▶ THE QUEEN OF SHEBA

One of the most famous figures of ancient Arabia is the Queen of Sheba, mentioned several times in the Old Testament (1 Kgs 10 and 2 Chr 9), who went to the court of King Solomon and was much admired there. In actual fact, the first trading contacts between south Arabia and the north did take place in the tenth century, although the historical authenticity of this queen is disputed. The Koran knows her as the wise Queen Bilqis (Sura 27). The Ethiopians consider their founding father, Menelik, to be a son of the liaison between King Solomon and the Queen of Sheba.

A caravan on its journey through the desert; the cities in the south of the Arabian Peninsula and along the Frankincense Road profited from the flourishing caravan trade.

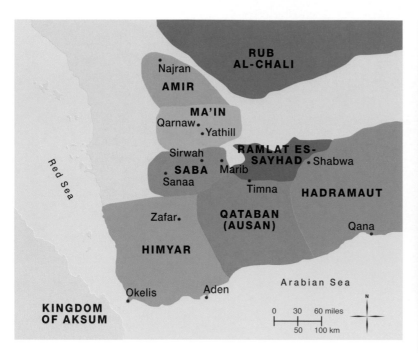

Saba

In the early days, the Kingdom of the Sabaeans, founded circa 1000 BC, with its capitals at Sirwah and later Marib, dominated the entire region and set up colonies in Eritrea. When in the fourth century BC the vassal states of Saba gained their independence, Saba lost control over a large part of the Frankincense Road. From the turn of the eras until around AD 140, it reestablished itself as a major power through joint rule with the state of Himyar, but after a series of conflicts was subjugated in around AD 260 by the Himyarites and slowly fell into decline; following several dam collapses, Marib was abandoned in AD 572.

Qataban, Ma'in, and Hadramaut

Qataban in the north of Yemen formed a kingdom from the eighth century BC and profited from sea trade with Africa and India; Hadramaut emerged as a kingdom in the seventh century BC and Ma'in, the Kingdom of the Minaeans, in the sixth century BC. Initially all subject to Sabaean sovereignty, these three vassal states formed an alliance against the Sabaeans in around 400 BC and freed themselves from their influence. Hadramaut and Ma'in

View over the city of Sana'a in the Yemen, still an important city today; in the foreground is a minaret in the characteristic south Arabian style of architecture.

were at times under joint rule; Ma'in, with its capital in Qarnawu, extended in the north into the Hejaz and reached as far as the Red Sea; Hadramaut, with its capital in Shabwa, controlled the beginning of the Frankincense Road in Dhofar. However, in the second century BC, Qataban succeeded in conquering Hadramaut and becoming the dominant power. The resurrected Kingdom of Saba, in alliance with Himyar, thus concentrated its attacks on Qataban, in particular. The newly independent Kingdom of Hadramaut initially profited from this, itself conquering Qataban in circa AD 150 and destroying its capital, Timna. In around AD 340, however, Hadramaut too was absorbed into the Himyarite Kingdom.

HIMYAR

The Himyarite Kingdom is the most recent of the ancient Arabian kingdoms, first becoming independent in 115 BC; around the turn of the eras it annexed parts of Saba, established the capital Zafar, and with the final occupation of Saba (AD 260) and the conquest of Hadramaut (AD 340) it became the major power in south Arabia. However, Himyar's control of trade routes, as well as conflicts with the local Jewish and Christian minorities, led on several occasions to interventions in the political affairs of south Arabia by the Ethiopians of Aksum. In order to safeguard his independence, King Du Nuwas of Himyar (AD 517–525), who made Sana'a his capital in AD 520, converted to Judaism. The persecution of Christians he instigated led in AD 525 to the occupation of the country by the Christian Ethiopians. The Himyarites then called on the Persian Sassanids (see p. 62) to help them throw off this foreign yoke; the latter did drive out the Ethiopians, but then in AD 597 they themselves occupied the country and annexed it as a province of the Persian Empire. From AD 630 onward, however, south Arabia was converted to Islam.

The Dar al-Hajar palace, built on top of a rock in Wadi Dhahr near Sana'a (Yemen).

The Nabataeans of Petra

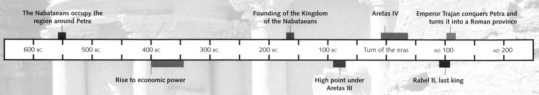

The Nabataeans occupy the region around Petra		Founding of the Kingdom of the Nabataeans		Aretas IV	Emperor Trajan conquers Petra and turns it into a Roman province

600 BC	500 BC	400 BC	300 BC	200 BC	100 BC	Turn of the eras	AD 100	AD 200

Rise to economic power	High point under Aretas III	Rabel II, last king

The Arab Nabataeans migrated in the first millennium BC northward from the Arabian Peninsula into the area between the Red Sea and the Dead Sea and from around 550 BC settled in east Jordan, where they established their royal city, Petra. From there, they controlled the northern trading posts of the Frankincense Road on its route to the Mediterranean coast.

THE NABATAEAN PEOPLE

The Nabataeans lived for many years as seminomads, raising livestock (mainly dromedaries) but not cultivating any crops,

and were not only successful traders, but in the early days were also feared on account of their attacks on caravans. After the fourth century BC, trade brought them considerable wealth and enabled the expansion of Petra into one of the most important and powerful cultural centers of the northern Arabian region. As well as frankincense, spices, and silver, the Nabataeans traded the finely painted ceramics that they themselves produced, and they also supplied Egypt with bitumen (tar) extracted from the Dead Sea, for use in embalming.

The Nabataeans spoke a Semitic language that was closely related to Arabic, and in the second

Background image: The façade of the Treasury in the valley of Petra (Jordan).

Above: Two of the royal tombs carved out of the rock in Petra, the Palace Tomb (left) and the Corinthian Tomb (right).

One of the most famous examples of their architecture, the "Treasury of the Pharaoh" (Khazne al Fara'un) is situated directly opposite the entrance to the gorge. Carved out of the glowing pink sandstone around the turn of the eras, in the Hellenistic-Roman style (the capitals of the magnificent façade were added later), it is probably the mausoleum of one of the later Nabataean kings. The enormous hangarlike rooms in the interior have high niches where sarcophagi may have stood.

century BC they developed their own consonant script, which can be seen as a forerunner of the Arabic script.

PETRA, CITY OF ROCK

Petra (in present-day Jordan, between the Gulf of Aqaba and the Dead Sea) lies hidden in a gorge about a mile (1.5 km) long and 650 ft. (200 m) deep, between precipitous, inaccessible rock faces; the city is only accessible from one side and the entrance at its narrowest point is only 6 ft. 6 in. (2 m) wide, so it could be sealed off and easily defended. The Nabataeans initially carved dwellings and tomb chambers into the soft, colorful rock; later, they also carved magnificent and monumental rock tombs and temples with huge columns in the Hellenistic style, such as the temples of the Royal Tombs. Houses once lined the central Colonnade Street. Ritual sites and shrines were built on the surrounding summits, which range between approximately 2,600 and 4,400 ft. (800 and 1,350 m) in height. Mountain streams and collected rainwater were channeled into Petra by means of a well-constructed system of channels hewn into the rock. Using a network of cisterns, they even cultivated the barren Negev Desert, where they set up staging points and caravanserais for their trade routes.

This obelisk of colorful sandstone is just one of the bizarre rock formations in the valley of Petra.

The amphitheater, hewn from the rock in the reign of King Aretas IV (9 BC–AD 40), clearly betrays Roman and Hellenistic influences.

PETRA—CITY OF ROCK AND CENTER OF TRADE

The impregnability of the rock city Petra was demonstrated in 312 BC, when the Macedonian leader of the Diadochi, Antigonos I Monophthalmos (*see p. 112*) tried in vain to annex the city and its people to his kingdom. In the following years, the Nabataeans' political power increased steadily; they enlarged their kingdom at the expense of the Syrian Seleucids and the Hasmoneans of Judah (*see p. 86*). In around 169 BC, with Aretas I, they founded a central dynasty that endured until the demise of the kingdom; from the time of Obodas III (28–9 BC), the kings were worshiped as gods along Hellenistic lines.

Under Aretas III (87–62 BC), the Nabataeans engaged in expansionist power politics; they conquered the north of Jordan and the south of Syria and in 85 BC captured Damascus, giving Petra a trade monopoly reaching as far as the Mediterranean coast. Aretas III called himself "Philhellen" ("Friend of the Greeks") and oversaw the eventual Hellenization of the Nabataean culture, minting coins with Hellenistic symbols. With the support of one of the pretenders to the throne, he exploited the fratricidal war between the Hasmoneans to expand his territory still farther and advanced with a large army on Jerusalem. This, however, brought the Nabataeans to the attention of the Romans under Pompeius Magnus, who arranged matters in Judea to suit their own purposes and forced Aretas to retreat. In 62 BC, in order to avoid a military trial of strength, the king came to an agreement with Rome.

Autonomy under Roman rule and decline

Although Petra maintained a high degree of autonomy over its internal affairs under this agreement, Roman influence over its culture and foreign policy became increasingly marked. The kings were heavily involved in the power struggle between Rome and the Egyptian Ptolemy Dynasty. Aretas IV (9 BC– AD 40) erected numerous buildings in the Roman style, such as the amphitheater in Petra, which could accommodate several thousand people in rows of seating hewn into the rock. During his reign there were up to 40,000 people living in Petra; following territorial gains, the kingdom was at its maximum size, extending as far as the Hejaz in the south and the Hauran in the north. In AD 36/37, Aretas took over large areas of Judea as far as Qumran, as compensation for the fact that his son-in-law Herodes Antipas of Judea had divorced his wife (Aretas's daughter). The last king, Rabel II Soter (AD 70–106), moved the capital of the Nabataean Kingdom from Petra to Bosra in Hauran, and subsequently Petra fell into decline. After the king's death, in AD 106, Emperor Trajan annexed the Nabataean Kingdom to the Roman Empire, naming the province Arabia Petraea. Following several earthquakes and conquest by Islam (AD 663), Petra was finally abandoned and sank into oblivion until the Swiss adventurer Jean Louis Burckhardt rediscovered the city in 1812; the systematic excavation of the city of rock began in around 1900.

Behind artistically arranged stone reliefs, a water conduit runs toward the narrow entrance to the valley of Petra (Jordan).

Persia

Rise of the Elamite city-states

Elamite Kingdom

Cyrus the Great conquers Media and establishes the Persian Empire

Darius I the Great

Sassanid Empire

Alexander the Great conquers Persia

High point under Khosrau I

Islamic Arab troops conquer Persia

| 3500 BC | 3000 BC | 2500 BC | 2000 BC | 1500 BC | 1000 BC | 500 BC | Turn of the eras | AD 500 |

Median Kingdom

"Persian Wars" against Greece

Parthian Kingdom (Arsacids)

Shapur I besieges Rome

Achaemenid Empire

Even before imperial times, Persia had already been the site of culturally significant amalgamations of smaller states and confederations of peoples.

THE KINGDOM OF ELAM

The native Elamites in southwest Iran, the breadbasket of Persia, were arable farmers and horse breeders who set up city-states in around 3500 BC. The capital, Susa, was founded as early as 4000 BC. The Elamites developed their own proto-Elamite pictorial script in around 3000 BC, which was replaced circa 2300 BC by a linear script and syllabary; approximately 1,600 clay tablets in Elamite were discovered when Susa was excavated.

From around 2300 BC, rulers who are known by name formed a centralized kingdom, whose history was closely linked to that of Mesopotamia, and immortalized their deeds in stone inscriptions. Under Shutruk-Nakhkhunte (1185–1155 BC), who conquered hundreds of cities, including Babylon, and exacted large tributes of gold and silver from his defeated foes, the Elamites expanded into Mesopotamian territory. The king abducted the Marduk statue and Hammurabi's stele from Babylon to Susa, where they were discovered in 1902. For this reason, the emerging empires of Babylon and Assyria viewed Elam as an enemy and in the centuries that followed made incursions as

Background image: The ruins of Susa (present-day Sush, Iran), the capital of the Kingdom of Elam.

far as Susa on several occasions. In 639 BC, Assyrian King Assurbanipal put an end to Elam's continuing political decline by conquering the kingdom; following the downfall of Assyria, Elam was incorporated into the Kingdom of the Medes and the Achaemenids.

THE MEDES

North of Elam, in the west of Iran, the Median Kingdom rose as the Elamite Kingdom declined. The Medes, who had originally formed two large tribes, were possibly descendants of the Scythians (see p. 172), with whom they were closely linked (this is evidenced by their way of fighting, as horse-riding warriors, as well as by their renowned horse-breeding skills), and are seen as the ancestors of the present-day Kurds. By circa 800 BC, they had moved to the region around their capital, Ecbatana. King Deioces (728–675 BC) founded a rapidly expanding empire and his son Phraortes (675–653 BC) unified the tribes of the Medes and the Persians and forced the Cimmerians (see p. 173) to sign treaties of alliance. Under Cyaxares II (652–612 BC), who threw off Scythian influence, the kingdom reached its greatest extent and in 614/612 BC took part in the destruction of the Assyrian Empire. In around 590 BC, the Medes occupied Urartu and advanced against the Lydians in Asia Minor; after the Battle of Halys (Anatolia) in 585 BC, that river was deemed to form the boundary of the Greek-Lydian sphere of influence. The last king, Astyages (585–550 BC), held the kingdom together and

This stone relief shows the conquest and destruction of the Elamite city of Khamanu by the troops of Assyrian King Assurbanipal (668–626 BC) in 640 BC.

married his daughter to the Persian vassal Cambyses; she became the mother of Cyrus the Great, who eventually waged war against his grandfather, deposed him in 550 BC, and annexed the Medes.

"Because my god Inshushinak stands by me, I, Shutruk-Nakhkhunte, have called upon him; he has heard my entreaties and shown my horned warriors their place . . . . O Inshushinak, my god! As you stood by me, I, Shutruk-Nakhkhunte, armed with horns, took the land under my protection."

From an inscription by King Shutruk-Nakhkhunte of Elam, circa 1150 BC

This relief shows Emperor Darius I (521–486 BC) on his throne, being approached reverently by a Mede officer and two Persian guards.

THE ACHAEMENID KINGDOM UNDER CYRUS AND CAMBYSES

In around 700 BC, the Achaemenid Persians, supposedly under the leadership of the progenitor who had given them their name, Achaemenes, moved from the area around Lake Urmia into central Iran, where they established a kingdom, initially as vassals of the Medes. Cyrus II, the Great (559–529 BC), broke up and took over the Median Kingdom (550 BC), united the Medes and the Persians, and in 546 BC annexed the Lydian Kingdom. In 539 BC he conquered Babylon, where he was greeted as a liberator, and allowed the Jews in "Babylonian exile" to return to Israel, which, like the entire Syrian and Phoenician regions, lay under his control. With the declaration he made in Babylon (539 BC) in particular, which is believed to be the first human rights charter in history, Cyrus established the Persian ruling principles of religious tolerance and of the religious sovereignty of annexed peoples.

He was seen, especially in the Old Testament (2 Chr, Dn) and in Greek historical writings (Herodotus), as an ideal ruler and a paragon of intelligence, moderation, bravery, and rectitude, who became a role model for generations of rulers.

His son, Cambyses II (529–522 BC), conquered Egypt in 526/525 BC and annexed it to his empire, making Persia the single major power in the Middle East.

DARIUS THE GREAT

Following some arguments over the succession (522/521 BC), a successor from a collateral line, Darius I, the Great (521–486 BC), came to power. He became the organizer of the first truly global empire, which at the height of its power covered Iran, Iraq, Afghanistan, Uzbekistan, Turkey, Cyprus, Greater Syria, Lebanon, and Egypt, as well as parts of Libya, Sudan, Greece, Bulgaria, and central Asia. As the Persians now formed a minority, he divided the empire into provinces (satrapies), whose governors were chosen from the local and as "viceroys" had wide-ranging cultural autonomy; they paid tribute to the emperor and provided contingents of troops for the Persian army. In a hitherto unprecedented leadership cult, Darius represented himself as the absolute ruler and king of the world. He erected vast palace cities and monumental buildings, notably in Susa, Persepolis, and Pasargadae. His "king's roads" provided the empire with well-built roads, mail, and trade routes, all under military protection. He strengthened religious tolerance through generous donations and sacrificial ceremonies for the gods of the peoples he had annexed. After numerous Greek cities in Asia Minor had voluntarily submitted to his rule from 494 BC, in 490 BC he embarked upon the "Persian Wars" (*see p. 98*) against the Greek city-states, which his son Xerxes I (485–465 BC) continued without success.

The western steps in the ruins of the palace city of Persepolis, which was destroyed by Alexander the Great.

"Thus says Darius, the king: The kingdom which had been snatched from our family, I have restored. I have reset it upon its foundations. I have restored the temples as they were before . . . . I have returned to the people their possessions, their flocks, their servants, and their houses . . . . I have reset the people on their foundations, both in Persia and in Media and in the other lands."

From an inscription by Darius I in Behistun, sixth/fifth century BC

Persian cuneiform text on a stairway in the palace of Emperor Darius I in Persepolis (sixth century BC).

The fire altar built in the reign of Darius I at Naqsh-i-Rustam (near Persepolis), a key ritual shrine of the ancient state-sponsored Persian religion.

became embroiled in altercations with the Greek cities; furthermore, Egypt succeeded in disengaging itself from the empire once again. The refined and luxurious court culture with its pomp and splendor and its complex rituals led time and again to palace intrigues, to which some of the emperors fell victim. The energetic Ataxerxes III (359–338 BC) restored the empire of old by conquering Asia Minor and Egypt (343 BC).

RELIGION

The original Indo-Aryan pantheon of the Persians started to move in the direction of monotheism with the increasing focus on the worship of the chief god Ahura Mazda, portrayed in the disk of the sun; the other gods were eventually demoted to "bounteous immortals" (*amesha spentas*) or attributes of the chief god, with the exception of the god of contracts, Mithras, who eventually became the focus of his own cult that spread across large swaths of Persia and even into the Roman Empire. With the reforms of Zoroaster (circa 630–553 BC) the cosmic

THE LATER ACHAEMENIDS

Darius's successors attempted to hold the empire together, but—despite strong contingents of Greek soldiers in the Persian army—repeatedly

THE ACHAEMENID KINGDOM
The Persian emperors ruled over the first real global empire in history that encompassed a wide variety of regions and peoples. These were all granted a high degree of cultural autonomy under indigenous satraps, but succession disputes and weaknesses in the central government led time and again to attempts by the annexed peoples to gain their independence.

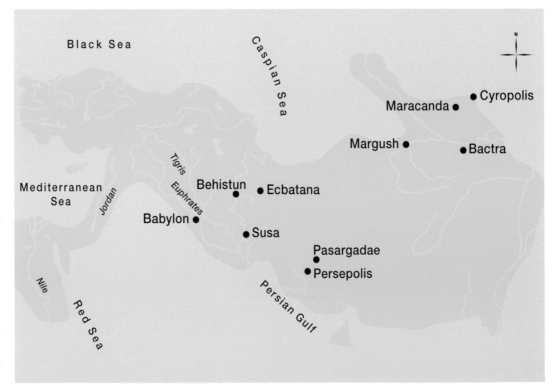

conflict between the duality of light and dark (*ormuzd* and *ahriman*), in which the behavior of people came to have a decisive role, was seen as critical. With its three principles of good thoughts, good words, and good deeds, Zoroastrianism had a decidedly ethical orientation. The idea of the final judgment at the "bridge of the separator" (*chinvat*), which separates the just and saved from the unjust and damned, was incorporated into many religions.

THE END OF THE ACHAEMENID EMPIRE

After the empire had once again been weakened by uncertainty regarding the succession to the throne, Darius III (336–330 BC) managed to stabilize the situation for the last time. Meanwhile, Philip II of Macedonia (*see p. 109*) had decided to put an end once and for all to the Persian threat to Greece and was preparing for war when he was murdered in 336 BC. His son, Alexander the Great, carried out Philip's plan and invaded Persia in 334 BC. At the battles of Granikos (334 BC), Issos (333 BC), and Gaugamela (331 BC) he defeated the numerically superior Persian army; Darius III fled to the east of his kingdom and was murdered in 330 BC by his satrap Bessos. Alexander occupied Persia, but allowed the Persians a great deal of autonomy. In 324 BC he married Darius's daughter and held a mass wedding between 10,000 of his officers and Persian noblewomen (in the face of strong resistance from the Greeks) with the aim of amalgamating the cultures of East and West in the progeny of these unions to provide a foundation for his world empire. When it was divided after Alexander's death (323 BC), most of Persia fell under Seleucid rule (*see p. 114*).

Representation of the chief Persian god Ahura Mazda with the winged sun disk (detail from the old parliament building, Majlis, in Tehran).

de nation
ique qui signifie
dy ou enfant perdu

Foundation and zenith of the Parthian Empire

The Parthians, whose original homeland lay in an area southeast of the Caspian Sea, formed a subclan of the Scythians (under the name Parni) and lived as horse-riding nomads until they occupied the Iranian province of Parthia between 250 and 238 BC and settled there. The founder of the Arsacid Kingdom and Dynasty, Arsaces I (247–217 BC), curtailed the power of the Seleucids and concluded treaties with the Graeco-Bactrian Empire in India. Mithridates I (171–138/137 BC) extended his rule across Persia, Media, and parts of Asia and also gained possession of Mesopotamia through a marriage of alliance with the Seleucids. The Parthians now deliberately fell in with the traditions of the Achaemenid Empire and showed themselves to be enthusiastic proponents of the Zoroastrian religion, for example, in the construction of fire shrines. Mithridates I made Ctesiphon his royal city and was the first to adopt the Iranian title Shah-in-Shah ("King of Kings").

Under Mithridates II (123–88 BC) the empire reached its zenith, making the Euphrates its western border and occupying Armenia, which became a vassal kingdom. The emperor gave the empire new structures and introduced a Hellenistic-Parthian style in government and in art. The Parthians embraced Hellenistic culture, but stressed their independence and saw themselves as its Persian-oriental counterpart. The empire was weakened by the uncertainty over the succession to the throne that set in after 88 BC, which at times even led to divisions of the empire and dual reigns.

The Parthians as antagonists of Rome

This uncertainty facilitated the advance of the Romans into Asia Minor and Armenia in the

Representation of a warlike king of the Parthians (copper engraving, 1662); the Parthians showed themselves to be serious opponents of Roman expansion in the East.

years after 70 BC; in the subsequent period, the situation in Armenia in particular became a constant bone of contention between the Parthians and the Romans. The peace treaty in 64 BC was followed by renewed acts of war in which the Romans initially suffered devastating defeats: in 53 BC the triumvir Crassus fell in battle against the Parthians, and in 36 BC Mark Antony suffered an annihilating defeat. Later, Arsacid rulers once more sought closer ties with Rome, but the Romans fomented internal disputes over the succession and brought Armenia under their sovereignty.

The Parthians grew stronger again under Vologases I (AD 51–78), who reconquered Armenia in AD 63 and introduced a Persian-Oriental reaction against Hellenism. In the

years that followed, several Roman emperors waged wars against the Parthians, for example, Trajan (114–117), Septimius Severus (197–198; they conquered the royal city Ctesiphon), and Caracalla (216–217). The Parthians' tenacity and resistance, however, always resulted in the Romans' having to give up what they had conquered. After a period of internal decline, the Parthian Empire was taken over by the Neo-Persian Sassanids in 224–226.

Below: The ruins of the great hall of the royal palace in Ctesiphon (present-day Iraq), the royal residence of the Parthians and the Sassanids.

Above: Silver coin of Parthian King Vonones II, shown with horned diadem; he died in AD 51 after a reign of just a few months.

PERSIA TEACHES ROME THE MEANING OF FEAR

The Sassanids, who came from the south of the Parthian Empire, traced their name back to their high priest Sassan (circa 200). The founder of the empire, Ardashir I (224–240/241), a satrap of Persis, rose up against the Arsacids, conquering Ctesiphon in 226 and the Mesopotamian Kingdom of Hatra in 240/241. He broke the power of the nobility in order to increase the power of the king—an ongoing power struggle that many of his successors also had to endure. His son Shapur I (240/241–272) led the empire to the first peak of its success, when he not only defeated the Romans several times, but also advanced far into Roman territory; in 260 he took Emperor Valerian prisoner at Edessa and humiliated him until his death in Persian captivity. Shapur was a supporter of the dualistic Manichaean religion founded by the Persian prophet Mani (216–276), who was persecuted by Shapur's successors and who strongly influenced Christianity. The Sassanids emphasized the Persian national culture and repudiated Roman Hellenism, but looked positively on ancient Greek philosophy. The Romans, who had always looked down on the Parthians as "barbarians," had to respect the Sassanids as being a cultural power of equal worth.

Under the long reign of Shapur II (309–379), the canon of Zoroastrianism was completed, and the first persecutions of Christians took place. In 363, Emperor Julian Apostata fell in battle against the Persians, whereupon Shapur dictated peace on terms that were favorable to

Stone reliefs in the grottoes of Taq-e-Bostan (Iran), in which the Sassanid great kings had themselves portrayed in the ancient Persian tradition; in the left-hand niche, the last important Sassanid ruler, Khosrau II (AD 590–628), can be seen on horseback.

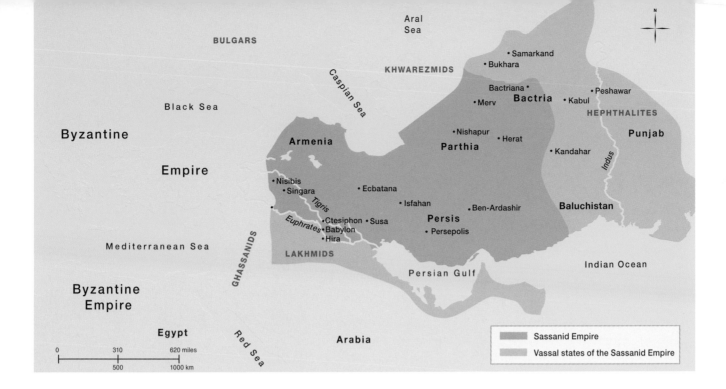

Aral
Sea

N

BULGARS

• Samarkand
• Bukhara

KHWAREZMIDS

Bactriana •

Bactria

• Peshawar

• Merv

• Kabul

HEPHTHALITES

Black Sea

• Nishapur

Punjab

Byzantine

Armenia

• Herat

Parthia

Empire

• Kandahar

Indus

• Nisibis

• Ecbatana

• Singara

Tigris

• Isfahan

• Ben-Ardashir

Baluchistan

Euphrates

• Ctesiphon • Susa

Persis

• Babylon

• Persepolis

• Hira

Mediterranean Sea

GHASSANIDS

LAKHMIDS

Indian Ocean

Byzantine
Empire

Persian Gulf

Egypt

Red Sea

Arabia

Sassanid Empire

0   310   620 miles

Vassal states of the Sassanid Empire

500   1000 km

him. His successors allowed Christians to settle there, but this subsequently resulted in a series of religious conflicts.

HEIGHT OF POWER AND DECLINE OF THE SASSANID EMPIRE

Khosrau I Anushirvan (AD 531–579) took on the threat from the Byzantine Empire. He occupied Antiochia in AD 540, and following a series of wars with mixed outcomes, reached agreement on the border with Byzantium. In the east, he put an end to the centuries-old threat from the Asiatic horse-riding peoples, and in 561/563 destroyed the Kingdom of the Hephthalites ("White Huns," *see p. 182*). Following this, he brought Yemen and Oman under Persian domination. Under his rule, Middle Persian literature and art flourished at his court. The last significant Sassanid, Khosrau II Parvez (590–628), proved himself a worthy opponent in the wars waged by Byzantine Emperor Herakleios against Persia: in 626 he besieged Constantinople, but in 627 suffered a crushing defeat. After his murder there was uncertainty over the succession to the throne; the empire had been exhausted internally by the long wars against Byzantium as well as those over Jerusalem. After 636,

THE SASSANID EMPIRE
The map shows the Sassanid Empire to be the Byzantine Empire's most significant opponent. The battles between them were to a large extent fought by the Arab vassal tribes of the Ghassanids and the Lakhmids.

the last emperor, Yazdegerd III (632–651), suffered several heavy defeats at the hands of the advancing Islamic Arabs, who captured Ctesiphon in 638 and by 640 had occupied most of Persia. Yazdegerd fled to Merv, where he was murdered in 651.

The stone relief at Naqsh-i-Rustam celebrates the victory of King Shapur I (AD 240–272) over the Roman army in 260; shown kneeling before Shapur (at left) is the captive and humiliated Emperor Valerian, who ended his life in captivity.

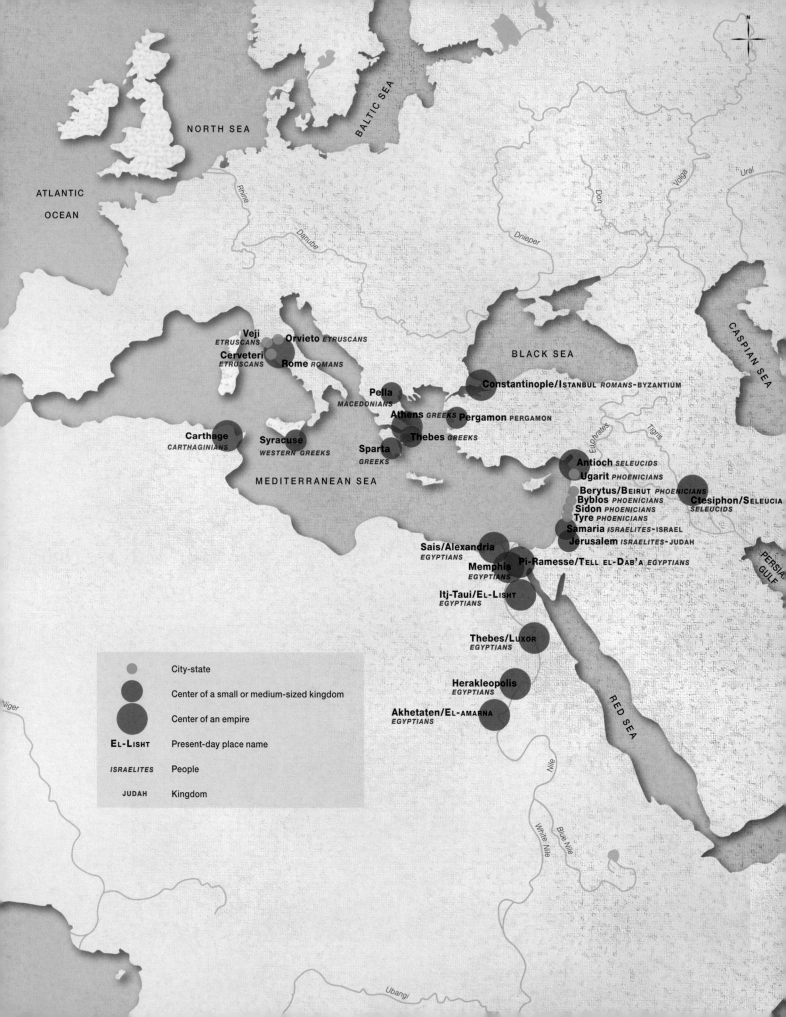

N

ATLANTIC
OCEAN

NORTH SEA

BALTIC SEA

Rhine

Danube

Dnieper

Don

Volga

Ural

CASPIAN
SEA

BLACK SEA

Veji *ETRUSCANS*
Orvieto *ETRUSCANS*
Cerveteri
ETRUSCANS
Rome *ROMANS*

Pella
MACEDONIANS

Athens *GREEKS*
Thebes *GREEKS*
Sparta
GREEKS

Constantinople/ISTANBUL *ROMANS-BYZANTIUM*

Pergamon *PERGAMON*

Carthage
CARTHAGINIANS

Syracuse
WESTERN GREEKS

MEDITERRANEAN SEA

Euphrates

Tigris

Antioch *SELEUCIDS*
Ugarit *PHOENICIANS*
Berytus/BEIRUT *PHOENICIANS*
Byblos *PHOENICIANS*
Sidon *PHOENICIANS*
Tyre *PHOENICIANS*
Samaria *ISRAELITES-ISRAEL*
Jerusalem *ISRAELITES-JUDAH*

Ctesiphon/SELEUCIA
SELEUCIDS

PERSIAN
GULF

Sais/Alexandria
EGYPTIANS

Memphis
EGYPTIANS

Pi-Ramesse/TELL EL-DAB'A *EGYPTIANS*

Itj-Taui/EL-LISHT
EGYPTIANS

Thebes/LUXOR
EGYPTIANS

RED
SEA

Herakleopolis
EGYPTIANS

Akhetaten/EL-AMARNA
EGYPTIANS

Niger

Viger

Ubangi

Nile

White Nile

Blue Nile

City-state

Center of a small or medium-sized kingdom

Center of an empire

EL-LISHT Present-day place name

ISRAELITES People

JUDAH Kingdom

Carthaginians   Romans   Egyptians   Phoenicians   Greeks

CULTURES AROUND THE MEDITERRANEAN

The history of Europe, the Middle East, and Upper Africa has been definitively shaped by the early Mediterranean cultures and empires. The enduring empire of the pharaohs in Egypt represented a developmental leap forward in almost all areas of culture, government, and art. In the Syrian coastal regions and in Upper Africa the Israelites, with their increasingly monotheistic religion, and the trading and seafaring peoples of Phoenicia and Carthage emerged from its shadow.

After early Minoan and Mycenaean times, the polis culture of the Greeks and of the western Greeks of Sicily, which was fragmented in terms of power politics but nonetheless seen as a cultural entity, formed the foundation of Western civilization and intellectual life. Led initially by Macedonia under Philip I and the world conqueror Alexander the Great, it sought to achieve a synthesis of East and West in Hellenistic culture. Politically, however, it disintegrated into rival kingdoms. All these cultures—including the Etruscans in Italy—finally fell under the influence and domination of the Roman Empire. Following the fall of Carthage, Rome, with its tightly organized army and administration during the strict Republican era as well as the late Hellenistic Imperial era, laid down the foundations of a functioning infrastructure in many areas for future government structures and legal systems. The christianization of the Roman Empire during late antiquity by Emperor Constantine and his successors was a step that was to have far-reaching consequences.

CULTURES AROUND THE MEDITERRANEAN
The map shows early cultures and kingdoms around the Mediterranean, from Egypt, Israel, and Phoenicia to Carthage, Greece (including Sicily), and Macedonia, as well as the Hellenistic kingdoms, the Etruscans, and the world power that was Rome.

Egypt

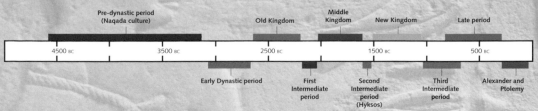

Pre-dynastic period
(Naqada culture)

Old Kingdom

Middle
Kingdom

New Kingdom

Late period

| 4500 BC | 3500 BC | 2500 BC | 1500 BC | 500 BC |

Early Dynastic period

First
Intermediate
period

Second
Intermediate
period
(Hyksos)

Third
Intermediate
period

Alexander and
Ptolemy

The Egypt of the pharaohs is among the most ancient and best-known human civilizations. Lasting for around 3,000 years, it was also the longest-lived advanced culture in history.

BEGINNINGS AND UNIFICATION OF THE KINGDOM

Egypt, which has had agricultural and trading settlements since Neolithic times, owed its civilization above all to the Nile and its fertile floodplains; in the pre-dynastic Naqada period (circa 4500–3150 BC) it was divided into two regions that later became kingdoms: Upper Egypt (the area on both sides of the Nile between Aswan and Luxor) and Lower Egypt (from present-day Cairo to the Mediterranean). In the Early Dynastic or Thinite period (circa 3100–2700 BC), Pharaoh Menes (circa 2980 BC), from Upper Egypt, united these two areas into one kingdom, symbolized by the Egyptian double crown consisting of the white crown of Upper Egypt combined with the red crown of Lower Egypt. From the capital, Memphis, the pharaohs of the first two dynasties attempted to unify the religion, script, calendar, and weights and measures used, thereby creating the first centrally administered state in history, although it continually had to counteract forces tending to pull it apart.

Background image: A relief showing men milking a cow, from the Mastaba (tomb) of the court official Ti in Saqqara (probably circa 2700 BC).

Above: The Chephren pyramid in Giza with the stone Sphinx in the foreground; the Sphinx was constructed in circa 2700 or 2600 BC, probably as a guardian of the Giza plateau.

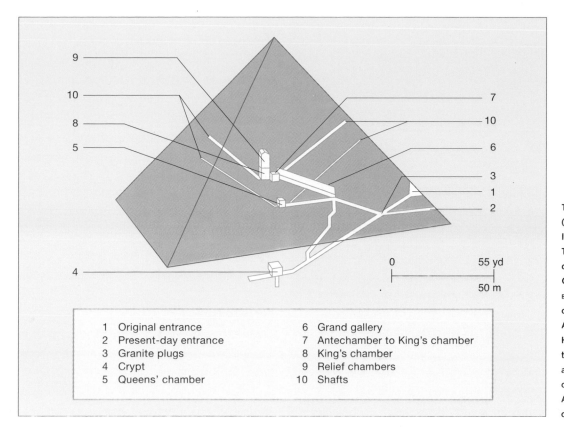

9
10
8
5
7
10
6
3
1
2

4

0   55 yd
|——————|
50 m

1	Original entrance	6	Grand gallery
2	Present-day entrance	7	Antechamber to King's chamber
3	Granite plugs	8	King's chamber
4	Crypt	9	Relief chambers
5	Queens' chamber	10	Shafts

THE CHEOPS PYRAMID (CROSSSECTION AND INTERNAL STRUCTURE) The tomb that was constructed for Pharaoh Cheops (circa 2620–2580 BC), with its chambers and corridors, carries the name Akhet-Khufu (Cheops's Horizon) and is the oldest of the three pyramids of Giza, as well as being the oldest of the Seven Wonders of the Ancient World and the only one that still survives.

THE OLD KINGDOM

The pharaohs of the Third to the Sixth Dynasties, who divided the kingdom into 38 nomes (administrative units), had to defend their initial godlike omnipotence as controllers of world events against the ever more popular cult of the sun (Ra, later Amun) as immortal chief god; the pharaoh was increasingly referred to as the "son of the sun"—a victory for the powerful priesthood. During this period, Egypt's characteristic culture, art, and religion were formed. The pharaohs demonstrated their "immortality" by means of vast tombs, the pyramids: beginning with the step pyramid of Zoser (circa 2690–2670 BC) in Saqqara, the bent and red pyramids of Sneferu (circa 2670–2620 BC), and the perfect pyramid of Cheops (circa 2620–2580 BC)—the oldest of the Seven Wonders of the Ancient World—through to those of his successors Chephren (circa 2572–2546 BC) and Mycerinus (circa 2539–2511 BC) in Giza. The pyramids were not, as was previously assumed, built by slaves, but by Egyptian artisans and builders who, as excavated workers' settlements show, were very well provided for.

> ▶ THE EGYPTIAN SCRIPT
> Hieroglyphs ("holy writing") remained an enigma for a long time and were deciphered in 1822 by the French archaeologist Jean-François Champollion. The earliest examples date from circa 3500 BC; they were in everyday use from circa 3100 BC, initially comprising some 700 characters, and rising in the late Ptolemaic period to almost 7,000 characters. Champollion recognized that the hieroglyphs represented not merely a pictorial script, but a combination of pictograms and a consonant script. The Egyptians also derived from them a cursive written and clerical script (hieratic script).

The gods: Isis and Osiris

Although the ancient Egyptian religion underwent many changes over the centuries, it exhibits the unity characteristic of a rich pantheon with developed mythologies, a particularly striking element of which are the gods with animal heads. The Egyptians and their pharaohs always held the gods in high esteem.

Papyrus showing a scene from the Egyptian Book of the Dead; from the tomb of Lady Cheritwebeshet (Twenty-First Dynasty, circa 1030–950 BC, Egyptian Museum, Cairo, Egypt).

In the early period, individual religious centers developed different families of gods, theogonies (divine genealogies), and creation myths in which various gods played the leading roles.

A pivotal myth tells of the divine siblings and rulers Isis and Osiris. Osiris, initially the ruler (pharaoh) and controller of worlds, is lured into a chest by his jealous brother Set, who then dismembers him and scatters the pieces all over the world. His loving wife Isis collects up all the pieces (with the exception of the reproductive organ) and puts them together again; Osiris, represented with green facial features, is now lord of the underworld, the realm of the dead.

Set and Horus

The falcon god Horus, the son of Isis and Osiris and the protector of the pharaoh and the cosmic order, has numerous adventures battling his uncle Set. The myth has clear political overtones: Set was originally the protective deity of Upper Egypt, lord of the desert and the nomadic elective kingdom, whereas Horus, on the other hand, was the god of Lower Egypt and the lord of permanent settlements, of fertility, and the (urban) order of the hereditary pharaonic lines. He is shown as overcoming the underlying hostility to life of the desert and "disorder."

Anubis, Thoth, and Khnum

Some of the animal-headed gods were accorded particular veneration, for example, Anubis, the black-headed jackal and son of the sun god Re or Osiris, who helped Isis put Osiris back together again and embalmed the corpse. He is the venerated guardian (especially in necropoles) of correct embalming and mummification rituals. Thoth, represented as an ibis or a baboon, is the god, worshiped particularly in Hermopolis, of knowledge and of scribes, record keeper for the judgment of the dead and the inventor of language and writing.

Representation of the divine trinity from the time of Pharaoh Osorkon II (874–850 BC): Osiris, flanked by his wife Isis and his son Horus.

The ram-headed lord of creation, Khnum, created gods, people, and all living things on his potter's wheel and brought them to life with his staff. Alongside each human, he created a double (identically represented), or *ka* (personality), a separate part of the soul that continued to exist as a protecting spirit even after death. The complex spiritual teachings of the Egyptians also recognized the *ba*, an independent part of the soul that after death left the body during the day but returned to it at night, and, particularly in the case of the pharaohs, the *akh*, the transfiguration from human to divine, the idealized form of all human attributes, the person's renown and reputation; in the chambers of the dead, the *akh* is represented as a pharaoh accompanying the body on the solar barque.

Mural of the jackal-headed god Anubis, protector of embalming the dead, from the tomb of the Pharaoh Haremhab (1319–1292 BC).

"O, my lord, who runs through eternity
who will be there forever;
Osiris, first of the westerners, the justified god,
lord of eternity, ruler of infinity.
Those who are are with you, gods as well as people."

From a prayer to Osiris

Mural showing the judgment of the dead, from the tomb of Ra Nentwy (circa 664–525 BC): the heart of the dead person is weighed against the feather of *ma'at* or divine justice.

THE MIDDLE KINGDOM: COLLAPSE AND REUNIFICATION OF THE KINGDOM

In the First Intermediate period (circa 2200–2055 BC), the unity of the Egyptian Kingdom was destroyed by competition from Thebes in the south and Herakleopolis in the north, each of which had their own pharaonic dynasties, hierarchies of gods, and cults.

In the era of the Middle Kingdom (circa 2055–1650 BC), Thebes under Nentuhotep II (circa 2046–1995 BC) initiated a reunification of the kingdom that was completed under Amenemhet I (circa 1976–1947 BC): the latter installed the cult of Amun as the chief god of the kingdom, moved the royal city from Thebes to Itj-Taui, and advanced far into Nubia and Libya, most of whose people became Egyptian vassals, mercenaries, and laborers. Under Amenemhet and his successors, who built pyramids as well as imposing royal palaces and temple complexes, Egypt became a world power with far-reaching trade links, especially in the Phoenician region (*see p. 88*), which was dominated by Egypt for centuries. Under Sesostris III (circa 1872–1852 BC), who conquered and fortified the whole of Nubia as far as the second Nile cataract, and his son Amenemhet III (circa 1852–1805 BC), Egypt was the leading economic and military power

The Ramesseum, the imposing temple complex of Ramses II (1279–1213 BC) in Luxor, in which he had his alleged victory at Kadesh in 1274 BC glorified.

▶ MA'AT AND THE PHARAOH

The concept of *Ma'at* was represented either in the person of a goddess (daughter of the sun god Re) with an ostrich feather on her head, or as the *ma'at* feather (as the gift of Re to the world). *Ma'at* was the expression of the principle of justice and truth, or the just world order that was pleasing to the gods; it was matched by the opposing principle of chaos (*Isfet*). The pharaoh's main task was to maintain *ma'at* by means of cult rituals balancing order and chaos; in order to do so, he himself had to rule "according to *ma'at*." At the judgment of the dead, the god Anubis weighed the heart of the dead person against the *ma'at* feather; the scale pans had to balance.

THE INVASION OF THE HYKSOS

The Second Intermediate Period (circa 1650–1540 BC) was dominated by the invasion of Semitic peoples from the east, who were called Hyksos. From their royal city Avaris (Tanis), they ruled over the Nile delta and Lower Egypt, but soon adopted Egyptian culture—they were far from being the barbarians they were for so long considered to be. However, some local Egyptian dynasties put up fierce resistance, and in circa 1540 BC, Pharaoh Ahmose (circa 1550–1525 BC) succeeded in driving back the Hyksos and bringing the kingdom under his control; in 1532 BC he occupied Avaris, thereby becoming the founder of the Eighteenth Dynasty and the illustrious New Kingdom.

in the entire Middle East; the intensification of agriculture through the building of dams and irrigation systems and the draining of wetlands brought the kingdom considerable prosperity.

Statue of the Pharaoh Sesostris III (1872–1852 BC); he strengthened the kingdom politically and economically, had numerous canal structures built, and extended Egypt's southern borders into Nubia as far as the second Nile cataract.

LIFE AFTER DEATH

If at the judgment of the dead the dead person was found to be just according to *ma'at* (*see box, p. 71*), they were led by Horus to everlasting life. Here, they would have the same status as on earth, whether as a farmer or a pharaoh; their needs in the life everlasting were seen as being the same as on earth. In order that the pharaoh, in particular, would have a pleasant life on the other side, his tomb was set out like a house, with connecting rooms that had (false) doors, murals, food, and rich grave goods such as gold, jewelry, clothing, furniture, and games. At first, the sarcophagus of the pharaoh was interred together with living people who were to function as servants and soldiers on the other side; later, these were replaced by small wooden figures (*ushebti*).

CHAMBERS OF THE DEAD, PYRAMIDS, AND *MASTABAS*

The most beautiful and splendid underground tomb chambers and complexes for pharaohs after the Eighteenth Dynasty are found in the Valley of the Kings; most notable among these is the complex of Sethos I (*see p. 78*). From the Third Dynasty, the pharaohs fitted out pyramids that may also have served ritual or astronomical purposes as tomb chambers with a system of passageways, often labyrinthine, false passageways, and shafts. The first dynasties, and some later ones, built so-called *mastabas* (literally: "stone benches") as tombs that were flat-topped, truncated pyramids on a rectangular base. The cult of the dead led to the establishment of entire cities of the dead, the necropolises; most of the pharaohs' tombs were plundered in ancient times, and some of them were even reused by subsequent rulers.

EMBALMING AND MUMMIFICATION

A particular feature of the Egyptian cult of the dead was the preservation and mummification of the corpse; it was based upon the idea of eternal life being a continuation of the bodily life on earth and the need for the *ba* soul (*see p.* 69) always to be able to find its undamaged body. The prototype of the mummy is taken to be the reassembled and bandaged body of the god Osiris, the lord of the realm of the dead.

In the Old Kingdom, the corpses of the pharaohs were merely anointed with herbs and oils and then wrapped in bandages; little thus remains of them. From the Fourth Dynasty, the conservation techniques improved: the internal organs were removed and put in four canopic jars—for the liver, lungs, stomach, and intestines—(the canopic gods were supposed to be the four sons of Horus). After the Middle Kingdom, the brain was also removed, and the body was desalinated with natron (mummified). Over a period of 70 days and in accordance with strict rituals (including the final "opening of the mouth" ritual, designed to "revive" the pharaoh for life on the other side), it was wrapped by the priests in linen bandages, in which amulets and figurines to bring good fortune were bound. The New Kingdom made mummification a real art form. Some of the best-preserved royal mummies date from this period, such as those of Sethos I and Ramses II; from these, it is possible to glean information about living conditions, diseases, and family relationships.

Mural showing an Egyptian pharaoh with scenes and hieroglyphs from tomb No. 24 in the Valley of the Kings; it is not known for whom it was built (Eighteenth Dynasty, circa 1532–1292 BC).

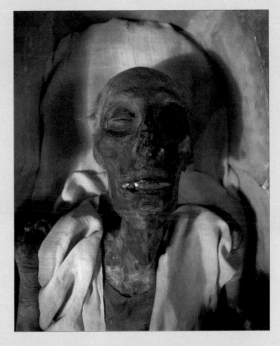

The well-preserved mummy of Ramses II (1279–1213 BC), who died at the age of about ninety and who, as a great builder and as the Pharaoh of the Bible, was one of the most famous rulers of Egypt (Egyptian Museum, Cairo, Egypt).

" I have not inflicted pain nor let [anyone] go hungry,
I have caused no tears.
I have not killed,
nor have I ordered others to kill;
I have caused no one harm . . . .
I am pure, I am pure! "

From the justification at the judgment of the dead, spell 125

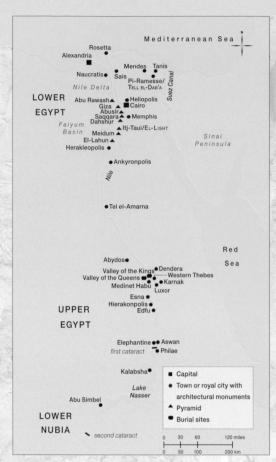

Mediterranean Sea

Rosetta
Alexandria

Mendes Tanis
Naucratis Pi-Ramesse/
Sais TELL EL-DAB'A

**LOWER
EGYPT**

Nile Delta

Abu Rawash Heliopolis
Giza Cairo
Abusir
Saqqara Memphis
Dahshur

*Faiyum
Basin*
Meidum Itj-Taui/EL-LISHT
El-Lahun
Herakleopolis

*Sinai
Peninsula*

Nile

Ankyronpolis

Tel el-Amarna

*Red
Sea*

Abydos
Valley of the Kings Dendera
Valley of the Queens Western Thebes
Medinet Habu Karnak
Luxor
Esna
Hierakonpolis
Edfu

**UPPER
EGYPT**

Elephantine Aswan
first cataract Philae

Kalabsha

■ Capital
● Town or royal city with
   architectural monuments
▲ Pyramid
■ Burial sites

*Lake
Nasser*
Abu Simbel

**LOWER
NUBIA**

second cataract

0   30   60   120 miles
0   50   100   200 km

(see p. 25)

THE EGYPTIAN KINGDOM
The map shows the
Egyptian Kingdom with
its various royal cities,
pyramids, and cult sites
dating from different
periods of its long and
checkered history.

constituted the golden age of Egyptian power and culture. Its rise began with Tuthmosis I (circa 1504–1492 BC), who in several military campaigns managed to reoccupy Nubia (Sudan) and advanced well into the Near East and Syria, where he made vassals of numerous trading centers and embarked upon the lengthy war against the Hurrian Kingdom of Mitanni (*see p. 25*); the well-organized Egyptian army with its various fighting units was subsequently to become an important power factor. Tuthmosis brought the gold and ivory trade with the African interior under his control, making Egypt immeasurably rich. During his reign, the theological amalgamation of Amun and Re into the chief god Amun-Re was completed, and by means of massive construction projects such as fortifications, mortuary temples, and obelisks, he began the process that was then continued by his successors whereby the pharaohs erected imposing monuments, over and above the pyramids, to preserve their memory for posterity. Tuthmosis was the first in a long series of pharaohs to be buried in the Valley of the Kings.

THE NEW KINGDOM: DISPLAY OF POWER UNDER TUTHMOSIS I

The New Kingdom of the Eighteenth to Nineteenth Dynasties (circa 1540–1070 BC)

HATSHEPSUT, THE "GREAT PHARAOH"

After the death of her sickly brother/spouse Tuthmosis II (circa 1492–1490 BC), the daughter of Tuthmosis I ascended the throne (circa

1490–1468 BC). Hatshepsut was aware of the unusual nature of this step: she had herself depicted as a man, the "Great Pharaoh," and sent out an expedition to the "land of gold" in the east, Punt (probably Ethiopia), that brought frankincense, myrrh, and cedar and ebony wood back to Egypt. The mortuary temple in Deir el-Bahari and the extended temple of Amun in Karnak are testaments to Hatshepsut's peaceful and stable reign and its architecture; she bequeathed a well-ordered kingdom to her stepson Tuthmosis III (see p. 76). However, in later times attempts were made to erase the memory of her by chiseling out her silhouette and her name cartouche—probably because she had been a woman on the throne.

View of the main hall of the great Amun temple of Tuthmosis III (circa 1490–1437 BC) in Karnak; this pharaoh, often described as "Egypt's Napoleon," was victorious in all his battles and led the kingdom to its greatest extent and power.

AMENHOTEP III, THE BUILDER

The greatest builder before Ramses II was Amenhotep III (circa 1388–1351 BC), who extended the temple complex at Karnak by adding a temple containing 700 statues of the lion goddess Sekhmet, who was believed to ward off plagues. He built the largest statue in Egypt as well as the largest Egyptian temple complex, in Kom el-Hatan (Thebes). The so-called Colossi of Memnon, statues of Amenhotep, survive to this day.

Amenhotep III favored the trends toward rationalism in religion and encouraged the centralistic sun cult of the god Aten—partly in order to diminish the power of the traditional priesthood and the local temples; in this way he prepared the ground for the cult revolution of his son Akhenaten (see p. 76). His reign was a stable period in which no wars occurred, and turned out to be a "golden age" of prosperity and art. He preferred realistic sculptures, again paving the way for his son's style of art.

The enormous mortuary temple of Hatshepsut (circa 1490–1468 BC) in Deir el-Bahari; this gifted ruler, aware of her power, had herself represented as the "Great Pharaoh."

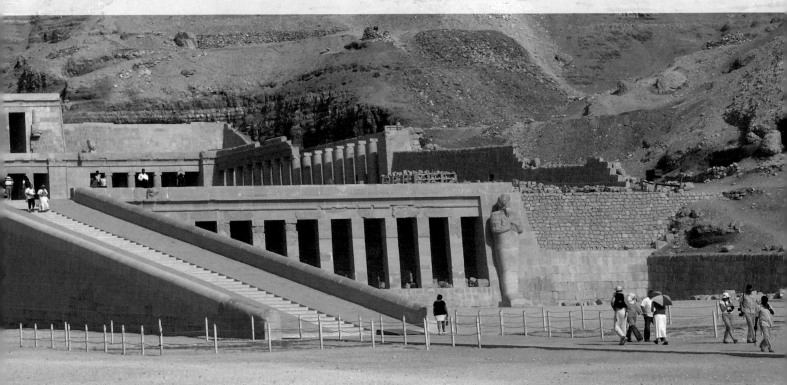

averting a Hurrian invasion, but also achieving, in 1457 BC, near the west Syrian town of Kadesh (in present-day Lebanon), a magnificent victory over a coalition of (allegedly) 330 Syrian princes, which gained him immeasurable spoils of war. Moreover, in 17 successful campaigns he forced the Syrian cities to capitulate and take the vassal's oath of loyalty, and then advanced farther east across the Euphrates, where the Hittites and Babylon also paid him tribute; he also occupied Nubia as far as the fourth Nile cataract, thereby bringing it completely under Egyptian control. He energetically set about remodeling the army and the administration of the kingdom and the occupied regions and split the role of the vizier into two top official posts, one for Upper Egypt and one for Lower Egypt. His powerful trading fleet expanded trade in the Mediterranean, especially in the Aegean; Egypt under Tuthmosis thus reached its greatest geographical extent and also its zenith not only in military but also in economic terms.

Amenhotep IV (Akhenaten) (1351–1334 BC) with his wife Nefertiti and his daughters: a family idyll under the protective rays of the sun god Aten.

TUTHMOSIS III, THE KINGDOM AT ITS ZENITH

Tuthmosis III (circa 1490–1437 BC), the most prominent military commander among the pharaohs, was initially co-regent with his stepmother Hatshepsut. He made astonishing advances, not only

The Colossi of Memnon, as they are known, in Luxor are colossal statues of the pharaoh and master builder Amenhotep III (1388–1351 BC).

AKHENATEN, THE "HERETIC KING"

Amenhotep IV, known under the name Akhenaten ("beloved of Aten") (circa 1351–1334 BC), carried out a religious revolution, for which his father Amenhotep III

(see p. 75) had paved the way. The myriad gods were replaced by the compulsory cult of the life-giver Aten, represented by the solar disk, and a new imperial and cult center was constructed at Akhetaten (El-Amarna). In this way, Akhenaten took power away from the traditional Amun priests at Thebes and placed himself and his co-regent wife Nefertiti (whose famous bust was found in AD 1912 and taken to Berlin) at the head of the cult. In art he also introduced a new realistic style of representation that at times openly caricatured its subjects (the "Amarna style"). Opinion is divided as to whether he introduced the first monotheistic religion in history, or whether he simply favored Aten; in any case, he acted decisively in defiance of the priesthood's opposition. His successors, however, vilified the memory of the "heretic king" and destroyed his statues.

THE LATE FAME OF TUTANKHAMUN

Tutankhamun (originally Tut ankh-Aten, circa 1333–1323 BC), probably a son of Akhenaten, ruled as a boy-king and undid Akhenaten's reforms; he died before reaching the age of twenty, as a result of either accident or murder. His personality and reign would hardly have left a trace on history, were it not for the fact that in AD 1922 the English archaeologist Howard Carter discovered his grave, the only pharaoh's tomb to be found undamaged, in the Valley of the Kings. The excavation of the site that included valuable grave goods and the nested sarcophagus containing the mummy, and most notably the golden death mask of the pharaoh, is regarded as the greatest archaeological sensation of the twentieth century.

"Everlasting is the being of Re,
Son of Re, Tuthmosis, beautiful to behold,
the justified one,
he knows these images.
His mouth is fashioned for the spirits,
he goes in and out of the Underworld.
He speaks to the living in all eternity."

Text of the wall papyrus in the tomb of Tuthmosis III, circa 1440 BC

The famous gold mask of the young Tutankhamun (1333–1323 BC) that Howard Carter found in the undamaged sarcophagus of the pharaoh in 1922 (Egyptian Museum, Cairo, Egypt).

RAMSES II AND HIS SUCCESSORS

The Nineteenth Dynasty (1292–1186 BC) provided Egypt with one final period as a great power: Sethos I (1290–1279 BC), builder of the Abydos temple complex, whose tomb is probably the most magnificent, occupied the west coast of Syria and brought the Hittite vassal cities of Amurru and Kadesh under his control, making conflict with the Hittite Kingdom unavoidable.

His son Ramses II (1279–1213 BC) advanced into Syria in 1276 BC, but two years later suffered a painful defeat against the Hittites (*see p. 44*) at Kadesh, following which he concluded peace in 1259 BC. Eventually he devoted himself to massive building projects, particularly in Karnak, Luxor, Bubastis, and Thebes (the Ramesseum), extended all the kingdom's important temples, and built the new royal city, Pi-Ramesse. Ramses II was highly gifted at self-portrayal, and wanted his fame to outshine that of all his predecessors, as is particularly evident from his colossal statues at Abu Simbel. He surrounded his royal household with hitherto undreamed of luxury and maintained trading relations with the entire known world of that time. The mummy of this pharaoh, who died aged around ninety, was discovered in 1881 and is one of the best researched. Ramses II (the biblical pharaoh at the time of the Israelite people's "Egyptian bondage") is one of the best-known characters in ancient history.

The last powerful pharaoh was Ramses III (1184–1152 BC) of the Twentieth Dynasty; he successfully repelled invasions by the Libyans and especially the attack on Egypt by the Sea Peoples. Nonetheless, Egypt lost the Syrian coastal region and with it important trading links. Under Ramses IV to XI (1152–1070 BC), central power was weakened by internal unrest; the empire went into decline.

Colossus of Pharaoh Ramses II (1279–1213 BC) in the great Temple of Amun at Luxor; the self-portrayals of this great pharaoh outdid even those of his predecessors.

The Late Period

The Late Period (circa 700–332 BC) was characterized by the dominance of the Amun priests of Thebes and of the military commanders; Tanis became the new royal city. From 853 BC, Egypt was besieged by the Assyrians several times. During the reigns of Piye (747–716 BC) and Shabaka (716–702 BC), the extremely successful Twenty-Fifth Dynasty of Kushite (circa 760–664/652 BC), "Black Pharaohs" from Nubia conquered Egypt from their kingdom of Napata (Sudan) (see p. 270); they made a show of taking on the traditions of ancient Egypt.

Taharqa (690–664 BC) took up the battle against the Assyrians, who conquered northern Egypt and Memphis in 671/669 BC and then installed the Twenty-Sixth Dynasty with Psammetichus I (664–610 BC) as pharaoh. In 653 BC, the latter made himself independent in his royal city of Sais and also successfully repelled the Babylonians. His son Necho II (610–595 BC) once again occupied the Phoenician region and created the Egyptian navy using Phoenician and Greek mercenaries. During the periods 525–404 BC and 343–332 BC, the Persians ruled over Egypt (as the Twenty-Seventh and Thirty-First Dynasties).

The seated colossi of Ramses II at Abu Simbel; in 1964–1968, when the entire site was threatened with flooding due to the construction of the Aswan high dam, an international rescue operation was mounted and they were dismantled into 1,036 blocks and reerected on a site farther inland that was 210 ft. (64 m) higher.

Alexander the Great
(356–323 BC); he conquered
Egypt in 332 BC and was so
fascinated by the Egyptian
cult of the ruler, that he
had himself portrayed as a
divine pharaoh (Hellenistic
sculpture, second/first
century BC)

THE LATER PTOLEMIES

Under Ptolemy II Philadelphus (285–246 BC), initially co-regent with his father, and his sister-wife Arsinoe II (circa 316–270 BC), Alexandria and the royal court became a world center for art and science. Ptolemy II, an important legislator, elevated his parents and his deceased wife to the status of gods, thereby founding the pharaonic ruler cult of the Ptolemy Dynasty. He pursued an active trade policy, especially with India, recognized the future greatness of Rome, and in 273 BC established trading relations with the Roman Empire. He expanded Egypt by adding significant territories in Ethiopia and Arabia. The long-running battle with the Seleucids (*see p. 114*) for control over the west Syrian coastal region was then won decisively by Ptolemy II Euergetes (246–221 BC), who took Antioch and pressed forward as far as the Euphrates, as well as gaining large areas of Asia Minor and Thrace. In 243 BC he became

ALEXANDER AND PTOLEMY I

Alexander the Great occupied Egypt in 332 BC. Upon his death in 323 BC, Egypt fell to a friend of his youth, the army commander and biographer Ptolemy I Soter (367–283 BC), who took on the title of king in 306 BC. The founder of the Ptolemy Dynasty steeped himself more than any other Diadochi in the cultural traditions of his kingdom, pursued farsighted financial and marriage policies, achieved conciliation between Egypt and Greece, and supported the arts and sciences in his capital city of Alexandria. In 299 BC he began construction of the Lighthouse of Alexandria (Pharos), which was completed by his son, of the Serapeon, dedicated to the bull cult of Serapis, and of the Library of Alexandria, founded in 284 BC, which became the center of Hellenistic intellectual life.

Cleopatra VII (51–30 BC), the last pharaoh, here represented as the goddess Isis; she put all her efforts into the power struggle against the Roman military commanders and eventually lost to Octavian. Her suicide ended the classical era of Hellenism.

hegemon of the Achaean League of Greek cities in Asia Minor; he left a legacy of administrative and calendar reforms.

The later Ptolemies had to quell rebellions in the territories that they had gained and are notorious for having engaged in unusually bloody battles with their siblings and other family members. These provided Rome with the opportunity to intervene. Ptolemy XII Neos Dionysos (80–58 and 55–51 BC) was totally dependent on Rome and decimated the state's finances with building projects in the pharaonic style.

CLEOPATRA'S POWER PLAY

In the struggle for power, Ptolemy XII's daughter Cleopatra VII (51–30 BC) removed her younger co-regent brothers Ptolemy XIII (51–47 BC) and Ptolemy XIV (47–44 BC); in 48 BC, thrown off the throne, she put herself under the protection of Julius Caesar, became his lover, and made

> **"However, her death happened extremely rapidly and without the guards assigned to her noticing the slightest thing. For as they came running and opened the door, they found Cleopatra already dead, adorned in her regal splendor, lying on a golden bed . . . . It is said now that a snake (cobra) had been brought in to her, hidden under figs and leaves in a basket . . . . "**
>
> From Plutarch's life of Mark Antony, first century AD

their son Ptolemy XV Caesarion her co-regent (47–30 BC). In the subsequent internal power struggle in Rome, Cleopatra allied herself in 41/40 BC with Mark Antony, whom she secretly married a few years later; the couple dreamed of kingdoms in the east for themselves and their three children. Following the defeat at Actium (*see p. 124*) in 30 BC, she committed suicide by allowing a cobra to bite her, in order not to fall into the hands of the victor, Octavian. The kingdom of the pharaohs then became a province of Rome.

The Lighthouse of Alexandria (Pharos), one of the Seven Wonders of the Ancient World (engraving by Joseph Fischer von Erlach, 1721).

Ancient Israel

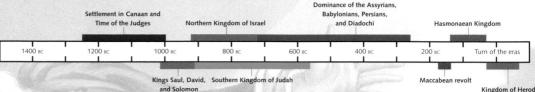

	Settlement in Canaan and Time of the Judges		Northern Kingdom of Israel		Dominance of the Assyrians, Babylonians, Persians, and Diadochi		Hasmonaean Kingdom	

| 1400 BC | 1200 BC | 1000 BC | 800 BC | 600 BC | 400 BC | 200 BC | Turn of the eras |

Kings Saul, David, and Solomon — Southern Kingdom of Judah — Maccabean revolt — Kingdom of Herod the Great and the Herodian Dynasty

The intention here is to trace not the spiritual/religious history of Judaism as the monotheistic religion of the "covenant with Yahweh," but the history of the ancient kingdoms of Israel, whose culture first blossomed under the biblical kings.

THE BEGINNINGS

The Semitic Israelites, who regarded Abraham of Ur (*see p. 20*) as their progenitor, were livestock-rearing nomads and seminomads, who later organized themselves into 12 tribes (of the 12 sons of Jacob in the Bible). Between 1250 and 1100 BC, the weakening of the Mesopotamian empires brought about by the invasion of the Sea Peoples made it possible for them to settle in Canaan. In the Bible, the Israelites were at first under Egyptian bondage—probably under Pharaoh Ramses II (*see p. 78*)—and then, under the leadership of their chief prophet Moses, who received the Torah, God's commandments, on Mount Sinai,

Background image: Abraham, out of obedience, offers his son Isaac as a sacrifice, which God ultimately prevents from happening (Bible illustration, circa 1860).

Above: King David leads a procession to the holy district of Jerusalem (painting by Luigi Ademollo, early nineteenth century).

moved to the land that had been "promised" to them. Once there, they had to hold their ground against other peoples and initially organized themselves under leaders called the judges; as advisors and preachers, their prophets also played an important political role. The last judge and prophet was Samuel (eleventh century BC).

SAUL AND DAVID

In around 1020 BC, Saul became the first military commander-king of Israel; he lived in Gibeah (El-Djib), and proved himself in battle against the Semitic Amorites and the Philistine Sea Peoples, against whom he ultimately fell in battle. The Bible describes him as being an unbalanced character who fails to live up to David, the hopeful fighter, to whom God's blessing is eventually transferred.

According to the Bible, David (circa 1000–965 BC) extended his kingdom against the Philistines in the north as far as Baalbek and Damascus, in the east as far as Moab, in the south as far as the Red Sea, and in the west as far as the Mediterranean coast. He brought the Ark of the Covenant, the Israelites' most sacred object, to Jerusalem, the capital city of the southern tribes, and made his city-state and the surrounding area the spiritual and religious center of the Israelites. In the Jewish history books he is depicted as a shining light, despite the personal failings mentioned in the Bible; the Jews believe that their future Messiah will come "from the house of David."

KING SOLOMON

It was not until the reign of David's son Solomon (circa 965–926 BC), who split the state into 12 districts and had a standing army, that the foundations for a kingdom with a well-developed public administration were laid. He traded intensively with all the neighboring states, especially with the Phoenician city of Tyre (see p. 90), and even traded with the south Arabian Queen of Sheba (see p. 47). Israel became wealthy, allowing its king a life

of luxury (frowned upon by the Bible) with a huge harem. Solomon had a magnificent temple for the Yahweh cult built in Jerusalem. The Bible praises his wisdom and righteousness (Judgment of Solomon, 1 Kgs 3:16–28), and several books of the Old Testament are ascribed to him (Proverbs, Ecclesiastes, Song of Songs, and the Book of Wisdom).

Moses, on his return from Mount Sinai, dashes the tablets of the law to the ground in his anger that the Israelites have in the meantime been worshiping the golden calf (Bible illustration by Gustave Doré, 1866).

" All the tribes of Israel came to David at Hebron and said, 'We are your own flesh and blood. In the past, while Saul was king over us, you were the one who led Israel on their military campaigns. And the Lord said to you, "You shall shepherd my people Israel, and you shall become their ruler."' . . . they anointed David king over Israel. "

From the second Book of Samuel, chapter 5, verses 1–3
(New International Version)

Divided Kingdom: The Northern Kingdom of Israel

Solomon's harsh treatment of the northern tribes led in 926 BC to the secession of the north to form the Kingdom of Israel under Jeroboam I (926–907 BC), who created a counterbalance to Jerusalem's central position in the cult by reviving the old Yahweh cult sites of Bethel and Dan. The high proportion of Phoenicians and Canaanites in the northern kingdom, together with defensive battles against the Moabites and Arameans, brought Israel times of unrest and violence. King Omri (882–871 BC) made Samaria his capital, and his son Ahab (871–852 BC) permitted the Baal cult in Israel. This led to Jehu (845–818 BC) overthrowing the Omride Dynasty, killing the Baal priests, and reinstating the Yahweh cult. While Israel was paying tribute to the Assyrians and following a period in which the culture and the economy flourished under Jeroboam II (781–742 BC), Israel became a target of Assyrian expansionism. When, in alliance with Egypt, the last king, Hoshea (731–722 BC), refused to pay the high levels of tribute, the Assyrians conquered and occupied the northern kingdom in 722 BC.

The Southern Kingdom of Judah

Solomon's son Rehaboam (926–910 BC) and his successors were recognized only in the southern

Model of the second temple of Jerusalem that was constructed in circa 520 BC near the old Temple of Solomon.

kingdom. The Bible tells of the lapse in faith of several kings and their conversion to the cult of Baal, of rebellions, and of mixed success in battles against the Arameans and the Edomites. Under Azariah (Uzziah, 783–742 BC), Judah developed into a strong power, but under Ahaz (735–715 BC) became a vassal of the Assyrians. Hezekiah (727–698 BC), who dared to rise up against the Assyrians, undertook a comprehensive religious reform, finally establishing the Yahweh cult in Judah. Jehoiakim (609–598 BC), who refused to pay tribute to the new great power, Babylon, was besieged by Nebuchadnezzar II (see p. 34) and was deported to Babylon. In 587 BC, following an attempted revolt by the last king, Zedekiah (597–587 BC), Nebuchadnezzar vanquished the southern kingdom, plundered Jerusalem, and destroyed the temple.

BABYLONIAN EXILE AND RETURN

While in exile in Babylon, some of the Jewish nobility converted to Babylonian cults. When Persian King Cyrus the Great conquered Babylon in 539 BC, he allowed the Jews to return to Judea, at the same time giving them complete religious freedom, and also rebuilt the destroyed temple in Jerusalem. In around 450 BC the Jewish priests there began editing the canon of holy writing (the Tanakh, the Hebrew Bible, which corresponds to the main books of the Old Testament) into its final form. The Israelites organized themselves politically and in relation to religious matters under the leadership of the high priests or priest-kings of the Zadokite Dynasty, and followed a holy law, the Torah, which they saw as a code for living. Under Ezra (circa 458 BC), with backing of the Persians, there was a fundamental reform of the cult and self-governing Jewish communities.

THE KINGDOMS OF ISRAEL AND JUDAH
The map shows the two rival kingdoms, Israel in the north and Judah in the south, with their capital cities of Samaria and Jerusalem. The southern kingdom was conquered in 721 BC by the Assyrians, the northern kingdom in 587 BC by the Babylonians.

A Samaritan village on Mount Gerizim (Samaria, West Bank): The Samaritans, who remain an independent religious community to this day, regard Mount Gerizim as their religious center.

"So Jehu destroyed Baal worship in Israel . . . . The Lord said to Jehu, 'Because you have done well in accomplishing what is right in my eyes and have done to the house of Ahab all I had in mind to do, your descendants will sit on the throne of Israel to the fourth generation.'"

From the second Book of Kings, chapter 10, verses 28 and 30
(New International Version)

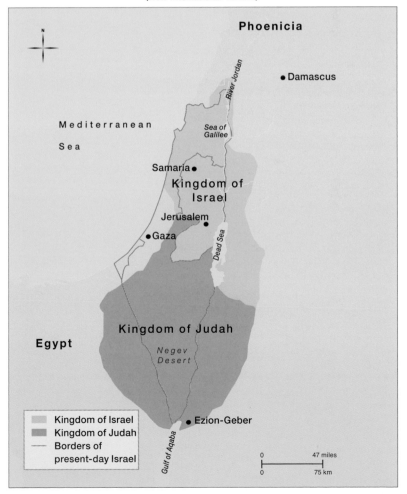

The Maccabean revolt

Under the Ptolemies (301–198 BC) and the Seleucids (after 198 BC), the Israelites enjoyed religious freedom. This changed when, in the wake of a struggle for power among the high priests, Seleucid King Antiochos IV Epiphanes (175–164 BC) raided the temple treasure of Jerusalem to finance his military campaigns and then attempted to enforce observance of the Hellenistic cult of the king in Judea and in the temple. The Judeans rose up in 167 BC under Mattathias and his sons Judas Maccabeus ("the Hammer," 166–160 BC) (who brought almost the whole of Judea, including Jerusalem, under his control and in 164 BC reinstated the exclusive position of the Yahweh cult—which is what the Jewish festival of Hanukkah remembers), Jonathan (160–143 BC), who continued the fight, and Simon (143–134 BC), who expanded the territory and in 141 BC became hereditary high priest.

The Hasmoneans

Simon's successors John Hyrcanos I (134–104 BC) and Alexander Jannaeus (103–77 BC) established the rule of the Hasmoneans; they destroyed the rival temple in Samaria and brought the whole of Idumea and Galilee under their control. The kingdom's elite turned to Hellenistic culture, which meant that there were repeated revolts by religious zealots, particularly by the Pharisees against the supporters of the Hasmoneans, the Sadducees. The Romans, who occupied Judea in 66 BC, used the internal conflict among the Hasmonean claimants to the throne after 67 BC as an opportunity to implement their policies, and installed their trusted ally, Antipater the Idumaean (48–43 BC), alongside the Hasmoneans, who were then reduced to purely priestly functions.

Herod the Great and the end of the kingdom

Antipater's son, Herod the Great (37–4 BC), got rid of the Hasmonean rulers and established a kingdom under Roman protection in which Jews and Greeks had equal rights. He succeeded in pacifying the religious camps and notwithstanding his denunciation as a "Roman vassal" by the Zealots, he had the mighty temple of Jerusalem built. He divided the kingdom between his three sons (tetrarchs). The execution of John the Baptist, as well as the ministry and crucifixion of Jesus, took place during the rule of the tetrarch of Galilee, Herod Antipas (4 BC–AD 39).

The fortress of Masada on the Dead Sea, erected by Herod the Great and symbol of Jewish resistance. After the destruction of Jerusalem (in AD 70), 973 Zealots ("zealous for God") entrenched themselves here; when, in AD 73, after a three-year siege, the Romans captured the fortress with the help of an enormous ramp, almost all the defenders committed suicide.

Herod Agrippa I (AD 41–44) once again united Judea under his rule, while Herod Agrippa II (50–70) lost control of the government due to his mismanagement of the economy and rebellions by the fanatical Zealots. The Jewish Revolt, led by the Zealots (66–70), resulted in the capture of Jerusalem and the destruction of the temple by the Romans, who in 73 had the country under their control. A final uprising under Simon bar Kokhba ("son of a star," 132–135) led to an imperial ban on Jews settling in Jerusalem and to the dispersal of Jewish communities throughout the world (diaspora).

Above: Judas Maccabeus, leader of the revolt of the Zealots (166–160 BC), before the battle against the Seleucid general Nikanor, whom he defeated at Emmaus in 165 BC (wood engraving by Gustave Doré, nineteenth century).

Below: The surviving western Wall of the Temple built by Herod in Jerusalem circa 20 BC, the Wailing Wall, a holy place of prayer for Jews.

The Phoenicians

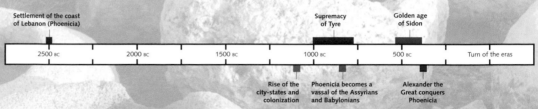

Settlement of the coast
of Lebanon (Phoenicia)

Supremacy
of Tyre

Golden age
of Sidon

| 2500 BC | 2000 BC | 1500 BC | 1000 BC | 500 BC | Turn of the eras |

Rise of the
city-states and
colonization

Phoenicia becomes a
vassal of the Assyrians
and Babylonians

Alexander the
Great conquers
Phoenicia

The northwest Semitic Phoenicians were the most famous seafaring and maritime trading people of antiquity. The name is a Greek exonym, derived from *phoenike* (purple country, from *phoinix*, purple-red), referring to an important item of export.

POLITICAL STRUCTURES, CULTURE, AND HISTORY

The Phoenicians, referred to in the Bible as Canaanites, established the first fortified settlements on the Mediterranean coast in around 2500 BC (in the region of present-day Lebanon) and fell under the influence of first the Egyptians, in

Background image: Stone troughs for catching rainwater in the Phoenician metropolis Byblos (present-day Jbeil).

Above: A Phoenician representation of a head. The significance or use of these artifacts, which were possibly associated with the cult of the dead, is not fully understood.

around 1800 BC, and then the Hittites, from circa 1400 BC. The invasion of the Sea Peoples allowed the rise from around 1100 BC of independent city-states, which did not feel themselves bound by any ties of unity, but rather competed against one another for trade and supremacy, with Tyre initially gaining the upper hand.

Most of the city-states were ruled by their own kings, with a council of elders as an advisory body; they worshiped their own pantheon of gods, headed by the city god Baal and the war and moon goddess Astarte. One of their most important achievements was the consonant script, probably developed by merchants, which was in general use from the eleventh century BC and an archetype of the modern alphabet (*see p. 28*). After their golden age (circa 1200–900 BC), from around 850 BC they became tribute-paying vassals of the Assyrians, who conquered the entire coastal region (apart from Tyre) in 745 BC, and subsequently of the Babylonians and Persians. The seizure of the whole region by Alexander the Great (in 333/332 BC) is generally seen as marking the end of the Phoenician civilization, which was absorbed into the Seleucid Kingdom (*see p. 114*).

TRADING AND MARITIME POWER

The Phoenicians used ships to colonize the coastal regions around the Mediterranean—by establishing colonies and trading posts in Upper Africa (Carthage), Cyprus, Sicily, and Sardinia, as well as on the Iberian Peninsula and the Canaries—and ventured as far as the northwest coast of England; their extensive nautical knowledge has frequently led to speculation that the Phoenicians may have been the first to discover America, before the Vikings and Columbus.

The Phoenicians traded in terracotta and glassware, precious metals, wine, olive oil, and textiles, as well as numerous goods that they obtained from other regions and trans-shipped into their port cities. Their principal exports, however, were textiles dyed with purple dye (extracted from the purple murex sea snail) that were exported to Greece, in particular, and the wood of the cedar of Lebanon that was mainly supplied to Egypt where it was used to build massive temple complexes, for shipbuilding, or for burning as incense; the cedar resin was also used in the embalming of mummies.

Depiction of a Phoenician trading vessel as they were built around the seventh century BC; with these ships, the Phoenicians dominated maritime trade.

Stone steles at a cult site (*tophet*) containing children's graves in Carthage (present-day Tunisia), possible evidence of child sacrifice. The Carthaginians adopted the gods and cults of their Phoenician homeland, particularly the worship of the chief god Baal (in Carthage Baal Hammon, *see box, p. 93*).

SHIPBUILDING AND NAVIGATION

The Phoenicians were among the greatest traders of their time and the secret of their power and prosperity lay in shipbuilding. The cedar stocks of Lebanon were felled on a drastic scale, which led to the desertification of whole areas of land; the original 1.25 million or so acres (approximately 500,000 ha) of cedar forest shrank, largely in ancient times, to the current level of only 845 acres (342 ha) of pure cedar stocks.

The Phoenicians built three types of ship, all of which could be rowed as well as sailed: round-hulled coastal ships for transporting heavy goods, warships with rams, and first and foremost the trading ships suitable for the high seas, with large holds and raised stem posts (extension of the keel). Phoenicians undertook the first circumnavigation of the African continent in circa 600 BC, at the behest of the Egyptian Pharaoh Necho II.

TYRE

Of the major Phoenician city-states—Tyre (Tur), Byblos (Jbeil), Sidon (Saida), Arados (Arwad), Tripolis (Tripoli), Ugarit (Ras Shamra), and Berytus (Beirut)—it was Tyre, made rich by the production of glass and purple dye, as well as the timber trade, which took the leading role between 1000 and 775 BC (including in the founding of Phoenician colonies), not least because of its position on a rocky island. King Hiram I (969–936 BC), who is mentioned several times in the Bible, delivered cedar wood to King Solomon for the construction of the Temple in Jerusalem (*see p. 83*). King Ittobaal II (887–856 BC) also achieved dominance over Sidon. From 858 BC, Tyre paid tribute to the Assyrians, but resisted Assyrian attempts to conquer it, and maintained its prosperity. Between 585 and 573 BC it withstood a 13-year siege by the Babylonians, but surrendered in 568 BC to Nebuchadnezzar II, who treated it leniently. Under Persian sovereignty from around 538 BC, Tyre made a stand against Alexander the Great, who conquered the city in 332 BC by building up a causeway.

BYBLOS AND SIDON

Byblos, which for a long time was called Gubla, was settled as long ago as around 5000 BC and had a city wall built around it in circa 2800 BC. It was predominantly the trade in cedar wood with Egypt, of which the city leaders were at times vassals, and the papyrus trade with Greece that made Byblos, the main access point to the Syrian/Phoenician trading region for the Egyptians, an early economic center to rival Ugarit from circa 1500 BC. Centuries later, in around 850 BC, Byblos became a vassal of the Assyrians.

Sidon was one of the first Phoenician centers to side with the Assyrians, but its kings rebelled several times against their demands for high tribute payments, which led to the destruction of the city by the Assyrians. Nebuchadnezzar II had Sidon rebuilt; the city achieved a late golden age as the key Mediterranean port of the Persian Achaemenid Empire from

approximately 570 BC. Although an attempted uprising in 350 BC led to its destruction by the Persians, the city was soon rebuilt again.

Ruins of an amphitheater in the important Phoenician port of Byblos (present-day Jbeil, Lebanon).

"This is the temple built by Jehimilk, King of Byblos. May Baal-Shamen and Baalat Gebal and the whole host of holy gods of Byblos extend his days."

From a dedicatory inscription in Byblos

One of the oldest cedar trees in Lebanon (photograph taken in 1955); cedar wood was used predominantly for shipbuilding and was one of the most important export items for the Phoenician cities, which at that time were trading throughout the known world.

Carthage

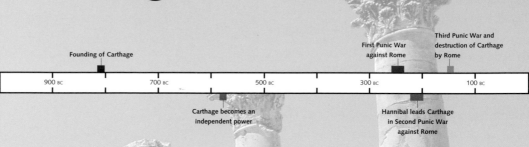

Founding of Carthage

First Punic War
against Rome

Third Punic War and
destruction of Carthage
by Rome

900 BC   700 BC   500 BC   300 BC   100 BC

Carthage becomes an
independent power

Hannibal leads Carthage
in Second Punic War
against Rome

The Carthaginians, descendants of the Phoenicians, called Punici by the Romans, made history primarily as a bitter enemy of Rome and through their great general Hannibal.

CITY-STATE AND ADMINISTRATION

Carthage, near present-day Tunis (Tunisia), was founded by Tyre as a Phoenician colony, probably after 814 BC. According to legend, the founding Queen Elissa (Roman: Dido) marked out the boundaries of the city with an ox hide cut into strips. The unhappy love affair between Dido and Aeneas related later by Virgil reflects the thorny relations between Carthage and Rome. Closely linked to its parent city of Tyre in the early days, Carthage became independent in around 580 BC, and in the battle for the Mediterranean against the Sicilian western Greeks it took over the Phoenician colonies on

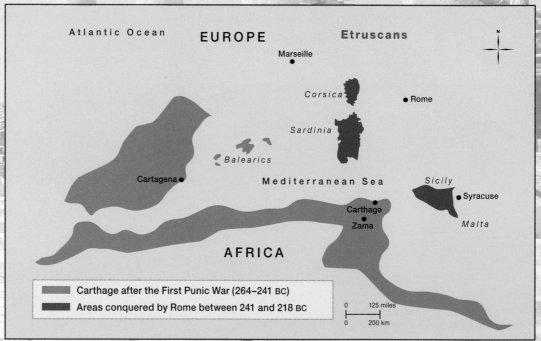

Atlantic Ocean   **EUROPE**   Etruscans

Marseille

Corsica

• Rome

Sardinia

Balearics

Cartagena •

Mediterranean Sea

Sicily

• Syracuse

Carthage
Zama

Malta

AFRICA

☐ Carthage after the First Punic War (264–241 BC)
☐ Areas conquered by Rome between 241 and 218 BC

0   125 miles
0   200 km

Background image: Remains of the mighty Thermae of Antoninus (constructed under Emperor Antoninus Pius, AD 138–161), a Roman development on the ruins of ancient Carthage.

THE CARTHAGINIAN EMPIRE

As a maritime power, at times the Carthaginians ruled the whole of the western Mediterranean and its coasts, but they engaged in fierce battles with the western Greeks on Sicily and eventually succumbed to Rome's superior forces when the latter's empire expanded into the Mediterranean region.

Sicily, Corsica, Sardinia, Upper Africa, and the southern coast of Spain.

The maritime and trading power was initially ruled by kings, but these were soon replaced by an oligarchy with democratic elements and a people's assembly. Its government was comparable to that of the Roman Republic. At its head stood two leading officials, elected every year (suffetes), then came the Senate, the most important state chamber, with a 30-strong executive body, and a supreme tribunal of judges consisting of 100 senators. At its height, the city of Carthage had 400,000 inhabitants, plus around 100,000 more in the surrounding agricultural areas (Megara).

The war fleet

The Carthaginian army consisted initially of native citizens, most of whom served in the navy, but later was increasingly supplemented with recruits from the Punic colonies and with mercenaries. During the battles with the western Greeks over Sicily, Carthage created a powerful war fleet, whose ships with their ram bows could hold up to 300 men and had up to 5 rows of oarsmen on each side.

Behind Carthage's large harbor was a circular harbor 1,066 ft. (325 m) in diameter that could be sealed off. It had an island in the center with sheds for 220 warships, where maintenance or repairs could be carried out at lightning speed. At times, Carthage had around 100,000 armed combatants at sea; the armed forces were under the command of the general, who was elected by the army leadership and approved by the Senate.

Aeneas bids farewell to the Carthaginian Queen Dido, who subsequently takes her own life out of grief. This myth reflects the difficult relations between Carthage and Rome, which eventually led to the downfall of Carthage (painting by Claude Lorrain, 1675).

> ### ▶ RELIGION AND CULT
> The religion of Carthage was based on that of the Phoenicians. At the head of their pantheon stood the fertility gods Baal Hammon and Tanit, who were worshiped in their own cult caves (tophets). Whether the Carthaginians actually carried out the sacrifice of firstborn children and boys described by some authors is still a matter of dispute; however, large numbers of bones from small children have been discovered in some tophets.

THE PUNIC WARS: BATTLES OVER SICILY AND HAMILCAR BARCA

Hannibal's crossing of the snowy Alps with a huge army and war elephants was a masterly logistical and tactical feat that caused a great deal of trouble for Rome (painting ascribed to Jacopo Ripanda, early sixteenth century).

Between 480 and 307 BC, the Carthaginians experienced mixed fortunes in battles over their trading centers in Sicily with the tyrants of Syracuse (see p. 106), who were attempting to force the Carthaginians off the island and who had signed treaties of friendship with Rome. However, Rome's intervention in Sicily provoked the First Punic War (264–241 BC) that took place almost exclusively at sea, and following a series of battles in which fortunes ebbed and flowed, forced the Carthaginians to retreat from Sicily (in 241 BC) and Sardinia (in 237 BC). This was General Hamilcar Barca's (241–229 BC) greatest hour. He put down a rebellion by Libyan mercenaries backed by the Romans, and in 237/236 BC crossed over to Spain with a large army and conquered the whole of southern Spain, which was a source of provocation to Rome; his son-in-law Hasdrubal (229–221 BC) continued the advance.

HANNIBAL, ENEMY OF ROME

Hamilcar's son Hannibal (246–183 BC), whose father made him swear eternal enmity with Rome when he was only a boy, took over the supreme command in Spain from his brother-in-law in 221 BC and during his conquest of the entire peninsula advanced northward over the river Ebro; this triggered the Second Punic War (218–201 BC). He hoped to preempt a Roman

THE END OF CARTHAGE

The tough peace terms dictated by Rome forced the city of Carthage to tear down its defenses and give up its war fleet. However, Roman senators surrounding Cato the Elder (234–149 BC) continued to warn of the danger from Carthage, so in the Third Punic War (149–146 BC), Rome used a technical breach of a treaty as an excuse to conquer and destroy Carthage totally following a three-year siege. The soil was formally cursed, and after several failed colonization attempts, Julius Caesar founded the Colonia Iulia Concordia Carthago here in 46 BC.

> "When the others surrounded the victorious Hannibal and wished him luck, . . . the cavalry commander Maharbal spoke, 'So that you know what you have achieved in this battle: in four days you will feast as a victor on the Capitol. Follow me! I will hurry ahead with the cavalry, so the Romans will learn that you have arrived, and not that you are about to arrive!'"
>
> From Livy's *History of Rome*, around the turn of the eras

Bust of Hannibal (246–183 BC), the brilliant general who had sworn eternal enmity with Rome (Naples Museum, Italy).

punitive expedition to Carthage by conquering Italy. In the fall of 218 BC, he crossed the Alps with his war elephants, forged alliances with the Celts and the mountain tribes of northern Italy, and used his tactical genius to defeat the Roman armies at the Battle of the Trebia (218 BC) and at Lake Trasimene (217 BC). The encirclement and destruction of virtually the entire Roman army at Cannae (216 BC) constituted Hannibal's greatest military victory. In 211 BC he advanced on Rome (*Hannibal ante portas!*—"Hannibal at the gates!"), but fell into difficulties from guerrilla warfare and Rome's evasive "scorched earth" tactic, which cut off his supplies. In 207 BC, the Romans thwarted his brother-in-law Hasdrubal's offensive with fresh troops in Italy, and in 203 BC Hannibal was recalled to Carthage after the Romans under their General Scipio had landed in Upper Africa. In 202 BC Hannibal was defeated by Scipio at Zama and fled across Syria to Bithynia (Asia Minor), where the Romans forced him to commit suicide in 183 BC.

A meeting between Hannibal and Scipio shortly before the decisive Battle of Zama (202 BC) failed to produce a solution, as the demands posed by Scipio on behalf of the Roman Senate were unacceptable.

Greece

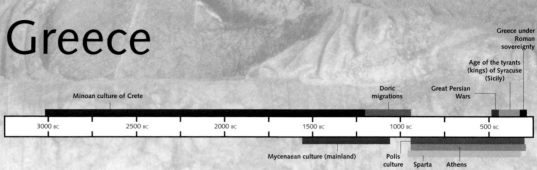

Minoan culture of Crete

3000 BC   2500 BC   2000 BC   1500 BC   1000 BC   500 BC

Doric migrations

Great Persian Wars

Age of the tyrants (kings) of Syracuse (Sicily)

Greece under Roman sovereignty

Mycenaean culture (mainland)   Polis culture   Sparta   Athens

Greek civilization, probably more than any other, has influenced all aspects of Western civilization. The Greeks themselves, whose original provenance is disputed, are an Indo-Germanic people and migrated to the Aegean Peninsula from the north in several waves.

CRETE AND THE MINOAN CULTURE

The earliest Greek culture on Crete, named after the fabled King Minos, had its golden age between the seventeenth and thirteenth centuries BC. It had vast palace cities; the latest and most important center was the palace complex of Knossos, comprising several hundred rooms, which was discovered and excavated from AD 1900 by the English archaeologist Sir Arthur Evans. The Minoans seem to have had a largely peaceful artisan, farming, and trading culture that had extensive contact with the Mediterranean and Phoenician regions; starting from a pictorial script, they invented two syllabaries, Linear A and Linear B. The discovery of numerous female

Background image: A sarcophagus from northwest Greece shows a scene from the *Iliad*, King Priam of Troy pleads with the Greek hero Achilles for the body of his son Hector.

Above: This fresco shows a peaceful harbor scene on Crete in Minoan times (sixteenth century BC).

statuettes (goddesses) led to speculation that their society may have been matriarchal; the symbol of the double-headed ax and the bull cult (as evident from battlements in the form of bulls' horns) also played a significant role. The murals in the unfortified palace complexes give the impression of an attitude to life that was cheerful, relaxed, and close to nature. The progressive decline of this culture from around 1375 BC, which also affected the Peloponnese, is linked to natural disasters (such as the volcanic eruption on Santorini in the seventeenth century BC) and the invasion of other Greek tribes and of the Sea Peoples.

MYCENAEAN CULTURE

The Mycenaean culture of the mainland Greeks in the south of the peninsula was influenced in artistic terms by the Minoans, but politically was significantly more warlike. Its hallmarks were shaft-and-beehive tombs (with weapons of war as grave goods), as well as fortified castle compounds around which cities grew up; various castle lords or city leaders from the Mycenaean ruling classes probably fought for supremacy over entire stretches of land together with the inhabitants, who also included the subjugated native populations. Homer's *Iliad* (see box) is a primary source of stories about these battles. The Mycenaean culture began to decline from around 1200 BC due to the Dorian migrations

(circa 1200–1000 BC), which affected the entire eastern Mediterranean region and led to the eventual settling of the Greek tribes.

▶ **HOMER'S EPIC POEMS**

In the *Iliad* and the *Odyssey*, Homer (eighth century BC) tells of the crusade by the armies of the Greek kings under the leadership of Agamemnon of Mycenae against Troy in Asia Minor, the remains of which were excavated from AD 1873 by the German archaeologist Heinrich Schliemann (1822–90). The *Iliad* (like other heroic epic poems, for example, the *Nibelungenlied or Song of the Nibelungs*) probably contains a germ of historical truth. However, this has been embroidered and enriched with legends; the historical accuracy of the texts remains a matter of controversy to this day.

The ruins of the palace city of Knossos, uncovered by Sir Arthur Evans after 1900; the huge complex with its elaborately decorated rooms, murals, and irrigation systems, together with evidence of the bull cult, demonstrate the high standard of Minoan culture.

"Sons of Atreus and you others, you radiant Achaeans,
May the gods, inhabitants of the Olympian heights,
Grant that you destroy Priam's city and return home safely;
But give me my daughter back and receive this ransom
Out of reverence for Zeus' far-shooting son Apollo.
The Achaean army, in agreement, demanded that
He honor the priest and accept the exquisite ransom."

From Homer's *Iliad*, eighth century BC

The Greek city-states: Polis culture

At the end of the Dorian migrations, the various Greek tribes had occupied all the countryside and formed urban communities (*polis*, pl. *poleis*) with surrounding land attached to each that were distinguished by a high degree of autonomy and self-government. The polis culture, particularly that of Athens (*see p. 100*), is considered to be the birthplace of democracy. After almost all Greek cities had rejected tyranny (dictatorship) as a form of rule, a system developed whereby the male full citizens of a polis met at a central meeting place (*agora*) to confer on political matters. However, full citizenship, which was linked to property and birthright, was possessed only by a minority; women and slaves were excluded, as were foreigners living in the polis (metics) and the inhabitants of the—originally subjugated—surrounding villages (helots, subordinate peoples), who were under the dominion of a polis and were called up for military service. Factional infighting, dependencies, and revolts meant that political relations in many poleis were extremely changeable and unstable.

The advantage of the polis lay in the high degree of participation by (full) citizens. Their disadvantage lay in the fragmentation and rivalry between the city-states that often manifested themselves in fighting. The only places where all Greeks were united were the shrines, such as the famous oracle at Delphi, in the areas around which several poleis would join together to form cult communities (amphictyons), and the Olympic games (from 776 BC), where representatives of the Greek cities competed against one another at various sports.

The Persian Wars

Joint action was necessary to prevent the expansion of the Persian Empire into Greek territory (*see p. 56*). After the Greek cities

A Greek amphora showing the capture and destruction of Troy by the Greeks; the Trojan War was a recurring theme in Greek art.

of Asia Minor had voluntarily submitted to the Persians in 494 BC in opposition to the dominance of Athens and Sparta and Athens had attempted to regain the lost territory, Emperor Darius launched a punitive expedition against Athens. However, in 490 BC the Persians were driven back at the Battle of Marathon by the Athenians under their General Militiades; a "marathon runner" brought the news of the victory to Athens, 25 miles (40 km) away, where he collapsed and died.

In 480 BC, Emperor Xerxes crossed the Hellespont with a huge army and against the heroic resistance of King Leonidas with his 300 Spartans (all of whom perished), captured the pass of Thermopylae; in 479 BC he occupied Attica and Athens. However, the previous year the Greeks, under the leadership of the Athenians, had been victorious at the naval Battle of Salamis, and now, under the leadership of the Spartans, they gained victory on land at Plataea in Boeotia and at sea off the Mycale Peninsula.

The defeated Persians had to retreat. However, after the Greeks' victory their unity was once more shattered, with the power struggle between the leading powers of Athens and Sparta manifesting itself even more openly.

Above: The mythical King Aegeus of Attica consults the Pythia (priestess) of the oracle at Delphi (Greek vase painting).

Right: The monument to Leonidas at Thermopylae exalts the self-sacrifice of the Spartans in the Persian Wars; the king is carrying a shield decorated with a head of Medusa.

The Temple of Poseidon in Sounion (Greece); for the Greeks, as a seafaring people, sacrifices to the sea god Poseidon, together with pleas for deliverance from storms and shipwreck, played an important role.

THE GREAT POWERS: ATHENS, CRADLE OF DEMOCRACY

In the classical age of Greece, Athens was the leading power in cultural, artistic, and political terms. The constitution drawn up in 594 BC by Solon the legislator that was aimed at achieving a balance between the nobility and the citizens, formed the basis for this. Athens had already become a leading economic power under the tyrant Peisistratos (560 and 546–527 BC), who supported the farmers with loans, and in 510 BC, with the help of Sparta, it overthrew the tyrants. In the subsequent power struggle the reformer Cleisthenes won in 507 BC. He divided the territory of Attica into ten phyles (clans, areas of the city) and these into 139 demes (urban districts and villages) with self-government and their own assets; by codifying the equality before the law of all full citizens (isonomy), he prevented a takeover of power by the nobility (oligarchy). The council

The Prytaneion—seat of government of a polis—located close to the central place of assembly (*agora*) in Ephesus (Turkey).

"Nonetheless, Pericles himself was very careful in his speeches, to such an extent that he never went up to the platform without first praying to the gods that he would not haphazardly let slip a word that would be inappropriate to the matter at hand."

From Plutarch's *Life of Pericles*, circa AD 50–120

of 500, comprising 50 representatives from each of the 10 phyles, became the real political decision-making body and gradually took power away from the traditional judicial body of the nobility (areopagus). This council flourished, particularly under Pericles (462–430 BC, Age of Pericles), who asserted the power of the people's assembly of all full citizens (ecclesia) over all other bodies. At the same time, however, Athens, as the leader (hegemon) of the Delian League, was harsh in the way it ruled over the allied or affiliated smaller poleis.

SPARTA: THE LEADING MILITARY POWER

The Spartans traced their constitution, the "Great Rhetra," established in 650 BC, back to the legendary lawgiver Lycurgus. The state was headed by two hereditary kings furnished by two families; the kings as military commanders were aided by a council of elders (gerusia), made up of 28 full citizens over the age of sixty, as well as the people's assembly of full citizens (apella). Later, a considerable number of functions were devolved to the five ephors, chief officials elected for one year, who were originally mainly responsible for the administration of justice.

The Spartans imposed heavy duties on the inhabitants of the surrounding area (perioikoi) and the helots (subordinate peoples) of Lakonia. It has to be noted that, as hegemon of the Peloponnesian League, they granted their allies greater rights than the Athenians did theirs. The Spartans' austere and disciplined way of life, entirely given over to military matters, became legendary. Boys were brought up not in the family, but in military communities, were drilled in enduring exertion and privation, and were expected to give their lives unconditionally to the service of the state; homosexual relationships were encouraged, and all meals were eaten communally. As the men were often away at war for years on end, the women of Sparta lived freer lives than women in the rest of Greece.

FROM *MYTHOS* TO *LOGOS*

Almost all Western sciences and literary genres have their intellectual roots in Greek culture; this is particularly true of the beginnings of philosophy. The Greek pantheon comprised families of gods with responsibilities for various spheres, who, like the love-stricken father of the gods, Zeus, behaved in an all-too-human fashion. Quite early on, Greek thinkers found this inappropriate. The Ionian natural philosophers, beginning with Thales of Miletus (circa 624–546 BC), Anaximander (circa 610–after 547 BC), and Anaximenes (circa 585–525 BC), therefore strove to find some basic cause underlying and supporting the multiplicity of things, an absolute principle, and found it in water, air, fire, or the *apeiron*, "the unlimited." Heraclites (circa 540–475 BC), with his state of flux (*panta rhei*) theory, asserted that movement was the principle behind all living things.

The three greatest Greek philosophers reacted to ethical crises, as explained by the rhetorically trained Sophists. These three were linked by a pupil-teacher relationship: Socrates (469–399 BC) called for self-recognition, critical thinking, and moral behavior, and paid with his life as an alleged "corrupter of youth," for his commitment to these ideas. Plato (427–347 BC), in his theory of forms, established goodness as a hierarchical order of what is and what should be; according to this, ideas are the ideal archetypes of all things, but real things, on the other hand, are to a varying degree part of the true being of the ideas underlying them in that they are representations of them. Aristotle (384–322 BC), Alexander the Great's tutor, developed a philosophy of order based on real things and placing them in ascending order in categories; his observations in almost all areas of knowledge laid the foundations of natural

Statue of the philosopher Socrates (469–399 BC), seated in contemplative pose, with a statue of the protective patron goddess Athena in the background, in front of the Hellenic Academy in Athens.

philosophy and natural sciences, including biology and medicine.

Above: Model of the Acropolis in Athens with its buildings from the Greek and Roman eras; the Acropolis of Athens served as a model for the layout of Greek citadels (*acropoleis*).

BUILDING AND ARCHITECTURE

The Greeks' intellect and creativity was always looking for new outlets. Early on, artists became masters at producing slender vases, amphorae, and dishes, mostly painted with scenes from Greek mythology. Greek architecture was also a formative influence in the West, and found particular expression in the design of temples and prestigious buildings with their Ionic and Doric columns. One of the most imposing complexes is the Acropolis (Upper City) of Athens that Pericles had rebuilt under the supervision of the sculptor Phidias, after its destruction by the Persians. Its most famous buildings are the temple of Athena Nike and the Parthenon temple, in which a statue of the city goddess, Pallas Athena, was erected, as well as the monumental gates to the sacred district, the Propylaea, and the

Erechtheum with its Porch of the Maidens supported by six larger-than-life caryatids. The Athens Acropolis in particular, with its classical elements, has influenced numerous Western building styles.

Right: The philosopher Aristotle (384–322 BC), one of the most important and systematic Western thinkers, is seen as the founder of the natural sciences.

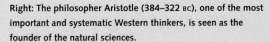

"Immortal Aphrodite on your brightly colored throne,
Wile-weaving daughter of Zeus, I call upon you:
Do not crush my heart, my lady,
With worries and distress.
But come to me, if ever from afar
You hear my call, and listen to my pleading . . . ."

From a poem by Sappho, sixth century BC

Greek tragedy

The Greeks loved theatrical productions, and every town that had any kind of pretensions built its own amphitheater. In the tragedies of the three great Greek tragedians, Aeschylus (525–456 BC), Sophocles (496–406/405 BC), and Euripides (485/480–406 BC), traditional myths about the gods, humans, and heroes were artistically reworked, often with a critical approach showing that people should take their fate into their own hands and not be content to be playthings of the gods—even if this meant becoming caught up in guilt and violence. The most prominent writer of comedies was Aristophanes (circa 448–385 BC).

The Peloponnesian War

The decline of classical Greece was brought about not by enemies from outside, but by a devastating fratricidal war. The Peloponnesian War (431–404 BC), between the major powers Athens and Sparta and their allies, was divided into two phases, the Archidamian War (431–421 BC) and the Decelean War (413–404 BC). Sparta initially enjoyed supremacy on land and Athens at sea. The shifting fortunes of the war resulted in destruction on a scale hitherto unknown, the smaller allies being the main victims of punitive actions by the major powers, including the burning down of cities and mass executions. Almost all the Greek colonies were severely affected by the war, including Sicily (see p. 106), where the Athenians suffered a catastrophic defeat at the hands of the Syracusians in 413 BC when they attempted to conquer it. After the peace party came to power in Athens, the Peace of Nicias (421 BC) provided a brief breathing space. In the second phase, following a series of defeats and the loss of its fleet at Aegospotami in 404 BC, Athens had to capitulate to the siege troops of Spartan General Lysander and open its ports. Lysander had Athens' fortifications razed to the ground; in the aftermath, the political system there was overthrown.

The exhausted Spartans, however, could not enjoy their hegemony over Greece for long. After further wars against an Athens that had regained strength, in 371 BC they suffered a crushing defeat at Leuctra against the Thebans under the leadership of the brilliant military strategist Epaminondas with his "oblique order" tactic. However, the Greek leadership soon fell to a new, unspent power, Macedonia under Philip II (see p. 109).

A mask from Megara Hyblaea, a Greek colony on Sicily, which would have been worn on the stage by tragedy and comedy actors (sixth century BC).

" It is thus clear that the state is of nature and more original than the individual. In fact, insofar as the individual is incapable of living independently, he will behave as otherwise a part will do in relation to a whole. However, he who cannot live in a community or in his independence does not need one, is not a part of the state, but a wild animal or god.*"*

From Aristotle's *Politics*, fourth century BC

► THE INTERPRETATION OF HISTORY

The Greeks also started Western written history, with Herodotus (circa 484–424 BC), the "father of history," leading the way, followed by Thucydides (circa 460–399 BC), who began the scientific approach to history, and Xenophon (circa 430–after 355 BC). Their writings show the desire not just to relate historical events, but also to interpret them and to indicate general historical trends. The great Greek historians were also historical philosophers.

Left: The historian Xenophon (circa 430–355 BC) wrote a history of Greece (*Hellenica*) and in his *Anabasis* (March of the Ten Thousand) described the military expeditions of Greek mercenaries in Persia, in which he was personally involved as one of the leaders.

Below: The amphitheater at Epidauros (Greece, fourth century BC); in every polis the theater was a central point for performing plays, songs, and poetry.

The ruins of the Temple of Olympian Zeus in Syracuse, Sicily, the tyrant-ruled center of western Greek civilization.

GREEK COLONIZATION

From as early as the eighth century BC, the Greeks were using ships to settle the coasts of the Black Sea and the Mediterranean, founding colonies as far away as southern France, although most were established in southern Italy and on Sicily. Overpopulation and supply crises in the motherland and a desire for adventure led to emigration and the foundation of colonies; although they were anxious to maintain their independence, these colonies retained close ties with their parent cities in terms of culture, religion, and form of government. Sicily, with its numerous, often magnificently designed cities, became the center of a dynamic western Greek civilization that asserted itself as a maritime trading power against the Carthaginians (*see p. 92*). In the early days, Sicily held in check the attempts of the Etruscans and the Romans to expand in southern Italy, for example, through the naval victory over the Etruscan fleet at Cumae (Campania) in 474 BC.

THE TYRANTS OF SYRACUSE

Tyranny as a form of government was more successful and survived longer in the Italian colonies than in the motherland. Syracuse, which was founded in 734 BC by Corinthians and rose to power under the brothers Gelon (485–478 BC) and Hieron I (478–466 BC), took the lead. Hieron brought poets like Aeschylus and Pindar to his court and made Syracuse the intellectual center of the western Greeks. The most famous tyrant of Syracuse was Dionysius I (405–367 BC), who subjugated the entire east of Sicily and attempted to drive the Carthaginians from the island. With an armed guard of mercenaries he usurped power and cleverly and unscrupulously drew on the backing of the nobility and the common masses in turn, in order to neutralize the influence of both. He brought the philosopher Plato to his court and himself made a mark as a poet, but his suspiciousness and slyness led to his being viewed by his contemporaries as an archetypal tyrant. His son Dionysius II (367–357 and 347–344 BC), on the other hand, was a weak character, given to luxury (*see box*). Later tyrants (kings, after 304 BC), such as Agathocles (317–289 BC) and Hieron II (269–215 BC), made Syracuse once again a significant and culturally important power in the western Mediterranean.

▶ **DION'S "RULE OF PHILOSOPHERS"**

Dion (409–354 BC) was foreign minister, brother-in-law, and later, son-in-law to Dionysius I, and in 388 BC became a pupil of Plato, who set his hopes on him. Dion induced his brother-in-law to bring the philosopher to the court at Syracuse. Faced with the loose moral conduct of his nephew Dionysius II, Dion, a strict moralist, seized power in 357 BC (at Plato's instigation) and attempted to transform the tyranny into a constitutional monarchy within the meaning of Plato's "rule of philosophers." The experiment failed when fierce resistance from the nobility and the Republican party led to Dion himself adopting tyrannical measures and he was murdered in 354 BC.

Above: The tomb of the famous mathematician and natural scientist Archimedes (circa 285–212 BC) in the Grotticelli Necropolis (Syracuse); the scholar was killed by a Roman soldier during the conquest of Syracuse.

Below: The ruins of the amphitheater of Taormina (Sicily), constructed in 474 BC.

Macedonia

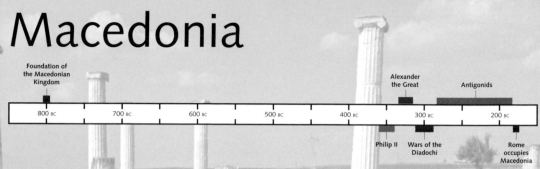

Foundation of the Macedonian Kingdom

| 800 BC | 700 BC | 600 BC | 500 BC | 400 BC | 300 BC | 200 BC |

Alexander the Great

Antigonids

Philip II Wars of the Diadochi

Rome occupies Macedonia

The Indo-Germanic Macedonians migrated into northern Greece in circa 1200 BC. At first, they lived austerely under the leadership of a military kingdom as farmers and shepherds and had scarcely any contact with the advanced Greek civilization; for a long time, the Greeks regarded them as semi-barbarians.

THE RISE

Of the kings who had been ruling since 805 BC, Alexander I (Philhellen, 498–454 BC) obtained permission to participate in the Olympic Games, set up his court at Aigai along Athenian lines, and began Macedonia's affiliation to Greek culture. The rise took place under Archelaos (413–399 BC), who moved the royal residence to Pella, covered the country with trade routes, brought Greek artists to his court, and developed Macedonia into a strong military power by restructuring the army. Amyntas III (393/392–370 BC) fought off the Illyrians and forged close ties with Sparta and Athens. These achievements seemed to be in danger of being lost when the young Perdiccas III (365–359 BC) fell in battle, along with 4,000 warriors, in a catastrophic defeat by the Illyrians in 359 BC. His brother, Philip II, subsequently usurped the throne.

Background image: The court of the palace at Pella (northwest of Thessaloniki, Greece), the royal residence of the Macedonian rulers until 168 BC.

Above: Huge clay amphorae for storing water or wine in the archaeological park at Pella; in order to keep the contents cool, the vessels were usually partially buried in the ground.

The battle-tested phalanx of Macedonian hoplites (heavy infantry): Philip II and Alexander the Great increased their strike capability still further with improved weaponry and tactics as well as by dividing them into divisions and regiments that were supported in battle by light infantry and archers.

PHILIP II OF MACEDONIA

Philip II (circa 382–336 BC) was not only a tough and cunning politician and brilliant military strategist, but also a highly gifted tactician. He defeated the Illyrians and played off the Greek cities against one another, while conquering city after city as far as the Greek coast. He seized possession of the rich gold and silver mines in the Pangaion Hills, captured Olynth in 348 BC, and advanced gradually toward Athens. By 346 BC he was *de facto* the hegemon of a large section of Greece; in 343 BC he concluded a nonaggression pact with Persia and occupied the whole of Thrace.

The unavoidable confrontation with the Greek cities ended in Philip's brilliant victory over the coalition led by Thebes and Athens at Chaeronea in 338 BC, with the help of his tactical innovation, the 18-ft. (6-m)-long pikes (sarissa) of his infantry (hoplites). In 337 BC, he united all the Greek cities (except Sparta) in the Corinthian League under his hegemony. He imposed lenient peace conditions on those he vanquished, particularly the Athenians, and respected their freedoms, as he was attempting to unite Greece and Macedonia into one Pan-Hellenic community by various means including establishing numerous foundations; his son Alexander continued this policy. Nonetheless, the Athenian orator Demosthenes (384–322 BC) warned repeatedly in his *Philippics* against "Philip the Barbarian's" craving for power. In 336 BC, Philip sent a large contingent of troops to Persia and was preparing for a large-scale campaign against the Persian Empire when, at his daughter's wedding, he was murdered—possibly with the cooperation of his wife Olympias, Alexander's mother.

Philip II of Macedonia elevated his kingdom to become the leading power in Greece, through a combination of superior political tactics.

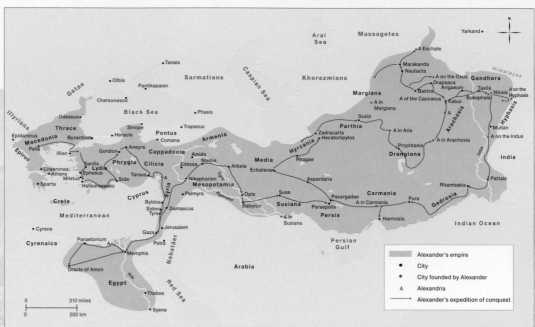

ALEXANDER THE GREAT'S EMPIRE: THE EXPEDITIONS OF CONQUEST

Philip's son Alexander III, the Great (356–323 BC), was an exceptional figure in history. In 336 BC he ascended the Macedonian throne, first completing his father's work by conclusively subduing the Thracians and the Illyrians, and in 334 BC crossing over to Persia with an army of Greeks and Macedonians. He conquered the Phoenician-Syrian region and in 332/331 BC entered Egypt without having to fight. There, he was greeted as a liberator and crowned pharaoh, and in 331 BC he founded Alexandria. By 330 BC he had occupied the entire Persian heartland; he advanced victoriously eastward and by 327 BC he had conquered Bactria and Sogdiana (present-day Afghanistan, Uzbekistan, Turkmenistan, and Tajikistan). In 326 BC he pushed forward into India, an area completely unknown to Europeans at that time. He occupied the Punjab and at the Battle of the Hydaspes River defeated Indian King Porus and his war elephants; however, poor morale

ALEXANDER'S EMPIRE

The map shows the route taken by Alexander the Great on his expeditions of conquest as far as India, as well as the numerous cities he founded (many of them are therefore called Alexandria) or whose fortunes he revived by establishing military bases and leaving behind settlers there.

and a threatened mutiny in the army forced Alexander (against his will) to turn back.

RETURN TO PERSIA

The return, through territories that had been formally conquered but not actually gained, turned out to involve heavy fighting and many losses; disastrously, the expedition passed through the Gedrosian Desert in Baluchistan, where many of the soldiers perished. Back in Persia in 325 BC, the following year Alexander organized the mass wedding at Susa (*see p. 59*) in order to merge the oriental and Greek/Macedonian cultures, although this met with some resistance from his old Companions. In 323 BC he moved to Babylon, where in June he fell ill and died of a fever (or possibly was poisoned) at the age of just thirty-three.

ALEXANDER'S PERSONALITY

Verdicts on Alexander have always oscillated between hero-worship and criticism. His

Background image: On the Kokcha River in Afghanistan lie the ruins of the city Dasht-e Qal'eh, one of the numerous cities founded by Alexander on his expeditions of conquest.

abilities as a brave general are undisputed; he also surrounded himself with gifted military officers and advisors. He was generous to the people he vanquished, tolerant of their religions and customs, and eager to learn from them; massacres of civilians and destruction of cities, such as Persepolis in 330 BC, remained the exception. His initial affability toward his soldiers, who regarded him as first among equals, gradually gave way to tendencies to self-deification along Egyptian/oriental lines; the Greeks and Macedonians in the army rebelled against the proposal to adopt proskynesis (prostration). After the death of his trusted friend and cavalry General Hephaestion (324 BC) he became increasingly reclusive and indulged in heavy bouts of wine drinking. His vision of a cultural union of East and West was bold and forward-looking, and in Hellenism was to an extent implemented by the Diadochi. His image lives on to this day in the oral traditions and legends of numerous peoples and cultures.

" And truly, to a just judge it is clear that his (Alexander's) good qualities arose from his nature, whereas his failings stemmed from his good fortune and his youth. His unbelievable strength of mind, his almost superhuman ability to endure privation, his . . . radiant bravery, . . . his generosity, which often dispensed more than was requested by the gods, his clemency toward the vanquished, the giving away of so many riches . . . . "

From *History of Alexander the Great* by Curtius Rufus, first century AD

This scene from the Alexander Mosaic in the so-called "House of the Faun" in Pompeii shows the horrified Persian Emperor Darius III (reigned 336–330 BC) turning to flee in the Battle of Gaugamela in 331 BC.

The Diadoch Kingdoms and Hellenism

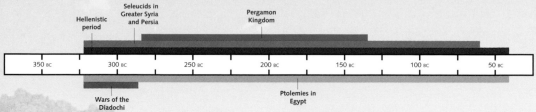

Hellenistic period

Seleucids in Greater Syria and Persia

Pergamon Kingdom

350 BC   300 BC   250 BC   200 BC   150 BC   100 BC   50 BC

Wars of the Diadochi

Ptolemies in Egypt

The era between Alexander's death and the Roman conquest of Egypt (323–30 BC) was characterized by the advance of Greek culture (Hellenism) in the West as far as Rome and in the East into the Orient across Asia Minor as far as Greater Syria and northern India— though the latter were also subject to oriental influences. Greek culture and art transcended their national boundaries, giving rise to a new ideal, that of cosmopolitans (citizens of the world) who were at home anywhere they encountered art and culture. The Hellenistic cult of the leader also had oriental features, culminating in the deification of the kings, who acted as patrons of the arts, donors, and benefactors (*euergetes*). Syncretistic amalgamations led to the formation of new religions.

Head of a *diadumenos* (diadem-bearer), a Hellenistic copy of an original by the Greek sculptor Polykleitos (circa 430 BC).

WARS OF THE DIADOCHI

Immediately after Alexander's death, his generals (Diadochi) started fighting against one another for power. Alexander's huge empire disintegrated irreversibly, and all the Diadochi who persisted in laying claim to the whole world empire failed; only those who limited themselves to individual regions succeeded. Of Alexander's energetic Companions, the following stood

out: firstly Lysimachus (360–281 BC), who conquered Asia Minor, Thrace, and later also Macedonia for himself and accumulated immense riches. When he fell in 281 BC at the Battle of Corupedium (Lydia) against Seleucus, however, his kingdom collapsed and the Wars of the Diadochi ended. Next came Antigonus I Monophtalmus (382–301 BC) and his son Demetrius I Poliorcetes (336–283 BC), who at times conquered the whole of the Asian

Background image: The city walls of Heracleia under Latmos (Turkey), which were probably refounded in circa 300 BC by the Diadoch ruler Demetrios Poliorketes (336–283 BC).

territories of Alexander's empire for themselves and acted as the protectors of the Greek cities, and in 306 BC were the first Diadochi to assume the title of king. When Antigonus, who wanted to reunite the empire, occupied Cyprus and attacked Syria and Babylon, a coalition of all the other Diadochi opposed him; Antigonus fell in battle against them at Ipsus in 301 BC. His son Demetrius acquired the crown of Macedonia in 294 BC, but ended his life as a captive of the Seleucids.

THE ANTIGONIDS IN MACEDONIA

Around Macedonia, a bloody power struggle had flared up between various Diadochi. This led to the extermination of the entire family of Alexander the Great by Cassander (319–297 BC), who was initially victorious until Demetrius Poliorcetes took power. Demetrius' son Antigonus II Gonatas (276–239 BC), who

> " Now the people, too, for the first time proclaimed Antigonus and Demetrius to be kings. Antigonus' friends immediately set the diadem upon his head, but he sent it over to his son Demetrius, giving him also the title of king in the letter he sent with it. In Egypt, when they heard this news, they also proclaimed Ptolemy to be king . . . . "
>
> From Plutarch's *Life of Demetrius Poliorcetes*, first/second century AD

developed a beneficent and humane style of government, was the first of a series of capable Antigonid rulers. Philip V (221–179 BC) tried to reinstate Macedonia's former hegemony over the Greek cities. He fought two wars and occupied Illyria in an attempt to drive the Romans out of Greek territory. A defeat in 197 BC forced him to give up his expansion plans. His son Perseus (179–168 BC) eventually succumbed to the advance of the Romans, who in 168 BC occupied Macedonia and turned it into a Roman province.

Colossal head of the Hellenistic ruler Antiochus I of Commagene (69–36 BC) on the hierothesion (cult sanctuary) of Nemrut Dag (Turkey). The rulers of Commagene combined Greek forms of ritual with Persian Zoroastrianism, as they saw themselves as the descendants of the Persian kings.

The great altar of Pergamon (present-day Bergama in Turkey) with its surrounding frieze of giants; Pergamon was a center of Greek culture and learning in Hellenistic times (built circa 165–156 BC, the altar is now in the Pergamon Museum, Berlin, Germany).

HELLENISTIC KINGDOMS: THE SELEUCID KINGDOM

After the Egyptian Ptolemies (*see p. 80*), the Seleucids were the next most successful Diadoch Dynasty. Their founder, Seleucus I Nicator (358–281 BC), who assumed the title of king in 305 BC, conquered the territory of the Persian Achaemenid Kingdom including Greater Syria, Judea, Mesopotamia, Media, Persia, and Asia Minor by successfully overthrowing other Diadoch. The Seleucid Kingdom (like the Achaemenid Kingdom) was ruled in a more decentralized manner, through several administrative centers with the various regions and peoples enjoying a high degree of cultural autonomy. The main stronghold of the Seleucids was the Syrian/ Phoenician region, with royal residences in Seleucia on the Tigris and in Antioch. In the legendary Elephant Battle of 275 BC, Antiochus I (281–261 BC) stopped the eastward advance of the Celtic Galatians (*see p. 144*) into Asia Minor, and then forced them to settle. His successors fought the Ptolemies with varying degrees of success for the Phoenician coastal territory.

Antiochus III, the Great (223–187 BC), wanted to create a world empire modeled on

Alexander's and conquered the whole of Asia Minor together with Armenia in the west and northern India in the east. When in 192 BC he attempted to bring Greece under his rule, he unleashed a bitter war with the Romans (192–188 BC), by whom he was defeated. After 160 BC the kingdom found itself facing a complex series of struggles for succession and became dependent first on the Ptolemies and then on Rome, later becoming part of the Great Armenian Empire of Tigranes the Great (83–69 BC). In 63 BC, Roman Commander Pompeius deposed the last Seleucid ruler and made the empire a Roman province.

Bronze bust of Seleucus I Nicator (358–281 BC), founder of the Seleucid Kingdom; the Seleucids realized Alexander's dream of uniting Greek and oriental culture, and ruled the greatest of the Diadoch Kingdoms.

THE PERGAMON KINGDOM

Pergamon (now Bergama, Turkey) stands out among the later Hellenistic small kingdoms in Asia Minor: the Macedonian fortress commander Philetairos (281–263 BC) declared independence in 281 BC; his son Eumenes I (263–241 BC) shook off Seleucid sovereignty in 261 BC. Attalus I (241–197 BC) fought off several attacks by the Galatians and, in alliance with Rome, conquered all the Seleucid possessions in Asia Minor. Under him, Pergamon thrived, its buildings, endowments, and monuments making it a cultural center with a wide sphere of influence, to which his sons Eumenes II (197–159 BC) and Attalus II (159–138 BC) added the acropolis and numerous temples. It was during their reigns that the famous Pergamon altar (now in the Pergamon Museum in Berlin, Germany) was erected, surrounded by a stone frieze depicting the struggle of the Greek gods against the giants as the victory of order over chaos. The library of Pergamon became the second largest in the Hellenistic world (after that of Alexandria). The last ruler, Attalus III (138–133 BC), bequeathed the kingdom to the Romans in his will and they turned it into the Roman province of Asia.

Athena, goddess of war and wisdom and patroness of sciences, fighting with the giants rising from the Underworld on the frieze of the Pergamon altar; the battle symbolizes the battle of the Pergamon rulers against the invasion of the Celtic Galatians, who were regarded as barbarians.

The Etruscans

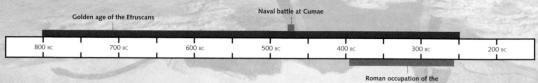

Murals in the so-called Tomb of the Leopard in the Etruscan necropolis of Tarquinia (Latium, Italy, circa 450 BC).

The origin of the Etruscans in northern Italy (then Etruria), whose golden age occurred between 800 and 250 BC, is still unclear. Evidence suggests that they were either a tribe of people related to the Greeks who had migrated across from Lydia in Asia Minor, or farmers native to central Italy—or possibly a mixture of both.

A finely worked Etruscan sculpture, head of a statuette (Museum Villa Giulia, Rome, Italy).

THE DODECAPOLI

Politically, the Etruscans were organized in a loose confederacy of a dozen city-states, ruled by monarchs or by annually elected officials, which were settlements established around communal cult centers. At first, they even ruled Rome. The Etruscans were farmers, but also worked copper, iron, and lead extracted from ore mines and traded in ceramic goods. In many areas they had close contacts with Greece, but as a naval power came into conflict with the western Greeks on Sicily (*see p. 106*) and were annihilated by them at the Battle of Cumae (Cuma, near Naples) in 474 BC.

The southern Etruscan cities, weakened by devastating military campaigns and havoc wreaked by the south Italian Samnites and most notably the Celts from the north in the fourth century BC, were gradually conquered by the expanding Romans, beginning with the destruction of Veii in 396 BC. The northern cities had to conclude treaties with Rome and allow the construction of numerous Roman settlements on Etruscan land. After heavy defeats when they attempted in vain to halt the Roman advance (in 303 BC at Rusellae, 280 BC at Vulci, and 264 BC at Volsini), the Etruscans became outsiders in their own country and in many

or carved into the rock. In the most important Etruscan cities (Cerveteri, Tarquinia, Orvieto, and Populonia), entire necropoles of family tombs came into being; the inner chambers of the tombs were painted with frescoes and contained furnishings and living rooms as well as opulent grave goods. Numerous urns for containing the ashes of the dead have also been found, often in the form of miniature houses.

cases became impoverished agricultural laborers on the estates of their Roman masters. In 90 BC they obtained universal Roman citizenship rights as auxiliary troops for Gaius Marius (156–86 BC), but their social position remained precarious; they also had to endure subsequent punitive action by Sulla (see p. 122). From the second century BC, the Etruscan culture was increasingly absorbed into the Roman culture.

THE NECROPOLES

The Etruscans' religion closely followed that of the Greeks, but they also had their own vegetation gods who were later incorporated into the Roman pantheon. One of its defining features was its distinctive cult of the dead: as early as around 700 BC there were burial mounds (tumuli); unlike the wooden buildings used for the living, the tumuli were constructed of stone

One of the most important necropoles is to be found in the ruins of the Etruscan settlement of Cerveteri (Lazio, Italy).

The Roman Empire

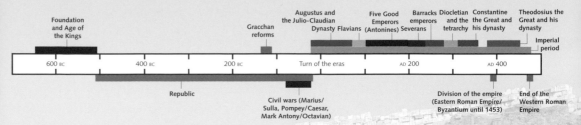

				Augustus and the Julio-Claudian Dynasty Flavians	Five Good Emperors (Antonines) Severans	Barracks emperors	Diocletian and the tetrarchy	Constantine the Great and his dynasty	Theodosius the Great and his dynasty

Foundation and Age of the Kings

Gracchan reforms

Imperial period

| 600 BC | 400 BC | 200 BC | Turn of the eras | AD 200 | AD 400 |

Republic

Civil wars (Marius/ Sulla, Pompey/Caesar, Mark Antony/Octavian)

Division of the empire (Eastern Roman Empire/ Byzantium until 1453)

End of the Western Roman Empire

The Roman Empire, with its two phases, the Republican and Imperial periods, evolved through deliberate military and cultural expansion from a city-state into what was probably the most significant empire in the history of the Western world. Rome's influence on the entire subsequent development of the West cannot be overestimated.

FOUNDATION MYTH AND BEGINNINGS

The city-state of Rome was founded, according to legend, in 753 BC but in actual fact probably around 650 BC, on seven hills in central Italy. Its legendary founders are supposed to have been Romulus and Remus, the twins suckled by a she-wolf (the heraldic animal of Rome). Romulus slew his brother when he dared to vault over the city walls that had just been built. The story is a clear warning to all invaders. Rome was initially dominated by the Etruscans, and its name is supposed to have come from the Etruscan Rumina family. In the history of Rome this was the period of the seven kings (beginning with Romulus, 753–510 BC), the first of which were glorified as cultural heroes; they were also supreme judges and cult leaders.

Background image: The Roman Colosseum was built by Emperor Vespasian (AD 69–79) as a large amphitheater.

Above: *The Rape of the Sabine Women* depicts one of the principal foundation legends of Rome, which the Romans also used to legitimize their rule over the Italian people (painting circa 1637).

The Roman she-wolf, according to legend, suckled the abandoned twins Romulus and Remus, and became the heraldic animal of Rome (bronze sculpture, circa 500–480 BC).

The seventh king, Tarquinius Superbus, is said to have shown, together with his sons, such insufferable arrogance that the Romans overthrew the monarchy in 509 BC. Lucius Iunius Brutus (*see box*) is thought to have been the leader of the resistance, founding hero, and first consul of the Republic.

THE EARLY PERIOD

Right from the early days, the Romans subjugated the surrounding Latin peoples (such as the Sabines) and established their dominion over numerous common sanctuaries in Latium. They soon exhibited the domestic structures characteristic of a "clan state" that imbued Rome's entire history (until well into Imperial times): a delicate and precarious balance between the noble upper classes (patricians) who formed the Senate, and the free lower classes (plebeians) who generally stood in an economically dependent client relationship vis-à-vis the patricians. In the army, the nobility provided the cavalry, the plebeians the infantry. In order to feed the fast-growing city, Rome needed more agricultural land and after 396 BC started to seize Etruscan territory in northern Italy,

> ### ▶ KISSING THE MOTHER
> Lucius Iunius Brutus is supposed to have been a nephew of the last king, Tarquinius Superbus, and to have made himself out to be stupid and harmless (Brutus = foolish). With his cousins, the king's sons, he visited the oracle at Delphi where they received the prophecy that power would fall into the hands of the person who was the first to kiss his mother. When they landed in Italy and his cousins all ran to their mother, Brutus fell to the ground, with feigned clumsiness, and quickly kissed the mother earth: he had understood the oracle.

gradually bringing it under Rome's control. In 387 BC Rome had to endure occupation and pillaging by the Celts under Brennus (*see p. 144*).

> " After Romulus had buried his brother with those who had raised him at Remonia, he continued with the building of the city [Rome], but first had men brought from Etruria who had to teach him how to proceed in religious mysteries, and had to arrange everything according to certain holy customs and written rules. "
>
> From Plutarch's *Life of Romulus*, first/second century AD

View of the Forum Romanum; to the right, the reconstructed building of the Roman Curia, the seat of the Senate, where decisions about the fate of the empire were made.

ROME'S REPUBLIC: THE OFFICES OF STATE

After 509 BC Rome saw itself as a republic and upheld Republican values; it therefore held annual elections for all important offices of state (annuity), with immediate reelection being ruled out. In order to accede to the highest offices, a fixed *cursus honorum* (ladder of honor) was prescribed; the highest offices were (in ascending order) the elected quaestors (aids to the consuls), aediles (overseers of

THE ROMAN EMPIRE UNDER TRAJAN
The map shows the empire at the high point of its expansion under Emperor Trajan (AD 98–117), with its numerous provinces that were administered by governors in provincial capitals. The city of Rome was dependent on tribute payments and food supplies from the provinces. With the collapse of central power (from AD 235), individual provinces or parts of the empire were able to gain their independence under usurpers.

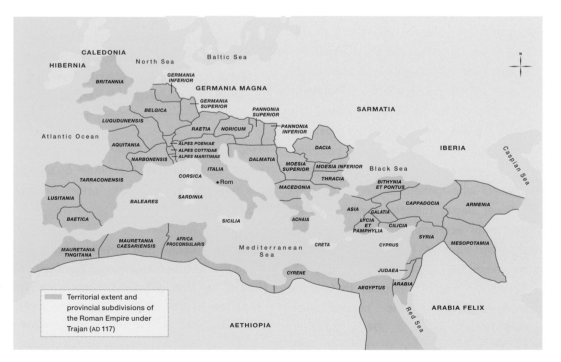

Territorial extent and provincial subdivisions of the Roman Empire under Trajan (AD 117)

markets and public life), praetors (justice), and finally the consuls. To control the exercise of power, each year two consuls having equal powers, who had to have reached the minimum age of forty-three, were elected as the highest state officials and *de facto* political leaders. Originally, only patricians were admitted as consuls, but in 367 BC the plebeians won themselves the right of access. The plebeians also decided one other of these high offices that was gaining increasingly in autonomy. They elected the people's tribunes (ten each year after 449 BC), who were the advocates of the plebeians against abuses by the patricians. Particularly in the late Republican period, this office was exploited by clever people's tribunes to push through social reforms or to whip up the restless masses.

ROMAN EXPANSION

After subjugating the Etruscans and Samnites and fighting off the Gauls, Rome set its sights beyond Italy and achieved dominance in and around the Mediterranean following tough battles—against the western Greeks in southern Italy and Sicily, fending off King Pyrrhus of Epirus (280/279 BC), who had landed in southern Italy, and in the Punic Wars against Carthage under Hannibal (*see p. 94*), which threatened Rome's very existence. After the destruction of Carthage (146 BC), Rome also occupied northern Africa and continued its irresistible advance into Greece and Asia Minor and from there into Syrian and Judean territories and defeated the Hellenistic kingdoms one by one. Rome's last great opponent was King Mithridates VI Eupator of Pontus in Asia Minor (120–63 BC), who was eventually vanquished by General Pompey in the Mithridatic Wars (89–63 BC); this victory made Rome a world power. Julius Caesar subsequently conquered

Gaul; his successors, however, did not succeed in subjugating the warlike Germanic tribes, so Rome built a frontier wall (*limes*) against the Germanic areas. Emperor Claudius eventually conquered a large part of Britain. The Romans never saw themselves merely as occupiers, but principally as bringers of culture, and in many areas set up the first infrastructures and economic administrative systems. One vulnerable area that historians see as the key to the fall of the empire was the increasing dependence of the center of the empire on deliveries of supplies from the colonies and peripheries, who exploited any weakness on the part of central government in their efforts to gain independence.

"Great men . . . let them be to us scholars and teachers of truth and virtue; only let not political science and the task of leading the people fall into disrepute, but respect these for what they are: knowledge of men, partly gained from manifold devotion to practical service to the state, partly treated literally as the fruit of their muses. Politics is the school of the people, which in the past often gave noble natures an almost incredible, almost divine energy to achieve, and still does today."

From Cicero's *On the Republic*, first century BC

The relief from the sarcophagus of Acilian (circa AD 282–285) shows Roman senators in their official garb.

THE REFORMS OF GAIUS GRACCHUS AND THE CIVIL WAR

The increasing social tensions in Rome culminated in demands by the people's tribunes Tiberius Sempronius (133 BC) and Gaius Gracchus (123/122 BC) for a comprehensive land reform in favor of the small farmers; their revolt was bloodily quelled, but triggered progress toward changes to and the expansion of civil rights (by Marius) and the allocation of land (particularly by Caesar).

Shortly afterward there was a bloody struggle for power between the generals Marius (consul in 107, 104–100, and 87/86 BC), who in 102/101 BC had chased the Cimbri and Teutons out of Italy and who was supported by the plebeians, and the patrician L. Cornelius Sulla (consul in 88 and 80 BC), who had distinguished himself as a general against Mithridates VI and was supported by the Senate. Power was initially seized in 87 BC by Marius (who died in 86 BC) and his comrade-in-arms Cinna (consul in 87–84 BC). After Cinna's murder (in 84 BC), Sulla returned to Rome and as dictator (82–79 BC) reinstated the role of the Senate, but took brutal action, including dispossessions and mass executions, against all his earlier opponents. The long-term consulships of Marius and Cinna meant that the previous time limit on consular office had become superfluous, and the government began to head in the direction of dictatorship, something that even Sulla's voluntary relinquishment of power in 79 BC failed to change.

FROM THE FIRST TRIUMVIRATE TO THE DICTATORSHIP OF CAESAR

The Republic degenerated into a caricature as everyone in Rome expected the brilliant general Gnaeus Pompeius Magnus (106–48 BC), a partisan of Sulla, to take over the

The murder of Pompey in 48 BC off the coast of Egypt; he had fled there from his rival, Julius Caesar.

Above: Gnaeus Pompeius Magnus (106–48 BC), one of the most prominent Roman generals, whose hesitation caused him to lose the power struggle against Julius Caesar.

Caesar, who was also a distinguished writer and was particularly popular with the people because of his shrewd social reforms, allowed himself to be proclaimed dictator in 48 BC. Opinion is divided as to whether he was actually seeking to establish a sort of monarchy. In 44 BC he proclaimed himself dictator for life, but shortly afterward fell victim to a murder plot by some of the senators ("on the Ides of March").

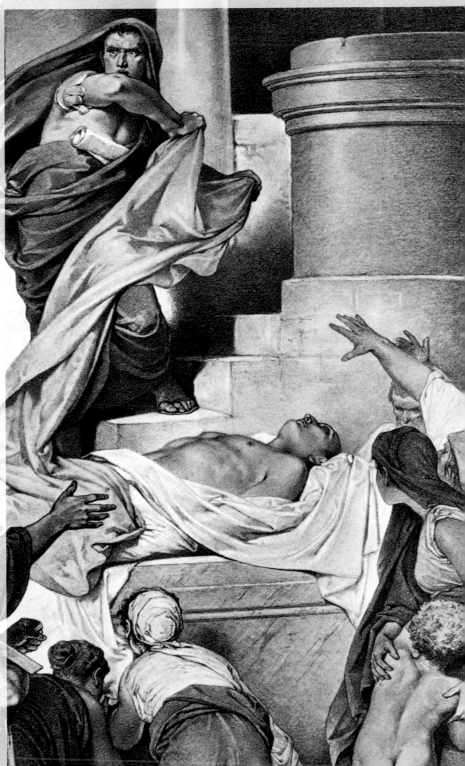

Below: Mark Antony and Julius Caesar after he was murdered by sections of the Senate on the Ides of March in 44 BC (scene from an illustration for William Shakespeare's tragedy *Julius Caesar*, circa 1885).

dictatorship. However, he hesitated, reinstated in 70 BC the people's tribunate that had been stripped of its powers by Sulla, and allied himself with the richest man in Rome, M. Licinius Crassus (115–53 BC) and the ambitious General C. Julius Caesar (100–44 BC), a relation of Marius and son-in-law to Cinna, to form the First Triumvirate (60–53 BC). These three divided up the empire into spheres of influence, each becoming lord of his own economic empire; at the same time, they were always scheming against one another—and together against the Senate. After Crassus fell in battle against the Parthians in 53 BC (see p. 61), there was an open struggle for power between the determined Caesar, who crossed the Rubicon with his troops in 49 BC and challenged the Senate with his march on Rome, and the indecisive Pompey, who retreated to Greece and Egypt, where he was murdered in 48 BC.

The Augustan Age: Second Triumvirate and Power Struggle

After Caesar's murder, his heir and great-nephew Octavian (63 BC–AD 14) allied himself with Caesar's leading general, Mark Antony (82–30 BC); they jointly defeated Caesar's murderers at Philippi (42 BC) and together with M. Aemilius Lepidus (90–13/12 BC) formed the Second Triumvirate (43–36 BC). After Lepidus had been stripped of his power (in 36 BC) there was a further bitter power struggle between Octavian (in the west of the empire) and Mark Antony (in the east). Mark Antony had allied himself with Cleopatra (*see p. 81*), but he also succumbed to a life of luxury. Eventually there was a decisive naval battle in September of 31 BC at Actium, when Octavian's fleet under the leadership of his friend and general M. Vipsanius Agrippa (63–12 BC)—whom Augustus later elevated to become *de facto* a co-regent—defeated the fleet of Mark Antony and Cleopatra; the couple subsequently took their own lives.

Principate of Augustus

Octavian was now the undisputed master of the empire and in 27 BC he received from the

---

▶ THE PAX AUGUSTA

Augustus saw preserving internal peace within the kingdom as his main task; he got the poets of whom he was the patron—Virgil, Horace, Ovid, and Sextus Propertius—and the historian Livy to propagate this idea. Architecturally, the principal expressions of this program in Rome were the Pantheon, founded in 25 BC by Agrippa as a temple for all the gods, and the Peace Altar, opened by Augustus in 9 BC and dedicated to peace, as well as subjects depicted in art.

The first emperor, Caesar Augustus (63 BC–AD 14), gave the Roman Empire a completely new direction.

The naval battle of Actium, on September 2 of 31 BC, ended with the flight of Mark Antony and Cleopatra and changed the course of history (anonymous artist's print).

Senate the titles *Princeps* (first) and *Augustus* (exalted); this marked the beginning of the Roman Imperial period. Augustus, however—warned by the fate of Caesar—used his power cautiously: he honored the Senate, saw himself as the first among equals (*primus inter pares*), and changed his politics completely, transforming himself from the vengeful Octavian into the peaceful Emperor Augustus. With energy and rigor he swept away all traces of the civil war and completely restructured the empire's administration, dividing Rome into 14 new districts (7 BC), introducing comprehensive allocations of land and grain as well as provision for veterans, tax laws, and criminal-law reforms, and building roads and temples. Furthermore, he implemented a strict moral code (to which he

also subjected his own family) and strengthened traditional family structures. Art, education, and literature enjoyed a golden age under his rule. When he died, deeply mourned, in September AD 14, in Nola in southern Italy, he was elevated to the status of a god by decree of the Senate.

"**Augustus' reputation for bravery and moderation reached even as far as the Indians and Scythians, who at that time were known of only by hearsay, and caused these peoples to send delegations to seek out his friendship and that of the Roman people. The Parthians, too, made no difficulties about conceding Armenia to him on his request . . . . When at one time there were several pretenders fighting over the throne, they recognized in the end only the one selected by Augustus as their king.**"

From Suetonius' *Life of Augustus*, first/second century AD

Portico of the Pantheon in Rome, founded in 25 BC by Agrippa and rebuilt between AD 118 and 125 by Emperor Hadrian (AD 117–138); it was erected for the state worship of all the gods and has been a Christian church since AD 608.

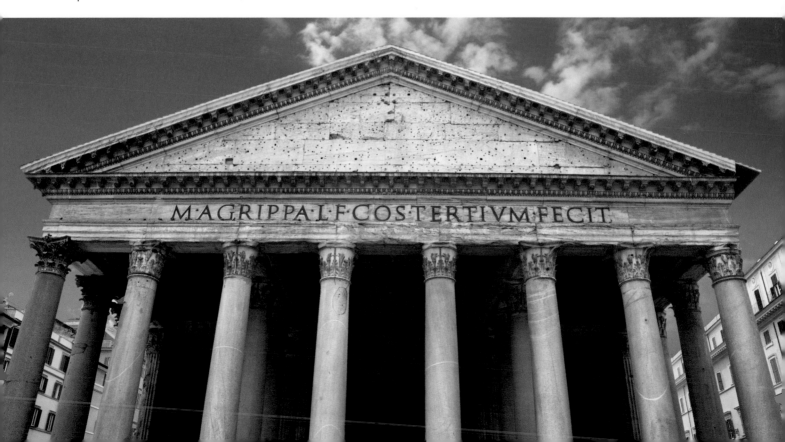

> "Anyone who thinks that Acerra stinks of yesterday's wine, of the wine which he gulps down unblended, is mistaken, because he always drinks until dawn."

From Marcus Aurelius' *Epigrams*, first century AD

EVERYDAY LIFE IN ROME: THE CITY AND ITS BUILDING

Rome, within whose walls lived 1.5 million people, had no comprehensive urban planning before the programs of building and social welfare introduced by Augustus and his successors, and grew to be a chaotic metropolis. Only the wealthy upper classes could afford villas and palaces; the poor mostly lived in cramped conditions that were disastrous in terms of hygiene. Mansions were arranged around a central courtyard (*atrium*), and the dining hall (*tablinum*), the central point for socializing, led out to a formal garden with porticos and pools. The crowded poor districts were prone to frequent fires and the collapse of buildings made out of flimsy materials. Life here took place mainly on the streets, with seedy bars, brothels, street bazaars, itinerant traders, and money changers, and the crime rate was high, particularly at night, as only the center had street lighting.

BATHS AND AQUEDUCTS

Although not all classes had access to it, as water supplies had to be paid for, Rome possessed a magnificent sewage system (*cloaca maxima*). The rich, particularly, and later the emperors, endowed numerous public baths and large spas that were accessible free of charge for all strata of the population and both sexes; at its height Rome had 11 spas (like that of Caracalla) and 856 baths. The bath, with its various pools and treatments, was also a place for socializing.

> ▶ THE ARMY
> The Roman army, guarantor of the security and expansion of the empire, was the best organized in the ancient world. Its tactical success lay above all in the separation of the Greek phalanx into individual units (maniples), which operated in a grid pattern in flexible formations. The length of a legionary's military service was set by Augustus at 16 years but was later extended to 20 years.

The Colosseum in Rome, a place for entertaining the masses: at its dedication in AD 80 there were 100 days of games, during which 2,000 gladiators and 5,000 wild animals lost their lives for popular amusement.

This is where debates were carried out and
deals were made. Rome at its cultural zenith
consumed around one million cubic m of water
a day for one million people; the first aqueduct
into the city was constructed as early as 312 BC,
and by late antiquity there were ten more.

BREAD AND CIRCUSES

The Romans loved shows, especially satires
and good comedies, but also tragedies. Games
(*ludi*) were social occasions, especially in the
Circus Maximus, put on by the emperor to
entertain the masses (*panem et circenses*:
bread and circuses). With the exception of
the chariot races, in which accidents often
occurred, sporting competitions along Greek
lines were less popular than gladiatorial
combats to the death, the heroes of which
rose to be the stars of the masses. Animal
fights or fights between condemned men and
wild animals (these, too, were always to the
death) were another popular spectacle.
The Colosseum, in the catacombs of which
the gladiators prepared for their fights, could
even be flooded in order for entire naval battles
to be enacted.

THE JULIO-CLAUDIAN DYNASTY

Augustus's stepson Tiberius (AD 14–37) ascended the throne as his successor. He attempted to transfer major functions to the Senate, but reacted to their reserve with bitterness and mistrust; during his temporary retreat to Capri, the praetorian prefect Sejanus ran a brutal regime. His great-nephew Caligula (37–41) was murdered because of his unpredictable megalomania, but Caligula's uncle Claudius (41–54) proved to be a capable regent and stabilized the imperial administration. Claudius's stepson Nero (54–68) began hopefully under the guidance of the philosopher Seneca, but then, obsessed with the idea that he was a gifted artist, neglected matters of government and lapsed into megalomania. In 64, he blamed the devastating fire in Rome on the Christians and initiated the first persecutions of Christians. His forced suicide in 68 terminated the Augustan Dynasty.

THE FLAVIANS

The turmoil of the years 68/69 was ended by the seizure of power by the governor of Judea, Vespasian (69–79); this energetic emperor extended the right of Roman citizenship to the Italian and western provinces, reinstated Augustus's blueprint for peace, and restored the health of the state finances through exemplary

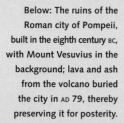

Below: The ruins of the Roman city of Pompeii, built in the eighth century BC, with Mount Vesuvius in the background; lava and ash from the volcano buried the city in AD 79, thereby preserving it for posterity.

Above: Statue of the god of war Mars in the garden of the Villa Hadrian in Tivoli; it was built as a summer residence and retreat for Emperor Hadrian (AD 117–138).

Wall mosaics in a villa in Pompeii (eighth century BC), which were preserved by the eruption of Mount Vesuvius.

frugality; he erected numerous public buildings such as the Colosseum. He was followed by his sons, the humane Titus (79–81), during whose reign the eruption of Mount Vesuvius in 79 buried the cities of Pompeii and Herculaneum, and Domitian (81–96). The latter was extremely capable, but his snubbing of the Senate and excessive power-consciousness (he replaced the imperial title *princeps* with *Dominus et Deus* ("Lord and God") resulted in his murder.

THE FIVE GOOD EMPERORS (ANTONINES)

Senator Nerva (96–98) introduced the principle of an emperor adopting the most capable person as his successor; this gave Rome a series of outstanding emperors. In 97, Nerva adopted the Spanish-born governor Trajan (98–117), who thus became the first emperor from the provinces. Under Trajan, who conducted successful campaigns against the Dacians (Danube), the Nabataeans (*see p. 50*), and the Parthians (*see p. 60*), the empire reached its greatest extent (although his successors were not able to hold onto the territory gained). Through his generous social endowments, Trajan made as much of a mark as the Hellenophile Hadrian (117–138) and the peace-loving Antoninus Pius (138–161). Under their peaceful reigns, Rome became a world center of a late Hellenistic epoch where art was appreciated and a magnet for scholars and artists from all over the world.

The tragedy of the philosopher-emperor Marcus Aurelius (161–180), who was also a famous writer, lay in the fact that he longed for peace but continually had to fight wars against the Germanic Chatti and Marcomanni, as well as against the Parthians. He broke with the principle of adoptive emperors and named his son Commodus (180–192) as his successor, who headed an exceedingly despotic regime and preferred performing as a gladiator.

" Make the attempt—perhaps you will succeed—to live like a man who is happy with his fate, and because he acts justly and is affectionately disposed, also possesses inner peace. "

From Marcus Aurelius' *Thoughts*, second century AD

THE SEVERAN DYNASTY

In the turmoil of the year 193, Septimius Severus (193–211), who came from Upper Africa, won out over his opponents and reestablished order in Rome by reorganizing the financial and judicial systems with an iron fist. He accepted Orientals into the Senate and, by favoring the praetorian guard (imperial bodyguards), transformed the empire into an openly military monarchy. The army thus became the deciding political factor. His son Caracalla (211–217), who wanted to establish a new Alexandrian empire through campaigns in the east, continued this policy. In 212, in the Constitutio Antoniana, he granted Roman citizenship to all free residents of the empire; this gave the empire an entirely new social structure.

Above: Emperor Diocletian (284–305), a gifted administrator, who with his tetrarchy restructured the administration of the empire. In 305 he abdicated and withdrew from public life.

Background image: Ruins of the amphitheater of the Syrian desert city of Palmyra, which rose up against Rome and was conquered and destroyed by Emperor Aurelian (270–275) in 273.

The Severan women, who came from a family of Syrian sun-priests, were instrumental in the increased prevalence of Syrian/oriental cults in Rome. Foremost among them were the influential mothers of the subsequent Emperors Elagabalus (217–222) and Alexander Severus (222–235). Elagabalus even tried, in a bizarre self-dramatization, to elevate the Syrian sun cult to the state religion, but this ended in chaos. Under the guidance of the outstanding lawyer Ulpian (murdered in 228), the serious Alexander Severus ruled strictly according to the law; both emperors, together with their mothers, fell victim to murder plots.

THE BARRACKS EMPERORS

Between 235 and 284, 26 emperors and around 50 usurpers were acclaimed as rulers, against a background of constant external threats and cut-throat civil wars; many of them were never in Rome, were officers or commanders put forward by their legions, or declared themselves independent in their particular provinces of the empire. The fall of this huge empire seemed imminent. Then the most important of the barracks emperors, Aurelian (270–275), surrounded Rome with a new fortified wall, destroyed the rebellious kingdom of Queen Zenobia of Palmyra (Syria, in 273) and made the state religion an amalgamation of the cult of the invincible sun (*sol invictus*) and the Persian Mithraic cult.

DIOCLETIAN AND THE TETRARCHY

When the officer Diocletian (284–305) seized power, he put an end to the turmoil and set the imperial administration on an entirely new footing. He recognized that the empire needed several centers and established the system of a tetrarchy (leadership of four): thus, the able officer Maximian (285/286–305/310) became co-Augustus in the west, with his capital in Milan, and Diocletian himself, as senior Augustus for the eastern

half of the empire, had his capital in Saloniki. In 293, each Augustus nominated a Caesar (assistant emperor), who later in his turn was himself to become Augustus and nominate a new Caesar. By means of a new taxation system, applicable to all classes, and the reduction in size of the imperial provinces (decentralization), Diocletian remedied the empire's disastrous financial situation and subjected the corrupt imperial officials to strict controls.

Representation of the Persian god of light, Mithras, performing a tauroctony, the ritual killing of a bull, to ensure the renewal of all life; this mystery cult, particularly prevalent in the Roman army, was linked to the cult of the invincible sun (*sol invictus*) and was in effect the official religion of the empire until Christianity won throughout.

"Remain at peace, enrich the soldiers, and to hell with the rest of it!"

Septimius Severus on his deathbed, to his sons Caracalla and Geta, in 211

Above: The head of a colossal statue of Constantine the Great (306–337), who accepted Christianity and paved the way for its rise to become the state religion (Rome, Capitol).

CONSTANTINE'S CONVERSION: THE COLLAPSE OF THE TETRARCHY

In 305, Diocletian announced that he and Maximian were abdicating; they were followed as Augustuses by the Caesars who had been in office since 293, Galerius (305–311) in the east and Constantius I Chlorus (305–306) in the west. When in 306 Constantius died in York, his son Constantine the Great (280–337) elevated himself to the position of emperor (306), in opposition to the rightful successor. Thereupon, Maximian returned to the throne, but in 310 was defeated by Constantine and forced to commit suicide. Following Constantine's example, Maximian's son Maxentius (306–312) also usurped the title of Augustus, and in the period that followed there were still other pretenders such as Licinius (308–324). In a gory power struggle (*see box*), Constantine and Licinius formed an alliance and by 313 had eliminated all the other emperors.

THE RULE OF CONSTANTINE THE GREAT

Meanwhile, there had been a change of policy toward the Christians, who had been subject to repeated periods of persecution but had a strong following in the army and outside it. In 311, Emperor Galerius issued the first tolerance edict that was followed in 313 by Constantine's Edict of Milan, which in practice guaranteed the Christians religious freedom.

Constantine in the west and Licinius in the east initially divided the empire based on Diocletian's model, but following escalating conflicts, Constantine defeated his co-emperor and forced him to abdicate. This made him sole ruler of the whole empire (324) and in 330 he elevated the city of Constantinople to the status of "second Rome" and capital of the eastern half of the empire. Constantine was increasingly attracted to Christianity, but was not baptized until he was on his deathbed (the alleged Donation of Constantine as the basis of the subsequent papal state never actually took place). He saw himself as the lord appointed over Christianity by God and for the good of

---

▶ **THE VICTORY AT THE MILVIAN BRIDGE**

The Constantine legend puts the date of the emperor's "conversion" at AD 312. Before the decisive Battle of the Milvian Bridge near Rome, against his brother-in-law and rival Maxentius (who drowned in the Tiber River during the battle), it is said that a cross appeared to him in the sky and he heard the words, "*In hoc signo vinces!*" ("With this symbol you will win!"). According to Christian tradition, Constantine owes his victory to the fact that he ordered the soldiers to mark the cross on their shield although the majority of them were pagans and he himself henceforth always wore the monogram of Christ on his helmet.

Left: Late Roman fresco of a woman with a child in her arms, surrounded by birds and flowers—the expression of a longing for peace.

the state subjected the young church to a harsh imperial regime; in 325 he presided over the Council of Nicaea and intervened heavily in the discussions over dogma. However, he endowed numerous churches, and Christian influences can clearly be seen in his legislation favoring the poorer classes.

This relief on the south side of the Arch of Constantine in Rome shows the Emperor Trajan's Dacian Wars. The chief of the Dacians has surrendered and is being brought before Trajan.

"Thus Licinius lay prostrate on the ground. Constantine, however, the mightiest of victors, distinguished by the virtue of godliness, took . . . possession of the east that belonged to him and so recreated, in the old way, a single and uniform empire of the Romans, in which they subjected all the countries of the globe, from the rising of the sun to the far west, together with the north and south, to their peaceful scepter."

From *History of the Church* by Eusebius of Caesarea, third/fourth century

Constantine's successors

In 337, Constantine bequeathed the empire to his three sons, who engaged in a murderous fratricidal war (until 350); eventually the middle one, Constantius II (337–361), won out. Like his father, he intervened in the church's internal disputes and brought the bishops, who formed under him the structure of an imperial church, into line with the state. With the institution of a court ceremonial, he created the foundations for the later Byzantine cult of emperor (with the emperor as the representative of Christ on earth, *Vicarius Christi*). His well-educated cousin, Julian ("the Apostate," 361–363), ultimately turned against Christianity and attempted to restore the ancient pagan religion, but failed and was condemned by Christian historians.

Valentinian and Theodosius

The open disintegration of the empire was initially halted by the energetic Valentinian I (364–375), who successfully drove back the invading Germanic tribes and implemented a thrifty administration. He lived in the west, mainly in Trier, and made his brother Valens (364–378) co-emperor of the east (in Constantinople). The latter fell in battle in August 378 at Adrianople against the invading Goths (Migration Period), who were flooding into imperial territories.

Faced with this situation, Valentinian's son Gratian (375–383) appointed Theodosius I the Great (379–395) as co-emperor of the east. The latter concluded peace with the Visigoths and allowed them, as federates, to settle south of the Danube (in 382). As far as domestic policy was concerned, he showed himself to be more amenable to the wishes of the church and in 391/392 made Christianity the sole state religion; this marked the beginning of the Christian persecution of the pagan cults.

Division of the empire and the end of the Western Roman Empire

Theodosius, who in the end (from 394) became emperor of the whole empire, allowed for the first time Germanic army commanders to hold high office (*see p. 150*) in an attempt, with the help of Germanic tribes, to strengthen the weakened Roman army and to prevent Roman generals from usurping the throne; through his actions, however, the western empire was also paving the way for its own downfall.

In 395, Theodosius divided the empire between his sons Arcadius (395–408) for the east and Honorius (395–423) for the west (capital: Ravenna); this marked the decisive splitting of the empire into the Western Roman Empire and the Eastern Roman Empire (later Byzantium). Now, it was Germanic commanders

Emperor Theodosius I, the Great (AD 379–395), elevated Christianity in AD 391/392 to the status of sole state religion and accorded the young church great privileges (portrait on the missorium (silver plate) of Theodosius, AD 388).

and courtiers who decided policy; the city of Rome was plundered in 410 by the Visigoths and in 455 by the Vandals. The Western Roman Empire, which was sunk in intrigue and corruption, achieved victory for the last time under imperial Commander Aetius (*see p. 185*), defeating the king of the Huns, Attila, on the Catalaunian Fields in 451. The last western Roman emperors were appointed or dominated by the Eastern Roman Empire, until Germanic Prince Odoacer unceremoniously deposed the last western emperor, Romulus Augustulus, in 476, thereby ending the rule of the western Roman emperors.

Alaric (circa 370–410), king of the Visigoths, overran Greece and Italy from the east and in 410 plundered Rome, sparing the Christian churches.

Relief from the Arch of Constantine in Rome, depicting the decisive battle between Constantine and Maxentius at the Milvian Bridge in 312. In Christian historiography, this event is linked to the emperor's "conversion experience."

ROMAN CIVILIZATION

Rome bequeathed a far-reaching civilizing legacy to the Western world. Initially it was the Germanic tribes that overran the empire during the Migration Period and took over the way of life and organizational structures of the empire and very soon carried these with them to the areas in which they settled. From the Middle Ages to early modern times, Latin became the language of educated people and of science, law, and government. In the areas of western Europe affected by Roman civilization, the imperial roads laid out by the Romans and the Roman forts that had developed into cities (e.g. Cologne, Trier, Regensburg, and Vienna) became the gateways and cultural centers for the civilization of the whole of the Western world.

IMPERIAL RULE

The idea of the Roman emperor as the ruler of the world (later the head of the Christian church), initially in the form of "Caesaropapism," as the spiritual as well as the secular head, had a formative influence on the Eastern Roman Empire of Byzantium (395–1453). Emperor Justinian I (527–565) restored the grandeur of Rome by conquering the entire Mediterranean coastal region and annihilating the kingdoms of the Vandals and Ostrogoths, and is seen by many historians as the "last Roman emperor." However, the ruler of the Franks, Charlemagne (*see p. 162*), and his successors also made a conscious link with the Roman tradition by crowning a second emperor in the west (800)— the designation of the western empire as the "Holy Roman Empire of the German Nation" (962–1809) is evidence of this. The Russian Czars (1547–1917) also drew on the Roman emperor ideas of Byzantium (after its fall), by proclaiming Moscow to be the "third Rome" and this is reflected not least in their title. "Czar"

A symbol of Roman civilization even in western Europe, the (reconstructed) temple in the garrison town of Castra Vetera (present-day Xanten, Lower Rhine, Germany).

The enormous Church of Hagia Sophia (Holy Wisdom), built in 532–537 in Constantinople (present-day Istanbul), demonstrated the claim to power of the eastern Roman emperor of Byzantium as the Christian heir to the Roman emperors.

is derived from "Caesar." The German Kaiser (Emperor) also bore the title *Semper Augustus* ("Forever Exalted").

ROMAN LAW

Perhaps the longest-lasting impression left by the Romans has been on Western law. Legal systems had played a decisive role in Rome since the oldest Law of the Twelve Tables of the Republic (circa 450 BC). The dissemination of Roman legal concepts was brought about principally through the Codex Justinianus, established in AD 534 by Emperor Justinian, later to become the Civil Law Code (*Corpus Juris Civilis*), as the most important collection of all Roman laws and ordinances. It became the guideline for jurisdiction in the West in all areas of law—criminal, civil, and procedural— and from the twelfth/thirteenth centuries was also incorporated into numerous national legal systems. Not only the content of law, but also legal institutions such as the attorney as the representative of the accused in court, the administration of justice by trained lawyers, the formalities of the conclusion of legal transactions, and principles of law such as *in dubio pro reo* (in doubt in favor of the accused) are all of Roman origin.

Justinian I (527–565), depicted here as the author of the Codex Justinianus, passed the legacy of Roman culture on to medieval Europe.

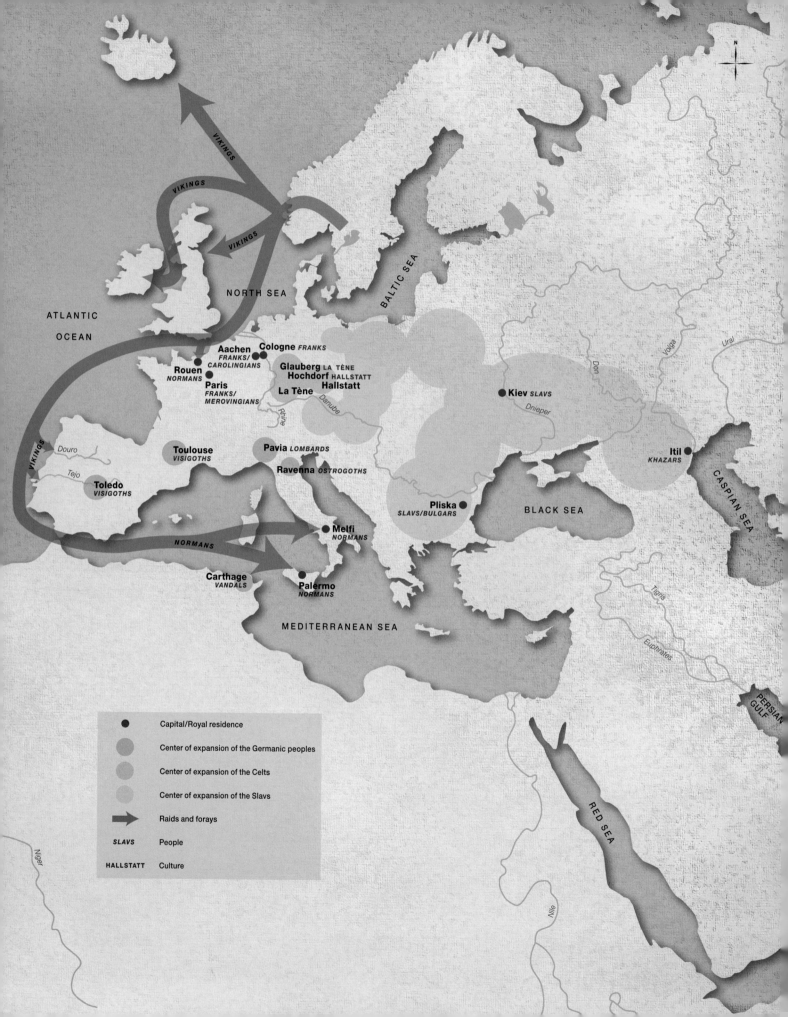

ATLANTIC
OCEAN

NORTH SEA

BALTIC SEA

VIKINGS

VIKINGS

VIKINGS

VIKINGS

VIKINGS

Aachen **Cologne** *FRANKS*
FRANKS/
CAROLINGIANS
Rouen
NORMANS
Paris
FRANKS/
MEROVINGIANS

Glauberg *LA TÈNE*
Hochdorf *HALLSTATT*
Hallstatt
La Tène

Rhine

Danube

Kiev *SLAVS*

Don

Volga

Ural

Dnieper

Itil
KHAZARS

CASPIAN
SEA

Douro

Toulouse
VISIGOTHS

Pavia *LOMBARDS*

Ravenna *OSTROGOTHS*

Tejo

Toledo
VISIGOTHS

Pliska
SLAVS/BULGARS

BLACK SEA

NORMANS

Melfi
NORMANS

Tigris

Carthage
VANDALS

Palermo
NORMANS

MEDITERRANEAN SEA

Euphrates

PERSIAN
GULF

● Capital/Royal residence

Center of expansion of the Germanic peoples

Center of expansion of the Celts

Center of expansion of the Slavs

→ Raids and forays

SLAVS People

HALLSTATT Culture

RED SEA

Niger

Nile

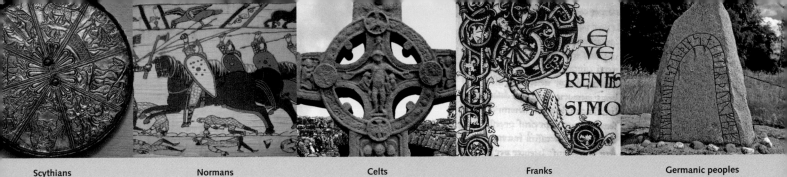

Scythians   Normans   Celts   Franks   Germanic peoples

CENTRAL AND NORTHERN EUROPE

Some of the earliest peoples in Europe north of the Mediterranean region were the Celtic tribes, who began to move after 400 BC, migrating toward the south and southeast; in western Europe they eventually integrated themselves into Roman culture. The various Germanic tribes initially offered greater resistance to the Roman world, spreading mainly through central Europe.

During the course of the Migration Period, which was set in motion by the invasion of Europe by the Huns, the Germanic peoples of eastern Europe were forced toward the west, where, not least due to their contact with Roman/Byzantine culture, they set up their own kingdoms: the Visigoths in France and Spain, the Ostrogoths—and later the Lombards—in Italy, and the Vandals in Upper Africa.

In the west, the Kingdom of the Franks under the Carolingian and Merovingian Dynasties grew to become a leading power. The high point of this development was the empire of Charlemagne, which was eventually divided into the territories of Germany and France.

For a long time, the north Germanic Vikings and Normans proved to be untamable and independent. They were fiercer than any pirate and no Roman fleet ever attempted to oppose them on their territory. On their forays through Europe they reached England, France, and southern Italy (Sicily), and were pacified only gradually.

The culture of the Slavic peoples developed in the east of Europe. After the Scythians and Cimmerians, nomadic horse-riding peoples from the steppes, had initially prevailed in the north of Asia Minor, Eurasian Turkic peoples following in the wake of the Huns managed to establish themselves in eastern Europe; they set up the kingdoms of the Avars, (proto-) Bulgarians, and Khazars, putting pressure on Byzantium, in particular.

CENTRAL AND NORTHERN EUROPE
The map shows the territories settled by the Celtic and Germanic tribes, of which the Visigoths and Ostrogoths, the Vandals, Lombards, and particularly the Franks established their own kingdoms; also the raids and settlements of the Vikings and Normans as well as the territories of the Slavs and of the Caucasian/Asiatic horse-riding peoples in eastern Europe.

The Celts

Beginning of Celtic civilization | 1300 BC | 1100 BC | 900 BC | 700 BC | 500 BC | 300 BC | 100 BC

Celtic migrations to Italy and eastern Europe as far as Asia Minor

Caesar vanquishes the Gauls

Hallstatt culture

La Tène culture

The numerous tribes and clans of Celts colonized the whole of central Europe, from northwest Spain (Celtiberians) and the British Isles to the central German uplands, Bohemia, and parts of Hungary, and migrated as far as Asia Minor (Galatians). Their languages formed a separate Indo-European language group.

TIMEFRAME AND SOCIAL ORDER

As early as the late Bronze Age (circa 1300–800 BC), the Celts left their mark on Europe through the urnfield culture, named after the rite of cremation and subsequent burial of the ashes in urns in the fields; their zenith, however, came in the Iron Age (circa 800–50 BC), with the defining cultural centers of Hallstatt and La Tène (see p. 142). Celtic clans were organized hierarchically around the (clan) princes, who controlled territories and trade, levied tolls, and formed alliances among themselves or waged war against each other; the status of noblemen depended principally on the ownership of extensive property and a

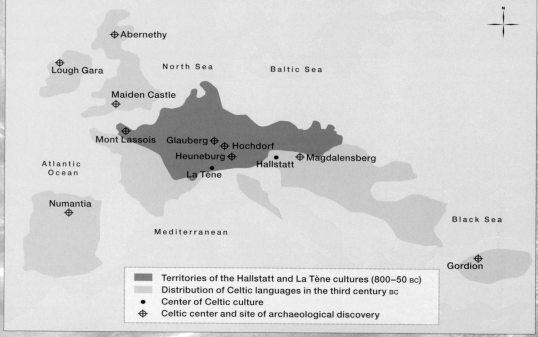

Territories of the Hallstatt and La Tène cultures (800–50 BC)
Distribution of Celtic languages in the third century BC
• Center of Celtic culture
⊕ Celtic center and site of archaeological discovery

Background image: Detail on the silver Gundestrup Cauldron (Denmark, first century BC); the representations of the gods suggest that it was used for ritual purposes.

THE CELTS IN EUROPE
The map shows the distribution of Celtic tribes, from the Celtiberians on the Iberian Peninsula to the Galatians in Asia Minor, together with the central European cultural centers of Hallstatt and La Tène.

Chief druid in ceremonial garb; the druids fulfilled priestly and judicial roles, preserved the lore of the Celtic tribes and were highly influential as political advisors.

large number of dependents, organized along strictly hierarchical lines. The Celts originally lived mainly in individual large farmsteads, then from the second century BC increasingly in defensively fortified *oppida*, surrounded by a protective wooden palisade, which were rather like villages or even small towns.

WAY OF LIFE AND ECONOMY

Their main source of food (apart from hunting for game) was agriculture; the Celts grew spelt, barley, millet, peas, beans, lentils, and herbs as well as cabbage and other vegetables, and raised livestock, particularly cattle (for milking) but also sheep and pigs; the horse was a status symbol of the nobility. Mining, extracting salts and ores, was becoming increasingly important, as was metal smelting, particularly for manufacturing weapons and for producing objets d'art, such as the famous Gundestrup Cauldron (Denmark). The Celts soon borrowed from the Romans the idea of making coins, which they also minted themselves, and traded throughout Europe. The main export items were salt, metals, textiles, wool, and timber, while the main goods they imported were glass and wine, as well as various luxury items for the elite.

The religion and mythology of the Celts were highly diverse in nature; while the mainland Celts, especially in the west, soon fused their cult beliefs with Roman gods (Gallo-Roman culture), the original English/Welsh and Scottish/Irish myth cycles, such as the Ulster Cycle, survived into the Middle Ages when they were put into written form.

Periods and centers of Celtic culture: The Hallstatt culture

This Celtic culture (circa 800–475 BC), named after the burial site discovered in 1846 at Hallstatt (Austria), a salt-mining center, extended over two areas (West Hallstatt and East Hallstatt) across eastern France, Switzerland, southern Germany, and Austria as far as Slovenia and Croatia. In the east it was characterized mainly by fortified hilltop settlements known as "princely seats"—large sites with a castle and an associated lower town—and located nearby, graves of princes with opulent grave goods (particularly ceremonial weapons and goods imported from the Mediterranean region); these provide evidence of the Celts' far-reaching trade links. In the grave of the Celtic Prince of Hochdorf (Baden-Württemberg, Germany), dating from the sixth century BC, the burial gifts also included wagons and harnesses.

Above: Celtic bronze shield (second/first century BC) with the typical circular motifs found in Celtic ornamental design.

The La Tène culture

The golden age of the Celts is considered to be that of the La Tène culture (circa 480–50 BC), which is named after the site discovered in west Switzerland and is divided into three periods, featuring an ever-widening proliferation of centers. The early period (circa 480–300 BC) has a series of magnificent graves, particularly the grave discovered in 1987 of the fifth century BC Celtic Prince of Glauberg (Hesse), whose burial mound is ringed with further graves; a life-sized sandstone statue of a ruler wearing a crown of leaves was also unearthed. The Glauberg may have been a Celtic cult center, as numerous cult objects and a 1,150-ft. (350-m)-long processional avenue to the grave have been excavated.

The middle La Tène period (circa 300–150 BC) fell during the time of the Celtic migrations (see p. 144); the late period (circa 150–50 BC) coincided with the time when larger *oppida* (see p. 141) were being established; with up to 5,000 or even 10,000 inhabitants, these were already urban in character and were distinguished by a high degree of social differentiation into separate artisanal and occupational groups.

Celtic art

It is principally the high level of artisanship of the La Tène period—for example, in terms of objects worked in gold, jewelry, or enamel, and weaponry components clearly based on Greek/Etruscan (or Scythian) models—which

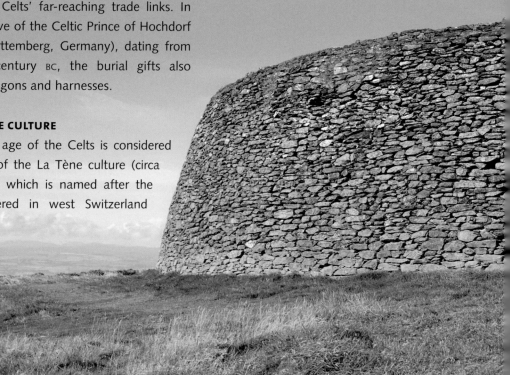

A Celtic bronze helmet with horns; it was probably not merely used for protection in battle, but also served representational purposes (first century BC).

has persuaded many historians to proclaim the Celts to have been one of Europe's advanced cultures. Such valuable articles would probably have been commissioned principally by the princes of the Champagne, Saar, Moselle, and central Rhine regions. Nearby, sacred sites and trade depots containing articles of everyday use, including elaborately worked pitchers, vases, and dishes, have also been excavated. The Celtic style of decoration transformed the rigid ornamental shapes of classical antiquity into flowing, soft, full, and undulating forms that produce an organic effect and are still seen as typically Celtic today.

Below: The stone enclosure of Grianan of Aileach in County Donegal (Ireland, built circa 170 BC); it served as a protective structure or a meeting place.

Celtic migrations and wars: The British Isles

In around 900 BC, the Celts began to migrate to the British Isles, where they lived in settlements as artisans and smiths and mixed with the native population.

Controversy still reigns today over their degree of independence. In around AD 350 they were beset by the Picts and Scots from the north as well as the Germanic Saxons and Frisians (Anglo-Saxons) crossing over from mainland Europe; some of them subsequently emigrated to Brittany.

Movement of Celts to Italy

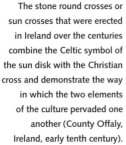

The stone round crosses or sun crosses that were erected in Ireland over the centuries combine the Celtic symbol of the sun disk with the Christian cross and demonstrate the way in which the two elements of the culture pervaded one another (County Offaly, Ireland, early tenth century).

After 400 BC, some Celtic tribes migrated—because of food shortages or limited availability of land—from the south German/Austrian region to Italy; the city of Milan, for example, can trace its origins to a Celtic settlement. Here, they initially overran the territories of the Etruscans (see p. 116), and after their victory at the Battle of the Allia in 387 BC captured Rome (with the exception of the Capitol), which was able to buy its freedom only with high tribute payments. The Celts in the Milan region were forced out of Italy by the Romans after 293 BC.

Caesar in Gaul

In 58 BC, Julius Caesar (see p. 122) began the subjugation of the Gauls (present-day Switzerland, France, and Belgium), defeated the Helvetii (Switzerland) at the Battle of Bibracte (in 58 BC), and after defeating the rebellious Suebi ruler Ariovist (57 BC), had occupied Belgium and France by 53 BC. The following year saw him confronted with a rebellion by Avernian Prince Vercingetorix, who had been proclaimed king and who had a following of numerous Gallic tribes. He engaged the Romans in a prolonged guerrilla war. His scorched-earth tactics resulted in supply bottlenecks for the Roman army. In 51 BC Caesar laid siege to Vercingetorix in Alesia, forced him to capitulate, and divided Gaul into Roman provinces. The subsequent period saw an extensive merging of the Celtic and Roman cultures.

The Galatians

The middle of the fourth century BC marked the beginning of the migration of the eastern Celtic tribes into Transylvania and Dalmatia, where some of them combined with the native Illyrians to create the mixed Japod people. After

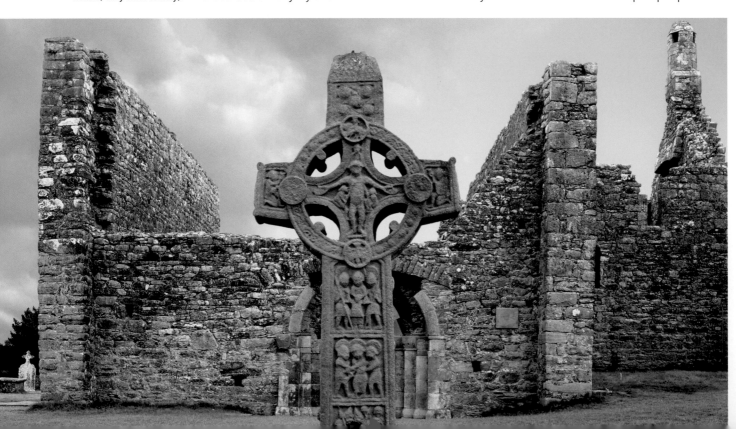

Above: A Celtic stone monument in Ireland; these constructions made of flat stones served as ritual sites or as burial places for eminent figures.

the death of Lysimachus (281 BC), who had fended them off in 279 BC, the Celts pushed forward into Greece as far as Delphi, but were prevented from plundering the oracle and were forced to retreat. Celtic tribes founded Belgrade, and others settled in Thrace (Kingdom of Tylis, up to 212 BC), but large groups continued to plunder the kingdoms of the Seleucids, Asia Minor, and Pergamon. One band that crossed the Bosphorus was defeated in the Elephant Battle by Antiochus I in 275 BC (*see p. 114*) and settled on the Phrygian plateau on both sides of the Halys bend (Turkey). They named this area, which was under Seleucid sovereignty, Galatia, and the inhabitants, the Galatians, merged with the native population there.

" Gaul consists of three main parts: one is inhabited by the Belgae, another by the Aquitani, and the third by a people who call themselves Celts in their language, but whom we call Gauls. All these people speak in different vernaculars and have different customs and laws. "

From *The Gallic Wars* by Julius Caesar, first century BC

Right: The well-fortified Kilmacdaugh Tower near Gort in Ireland bears witness to warring times on the Emerald Isle.

The Germanic peoples

Merging of the
Germanic tribes

Era of Germanic military commanders
in the Roman Empire

Ostrogothic
Kingdom in Italy

Visigothic Kingdoms in
France and Spain

| 100 BC | Turn of the eras | AD 100 | AD 300 | AD 500 | AD 700 | AD 900 |

Italian migrations of
Cimbri and Teutons

Battle of the
Teutoburg Forest

Vandal Kingdom in
Upper Africa

Lombard Kingdom
in Italy

A large number of Germanic tribes and peoples with Indo-European languages settled in central Europe and southern Scandinavia; evidence of their existence in the early days comes exclusively from Greek and Roman sources. Nowadays, they are referred to as the Germanic tribes only from around 100 BC; in late antiquity some of them established kingdoms based on the Roman model.

WHO WERE THE GERMANIC PEOPLES? TRIBES AND WAY OF LIFE

Research into the history of the Germanic peoples was for a long time fraught with ideological difficulties; in particular, German nationalist interests saw them as a uniform people or tribe; by contrast, the latest research emphasizes the heterogeneous nature of the tribes.

Early settlement of central Europe by the people of the Funnel Beaker culture (circa 4200–

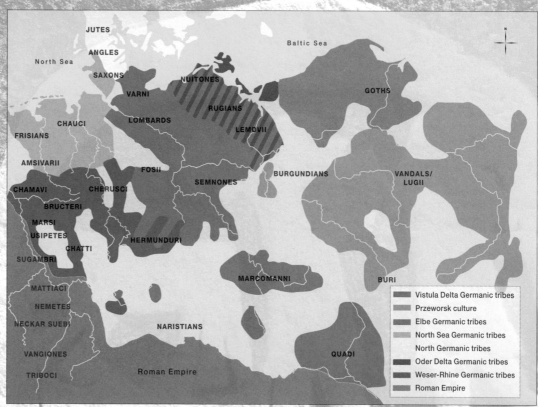

Legend:
- Vistula Delta Germanic tribes
- Przeworsk culture
- Elbe Germanic tribes
- North Sea Germanic tribes
- North Germanic tribes
- Oder Delta Germanic tribes
- Weser-Rhine Germanic tribes
- Roman Empire

Background image: Scene from Valhalla; the Germanic peoples believed the paradise for warriors killed in battle to be a feast at Odin's table with epic songs and contests (stone relief from Gotland Island, ninth century AD; Historika Museet, Stockholm, Sweden).

GERMANIC TRIBES CIRCA AD 100 (EXCLUDING SCANDINAVIA)
The map shows the areas settled by various Germanic tribes, before some of them colonized new regions during the Migration Period.

2800 BC) is no longer attributed to the Germanic tribes, whereas the people of the subsequent Corded Ware culture (circa 2800–2200 BC) were possibly ancestors of the Germanic, Baltic, and Slav peoples, who had migrated in from the east. At any rate, the Nordic Bronze Age (circa 1800–500 BC) is now seen as being a "proto-Germanic" period.

The Germanic tribes, who were often hostile toward one another, lived mostly by hunting, gathering wild herbs, cultivating crops (e.g. oats, wheat, rye, and millet) with plows, harrows, spades, and hoes, as well as from forest clearance and fallow cropping, but also raised cattle and domestic livestock; they engaged in less trading than the Celts. The main forms of settlement were fenced small scattered villages and large farmsteads with three-aisled longhouses. Their religion and the Old Norse mythology celebrated the fighting of free men and depicted the warrior paradise (Valhalla) as an endless feast with contests at the table of Odin (Wotan)—the chief of the Æsir (the Germanic family of gods). Even early authors emphasize the untamed character and closeness to nature of the Germanic peoples, and the Romans viewed them with a mixture of revulsion at their "barbaric customs" and admiration of their endurance and fighting ability.

THE PEOPLE'S THING—ARCHETYPE OF DEMOCRACY?

The Germanic social order was patriarchal and emphasized the extended family or clan; the head of the house, as a free man, was in command of not only his family, but also the semi-free (servants) and slaves (mostly prisoners of war from other tribes). The most important assembly was the three-day-long People's Thing—a religious, advisory, and judicial assembly of the free men, with the opportunity to speak openly to all, which took place at a (ritually significant) Thing site and was presided over by the tribal prince. During the meeting, Thing Peace reigned; this was particularly true for political and military consultations, but malefactors were declared "peaceless and free as a bird," that is, banned from the community (outlawed). The charismatic leadership of a Germanic prince could be demonstrated not just by success in battle (the *Sieg-Heil* or victory hail), but also by wise speeches at the Thing (the *Rat-Heil* or counsel hail). German nationalist interests in the nineteenth and early twentieth centuries, in particular, saw the Thing, which was retained for a long time in Iceland and Norway, as the "archetype of clan democracy" and glorified it accordingly.

Bronze statuette of the god Thor with his hammer Mjölnir, a symbol of power, fighting ability, and fertility; Thor or Donar ("the Thunderer") was worshiped as the weather god, but also as the god of fertility (Iceland, tenth century AD; National Museum, Reykjavik, Iceland).

THE GERMANIC PEOPLES AND ROME

In around 120 BC, the tribes of the Cimbri, Teutons, and Ambrones were caught up in the movements of the Celtic migrations (see p. 144) and invaded Italy from Jutland via Gaul and Bohemia; however, they were driven back by the Romans under Marius (see p. 122) in 102/101 BC. In 72 BC, the Suebi under Ariovistus settled in Gaul, but were defeated by Caesar. The subjugation of Gaul by Caesar (58–51 BC) also affected some Germanic tribes that were colonized by the Romans. Caesar made the Rhine the frontier against the "unpacified" Germanic territories, particularly the warlike Chatti (ancestors of the Hessians); many Germanic tribes, however, continued to invade Roman Gaul on pillaging raids. Just before the turn of the eras, in present-day Bohemia, the Marcomanni established a tightly organized kingdom under their king, Marbod, who had been brought up in Rome. The Romans tried in vain to conquer it in AD 6, but in the year AD 19 it succumbed to an invasion by the Cherusci under Arminius.

The reconstructed Roman castle of Saalburg on the Upper Germanic Rhaetian Limes; *the Roman settlers and their Germanic allies safeguarded their cities from attacks by unpacified tribes from the interior of Germania, but also maintained trading links with them.*

A stone with engraved runes near Holo (Sweden); most surviving rune inscriptions are found in northern Europe.

THE BATTLE OF THE TEUTOBURG FOREST AND THE *LIMES*

From 12 BC, Emperor Augustus charged his stepsons Drusus and Tiberius with "pacifying" the Germanic peoples and clearing them out of Gaul. They exploited the rivalries between the tribes and their princes; in AD 5 Tiberius advanced to the

mouth of the Elbe and into Marcomanni territory, and established the Roman province of Germania. The year AD 9 turned out to be a traumatic one for the Romans when the allied Cherusci ruler Arminius lured the Roman army into an ambush at Kalkriese (near Osnabrück, Germany) and defeated them in the Battle of the Teutoburg Forest. Rome relinquished its territories on the right bank of the Rhine and increased the defenses of those on the left bank and of the legionary fortresses there against the Germans. From AD 83, Emperor Domitian began the construction of the Upper Germanic *limes* in Wetterau with a series of walls and forts; Antoninus Pius (138–161) upgraded it to a closed palisade wall with stone towers, and it was not abandoned until the Alamanni invasions of 259/260.

▶ **THE RUNES**

Runes (Germanic *Run*: mystery, secret) are the oldest Germanic forms of writing, dating from circa AD 150, which, particularly in southern Scandinavia, were etched on stone or laid out in wood and probably did not represent a continuous written script. Runes were seen as a gift from the god Odin, charged with magic power (this makes them the focus of esoteric cults to this day). They were principally used for prophecies and spells (e.g. for warding off disease and for blessing animals); short rune inscriptions record dedications or ownership. The oldest rune script (*futhark*) comprises 24 symbols that were later increased to 33 by the Anglo-Saxons and in Scandinavia reduced to 16 symbols. With the spread of Christianity and the widespread use of the Gothic script, runes fell into disuse in around 700 in central Europe, and in England and Scandinavia in circa 1000.

The victorious Cherusci leader Arminius was acclaimed as "Hermann the German," by German nationalists in the nineteenth century as a pioneer of the unification of all Germans.

Roman settlers in the occupied Germanic provinces paying their taxes (relief from Neumagen, near Trier, Germany, third century AD); the Roman administrative system functioned even in far-flung provinces.

GERMANIC PEOPLES AND ROMAN CIVILIZATION

Despite numerous battles Romans and Germanic peoples were soon peacefully exchanging cultural ideas and trading goods, especially in the *Agri Decumates* between the Rhine and the *limes*. The legionary camps were enlarged to form Roman towns with all modern conveniences which became the nuclei of numerous central European cities. Allied Germanic princes sent their sons to be educated in Rome, where they became familiar with Roman lifestyle as well as wine-growing and arts and crafts. Since the time of the Five Good Emperors (*see p. 129*), Germanic mercenaries

and protection troops had become increasingly popular in Rome, and the reign of Emperor Theodosius (*see p. 134*) saw the beginning of their promotion to the highest offices in the army.

THE GERMANIC ARMY COMMANDERS

Germanic army commanders took advantage of the rapid weakening of government power in both parts of the Roman Empire after 395 and from this time on it was they who determined policy. In the Western Roman Empire, the Franks Arbogast (388–394) and Stilicho (394–408), as army commanders and imperial administrators, dictated overall policy and warfare, and controlled who was acclaimed

The Porta Nigra (Black Gate) was constructed in around AD 180 as a city gate for the Roman city Augusta Treverorum (present-day Trier), and is one of the most significant examples of Roman architecture on German soil.

emperor; Suebi Chief Rikimer (AD 456–472) deposed several emperors and acclaimed others who were more to his liking. His successor, Odoacer, dethroned the last Western Roman emperor in 476, and ruled himself as king of Italy until his murder by Theodoric in 493. In the Eastern Roman Empire, the sovereignty of the Germanic peoples eventually came to an end in 471 with the murder of the powerful army commander and patrician Aspar.

THE CHRISTIANIZATION OF THE GERMANIC PEOPLES

Contact with the Roman world also brought the Germanic tribes into contact with Christianity. A pioneer in this area was Bishop Wulfila (Ulfilas, circa 311–383), who acted as a missionary among the Visigoths in the Lower Danube region (*see p. 152*); he developed a Gothic script and used the Wulfila Bible to teach them Christianity, albeit in an Arian form (*see box*); this subsequently led to ongoing conflicts between the Christian Germanic peoples and the Roman Pope. Later, the Ostrogoths, Vandals, Lombards, and Burgundians also took over the Arian form of Christianity.

> The Roman amphitheater in Trier held 20,000 spectators; the inhabitants of the Germanic provinces occupied by the Romans also surrounded themselves with all the comforts of urban civilization.

▶ ARIANISM

The teachings of Presbyter Arius (circa 260–336) were prevalent under Emperors Constantius II (337–361) and Valens (364–378) and emphasized, in contrast to the Christian idea of the Holy Trinity, a radical monotheism: God the Father as the only god, with Jesus Christ—an intermediate being—being created (not begotten) by God as the *logos* (word of God), intermediary, and image of God, in order to create and redeem the world. For the Arians, Christ is merely of a similar substance to God the Father (Greek: *Homoiousios*), not consubstantial, or more literally of the same substance (Greek: *Homoousios*), as in Catholic doctrine.

> "The Germanic peoples go into battle naked from the waist up, or at most wear a light cloak that hinders them little. They eschew all show of decorative weapons; only their shields are painted in bright colors. Very few wear armor, hardly any of them have a metal or leather helmet."
>
> From *Germania* by Publius Cornelius Tacitus, first/second century AD

Visigoth King Alaric
conquered and plundered
Rome in 410 and
also carried off huge
amounts of treasure from
the city. A few years
later, in 455, the Vandals
under Geiseric once more
plundered the former center
of the empire, which was by
then half in ruins.

THE KINGDOMS OF THE GOTHS

The Goths, who may have originated in Scandinavia, settled in the area of the Vistula Delta around the turn of the eras, and in circa 200 moved southward into the Ukraine and the areas around the Black Sea and the Danube. After 238 they made several incursions into Roman territory and in circa 290 split into the Visigoths and the Ostrogoths.

THE VISIGOTHS

Visigoth tribes (from the Gothic *visigothi*: noble Goths) settled in Dacia as Roman federates, probably from 369 onward; when they crossed the Danube in hordes, they were confronted by Emperor Valens, who fell in battle against them in 378 at the Battle of Adrianople (*see p. 134*). In 382, Theodosius eventually made the groups who were flooding into imperial territory federates. Under pressure from the Huns (*see p. 182*), they moved westward during the Migration Period, from 391, and invaded Italy, plundering as they went; under Alaric (394–410), they besieged and plundered Rome in 410. They were then forced northwestward and colonized Gaul (Kingdom of Toulouse, with its capital in Toulouse). Under King Theodorid (418–451), who fell at the Battle of the Catalaunian Fields (between Troyes and Châlons-sur-Marne, France), the Visigoths fought on the side of the Romans against Attila's Huns. The Kingdom of Toulouse, particularly during the reign of Euric (466–484), established a functioning administration along Roman lines and also occupied the Iberian Peninsula after 490. Forced out of Gaul by the Franks by 507, the Visigoths made Spain their homeland and kingdom (Kingdom of Toledo, with its capital in Toledo); under Reccared (586–601), the Visigoths converted from Arianism (*see box, p. 151*) to Catholicism after religious conflicts in 587. Following disputes about the last King Roderic's claim to the throne, their culturally significant kingdom fell victim in 711 to invasion—abetted by some of the Gothic nobles—by the Islamic Arabs and Berbers who had crossed over to Spain.

THE OSTROGOTHS

The Ostrogoths (Gothic *ostrogothi*: shining Goths), who settled in the Ukraine together with other Germanic tribes, were conquered in 375 by the Huns, in whose wake they traversed central and western Europe. After Attila's death (in 453), they became independent and settled

under Byzantine sovereignty in Pannonia (between the eastern Alps, the Danube, and the Sava). In 474, Theodoric the Great (circa 454–526), who was brought up at the imperial court in Constantinople as a hostage, became their king, and in 488 he was sent by the emperor to Italy, in order to subjugate the Germans there. After besieging Ravenna and murdering Odoacer (*see p. 151*), Theodoric ruled as king from 493. His severe but largely just rule led to a conciliation between the Goths and the ancient Italians, and to a final flowering of late Roman culture and administration. The disputes about the succession after his death gave the Byzantines the opportunity to intervene directly; after 535, Emperor Justinian's generals conquered the Kingdom of the Ostrogoths, which ended in 552 with the death in the battle of the last ruler, King Totila (542–552), and incorporated it into their empire.

Above: Ostrogoth King Theodoric the Great (circa 454–526) conquered Italy in 493 and based his kingdom on Roman models of administration and culture.

Right: The mausoleum of Theodoric in Ravenna; he made this city the seat of his government and built it up into a significant center of culture.

A Lombard stone relief with animal and plant motifs (eighth century AD); the Lombards, too, adopted numerous elements of Roman culture, but their elective kingship frequently led to brutal power struggles.

THE KINGDOM OF THE VANDALS

The Vandals, so often unfairly maligned (the term "vandalism" for cultural destruction is a term that was coined during the French Revolution), probably originally settled in Silesia, Hungary, and Romania in various tribal groups; in around 400 they were forced westward by the Huns and in 406, together with the Alans and the Suebi, crossed the Rhine to Gaul, moving on to Spain in 409. Under pressure from the Romans and other Germanic peoples, their paramount King (since 428) Geiseric (389–477) crossed over to North Africa via Gibraltar with around 80,000 Vandals and Alans in 429. With the conquest of Carthage (in 439) they took over the agriculturally rich territories and the Roman government of North Africa; Geiseric built up a powerful fleet, conquered Sardinia, Corsica, the Balearics, and parts of Sicily, and sailed up the Tiber to sack Rome in 455. His successors, fervent Arians (see box, p. 151), persecuted the North African Catholics. During Thrasamund's reign (496–523) the kingdom was hard pressed by Byzantine and Berber rebellions, but internally demonstrated a refinement and romanization of culture and art and became more religiously tolerant. The last king, Gelimer (530–534), was eventually forced to capitulate to the troops of

Byzantine General Narses. Byzantium annexed the Vandal kingdom in North Africa, and the Vandals gradually merged with the native Berbers.

The Kingdom of the Lombards

The Lombards—the name is not fully understood, but probably stems from their long-handled battle axes and not (as is widely thought) from "long beards"—originally settled the region of the lower Elbe. They were a particularly warlike Germanic tribe and invaded Roman imperial territories during the Marcomannic Wars (166–180). In around 485, some groups settled the middle reaches of the Danube, others in Moravia and Pannonia; in 510 they annihilated the Kingdom of the Heruli and in 567, together with the Avars (*see p. 174*), the Kingdom of the Gepids. Themselves ousted by the Avars, in 568 they conquered Upper and central Italy under their leader Alboin (circa 560–572/573) and captured their future capital, Pavia. Their settling down coincided with the end of the Migration Period. The Lombard Kingdom consisted of strong, relatively autonomous duchies of Upper Italian cities, from which the kings were chosen; this continually led to disputes about the succession to the throne. Under Liutprand (712–744) they reached the zenith of their power and in 751 captured the Byzantine city of Ravenna. As devout Arians, the Lombards were continuously in conflict with the western Roman Pope and always having to defend themselves against attacks by the Byzantines and Franks, who at the request of the Pope repeatedly intervened in Italy after 754. The last king, Desiderius (757–774), was besieged in Pavia and deposed by Charlemagne in 774, whereupon Charlemagne crowned himself king of the Lombards in Pavia and annexed Upper Italy to Francia.

Lombard King Alboin (before 526–572/573) led his people to Italy in 568 and after capturing the city of Pavia in 572 made it the seat of government.

An early handwritten example of *History of the Lombards* by Paul the Deacon (circa 725–797); he has provided us with the most detailed chronicle of the Lombards.

"Now when King Alboin came with all his warriors and a huge crowd of all sorts of people to the Italian frontier, he climbed up the mountain that rises in that area and looked down on as much of Italy as he could see. For this reason, the mountain has since that time been called the King's Mountain [Monte Maggiore]."

From *Historia Langobardorum* (*History of the Lombards*) by Paul the Deacon, eighth century AD

The Franks

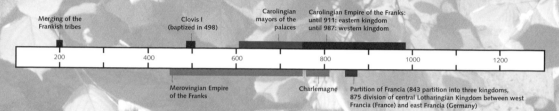

Merging of the Frankish tribes		Clovis I (baptized in 498)		Carolingian mayors of the palaces	Carolingian Empire of the Franks: until 911: eastern kingdom until 987: western kingdom		
200	400		600	800		1000	1200
		Merovingian Empire of the Franks			Charlemagne	Partition of Francia (843 partition into three kingdoms, 875 division of central Lotharingian Kingdom between west Francia (France) and east Francia (Germany)	

Ruins of the Benedictine Abbey at Jumièges (France), which was founded in 653 by St. Philibert (617–684); Philibert held high rank at the court of the Merovingians before he retired to a cloistered life, repelled by the intrigues of the court.

In around 200 the western Germanic tribes formed a confederacy, initially to the east of the Roman frontier of the Lower Rhine; in around 355 the Franks crossed the Rhine and advanced into Roman Gaul (Brabant). Franks from the Middle Rhine, the Bructeri from the Ems-Lippe region, the Sugambri from the Ruhr and Sieg, and later also the Chatti from Hesse. During the course of the Migration Period (and eventually with the collapse of the Roman Rhine frontier in 406/407) they occupied core

THE TRIBAL CONFEDERATION

After 250, Roman sources begin mentioning the Francii ("the valiant ones" or "the free"). Their confederation also included the Salian Franks (Salii) in north Brabant (Toxandria, settled in 358 by Emperor Julian the Apostate), the Ripuarian

Frankish territories (Francia, Hesse, Rhineland-Palatinate, Alsace-Lorraine, Luxembourg, Holland, and eastern Belgium) and made the area around Cologne their center. Under them, the Salian Franks immediately took over the leadership in Brabant; their tribal kings (dukes)

Merovech (447–457), who gave his name to the Merovingian Dynasty, and his son Childeric (458–482) were at the same time Roman military commanders (generals).

CLOVIS AND CHRISTIANITY

Childeric's son Clovis I (482–511) defeated the last Roman military commander in 486 and made himself to all intents and purposes independent in the Netherlands/north Belgium region (with his capital in Tournai). Ambitious and ruthless, he eliminated all his rivals for the leadership of the Franks and in two battles (in 496 and 506) subjugated the Alemannii in the region of Alsace/western Switzerland. In the Battle of Tolbiac (in 496) he is supposed to

became. Clovis, however, made the role of the church subordinate to that of the state, reserved for the king the chairmanship of the synods and the nomination of bishops, and made the clergy subject to royal tax legislation. He thus established the independent development of the Frankish church (which later led to Gallicanism in France) and the considerable sway held by the Frankish and later the Roman/German kings and emperors on church matters until the Investiture Controversy in the eleventh/twelfth century. However, he laid the foundations of the Frankish tradition of endowing churches and abbeys and

Right: Idealized portrait of Clovis I (466–511), who was revered as the founder of the Frankish Kingdom (painting by Pierre Duflos, 1780).

have pleaded for the first time for help from the Christian God; in 498 he had himself baptized, together with 3,000 Frankish nobles, in Rheims Cathedral. Unlike the other Germanic peoples, the Franks became Catholics and thus allies of the Roman Pope, whose protectors they later

the Benedictine abbeys, in particular, became influential centers of education. In 507, with his victory at the Battle of Vouillé (near Poitiers), he drove the Visigoths out of France to Spain (see p. 152) and annexed most of Gaul to Francia, which then became a major European power.

MEROVINGIAN SOCIETY

The majority of the Frankish population consisted of farmers with their servants and maids. The noble class was very small, and there were scarcely any urban centers—these grew up around the residences of counts and bishops. Kings and nobles were initially large landowners descended from the Roman *latifundia* owners; their holdings were cultivated by peasants, who as bondsmen (dependents) were classed as free or unfree and were obliged to serve in the army. An increasing number of unfree peasants became serfs, who as hereditary servants of their masters were forced to perform feudal duties and specified tasks; they became more and more dependent and their freedom of movement was significantly restricted. Until the Middle Ages, the Frankish rulers and their successors were "itinerant kings," who with their retinue traveled the country to court assemblies and judicial hearings, taking up residence in various royal *palatia* or palaces.

THE HISTORY OF THE MEROVINGIANS

In 511, Clovis divided the empire among his four sons; the youngest, Chlotar I (511–561), ruler of Laon and the Meuse region, reunited all the territory in 558 and also acquired Thuringia and Burgundy. He, too, divided the empire among his four sons,

"The King [Clovis] was the first to be baptized by the bishop [Remigius]. A second Constantine, he stepped into the holy bath, in order to . . . cleanse himself in the cool water. As he went to be baptized, the saint of God spoke to him eloquently, 'Gently bend your neck, Sigamber; worship what you have burned; burn what you have worshiped.'"

From Gregory of Tours's *A History of the Franks*, sixth century

Illustration from a fourteenth century medieval manuscript showing the baptism of Clovis by Bishop Remigius of Rheims in 498.

creating the regional kingdoms of Burgundy (merged with Austrasia from 632), Austrasia (Austria, eastern empire), and Neustria (western empire). The eastern empire, whose kings were at times overall rulers, survived until 751, but the Carolingians (*see p. 160*) seized power in the western empire in 737. The various clans of the Merovingians were constantly engaged in unusually bloody and violent family and fratricidal wars against one another. The last Merovingian overall ruler, Childeric III (743–751), was deposed in 751 by Pepin the Short with the consent of the Pope and was banished to a monastery.

FREDEGUND AND BRUNHILDA

The wives of the Merovingian kings also resorted to violence in the power struggle. In order to be able to marry his mistress Fredegund, Chilperic I of Neustria (561–584)

Engraving of Merovingian King Chlotar I (circa 498–561); he reunited Francia in 558, but then divided it up again among his sons.

strangled his wife Galswintha in 567. In 575, the couple had Chilperic's brother Sigibert I of Austria (561–575) murdered, whereupon his widow Brunhilda, Galswintha's sister, ruled with an iron hand as regent, initially for her son, then for her grandchildren and her great-grandson. In 584, Chilperic, too, fell victim—possibly with Fredegund's cooperation—to a murder plot; Fredegund then ruled Neustria until her death in 597. Her regime was just as power-conscious as Brunhilda's, and she was not afraid to blackmail and murder bishops. Brunhilda, probably the model for the Brunnhilde in the *Nibelungenlied*, was dethroned in 613 by the Austrian nobles; they crowned Fredegund's son, Chlothar II (584/597–629) of Neustria, king, making him once more ruler of the entire empire—and the hated Brunhilda was dragged to her death behind a horse.

This page from a Merovingian manuscript shows the high standard of illustration of the scribes and copyists, most of whom were monks, as well as their love of detail.

Within the image: **karolus impaint** · **magnus Annis.14 2**

Charlemagne (742–814), the "father of Europe," depicted as the perfect model of a Christian ruler (copy of a painting by Albrecht Dürer, circa 1600).

THE RISE OF THE CAROLINGIANS

The power of the Frankish Dynasty that arose in the seventh century was directly linked to Chlotar II's victorious unification of the empire (*see p. 159*). The Frankish nobility, which had enabled him to do this, extracted from him in the *Edictum Chlotharii* of 614 major concessions favoring the landowning nobility and feudal society. In Austria and Burgundy, mayors of the palaces (*majordomus*) were installed, who soon wielded the real political power. The Carolingians came into being as the result of marriages allying the two leading noble families, the Arnulfings (after Arnulf of Metz, bishop until 640 and Chlothar II's main political advisor) and the Pippinids (after Pepin the Elder, who from 615 to 640 was the Austrasian mayor of the palace and ultimately became the *de facto* ruler of Austrasia, and was also the initiator of the Carolingian uprising of 613). Pepin's grandson Pepin of Herstal (679/688–714), as mayor of the palace of Austrasia in 679 as well as of Neustria and Burgundy in 688, succeeded in securing a position of unparalleled power for the Carolingians, from which they could then no longer be dislodged.

CHARLES MARTEL AND PEPIN THE SHORT

Charles Martel ("the Hammer," 686–741) inherited all his father Pepin's titles unchallenged in 714 and from 737 onward was even head of state of Francia. In successful military campaigns against Saxony, Frisia, and Bavaria, he enforced the unification of the kingdom and the sovereignty of Francia in the Germanic territories. In 732, at Tours and Poitiers, he defeated the Arabs and Berbers invading from Spain and halted their northward advance; this deed was later declared to be "the salvation of the West."

In 741 Charles handed over power to his sons Carloman and Pepin the Short (714–768). After the Alamannic ruling classes had been annihilated at the Blood Court at Cannstatt

Left: Mosaic of the throne of Christ as the center of the cosmos in the Palace Chapel of Aachen Cathedral, built in the reign of Charlemagne circa 792–805; under this symbol of Christian world domination, the emperor was enthroned as the representative of Christ on earth.

Below: Depiction of a Carolingian ruler at the center of a city; the Carolingians were itinerant kings, who constantly moved through their territories to deliver justice, generally staying in their own royal or imperial palaces.

▶ THE DONATION OF PEPIN

In 756, Pepin handed over the conquered exarchate of Ravenna (the Byzantine administrative district) and the duchies of Spolento and Benevento to the Pope and promised him sovereignty over all the Italian territories conquered by the Lombards. This "donation of Pepin" formed the basis of the later Papal States and of the temporal power of the Pope in Italy.

in 746, the ambitious Pepin placed Bavaria under Frankish sovereignty and in 751, having deposed the last of the Merovingians, took the title of king for himself and his successors. Subsequently, in 755, at the request of the Pope, Pepin laid siege to the Lombards in Pavia, taking Ravenna from them in 756 (see box). In successful campaigns against the Saxons and in Aquitaine, he enlarged the Frankish sphere of power and with the conquest of Narbonne finally forced the Arabs to retreat beyond the Pyrenees. Together with Boniface (672–754), the "Apostle of the Germans," he carried out a thorough reform of the Frankish national church.

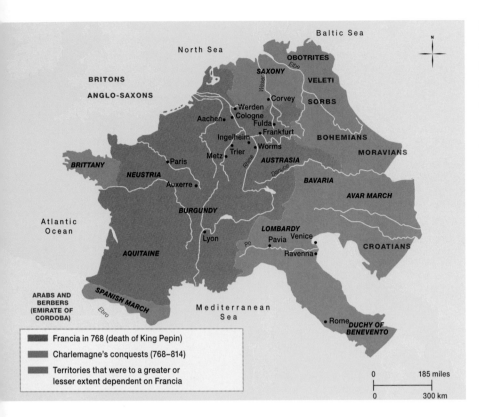

North Sea · Baltic Sea · OBOTRITES · SAXONY · VELETI · BRITONS · ANGLO-SAXONS · Werden · Corvey · SORBS · Aachen · Cologne · Fulda · BOHEMIANS · Ingelheim · Frankfurt · MORAVIANS · Metz · Trier · Worms · BRITTANY · Paris · AUSTRASIA · NEUSTRIA · Danube · AVAR MARCH · Auxerre · BAVARIA · Atlantic Ocean · BURGUNDY · LOMBARDY · AQUITAINE · Lyon · Po · Pavia · Venice · CROATIANS · Ravenna · ARABS AND BERBERS (EMIRATE OF CORDOBA) · SPANISH MARCH · Ebro · Mediterranean Sea · Rome · DUCHY OF BENEVENTO

Francia in 768 (death of King Pepin)

Charlemagne's conquests (768–814)

Territories that were to a greater or lesser extent dependent on Francia

0   185 miles
0   300 km

CHARLEMAGNE'S EMPIRE
The map shows the Carolingian Empire under Pepin the Short as well as Charlemagne's additions, together with territories that were largely under Frankish control.

CHARLEMAGNE: THE FATHER OF EUROPE

In 768, Pepin bequeathed to his sons Charles and Carloman (d. 771) a consolidated empire that Charles, who was to become known as Charlemagne (742–814), expanded to make it the leading power in central and western Europe. In bloody campaigns between 772 and 804, Charlemagne subdued and christianized the rebellious Saxons under their duke, Widukind; during the course of these campaigns, 4,500 Saxons were executed at the Blood Court at Verdun on the Aller. He deposed the last Lombard king in 774 (see p. 155) and in 788 he got rid of the last Bavarian duke and annexed Upper Italy and Bavaria to his empire. In 778, at the request of Arabian emirs, he intervened in Spain and established the Spanish March of the Franks in northern Spain and the regional kingdom of Aquitaine. After 800, Charlemagne enlarged the empire by means of military campaigns in the north against the Danes and in the east against the Bohemians, who submitted to his sovereignty in 805/806 and soon after converted to Christianity; by 803 he had also destroyed the Avar kingdom in Pannonia (see p. 174).

The high point of Charlemagne's reign was his imperial coronation by the Pope on December 25, 800, in Rome, marking the establishment alongside the Byzantine Empire of a second, western empire, which was to form the basis of the "Holy Roman Empire of the German Nation" (962–1806).

Besides his military successes, Charlemagne decisively remodeled the Frankish Empire,

Memorial to the Battle of Roncevaux Pass in northern Spain; here, the Frankish rear guard under the command of Breton Count Roland (Hruodland) were attacked and annihilated by Basques as they marched back from establishing the Spanish March in August 778. In the *Song of Roland*, which originated in around 1100, the dying Roland sounded his horn to call on the emperor for help, whereupon the latter turned around and inflicted a devastating defeat on the "heathens."

> **"** Charlemagne's manner of speech was fluent and effusive; he could express what he wanted clearly and articulately. He was not content with his mother tongue alone, but took the trouble to learn foreign languages. Of these, he learned Latin so well that he could speak it like his mother tongue . . . . He cultivated the liberal arts enthusiastically, held their teachers in great esteem, and conferred great honors upon them. **"**
>
> From Einhard's *Life of Charlemagne*, eighth/ninth century

Charlemagne lays a donated reliquary on the altar of Aachen (scene from a window in Chartres Cathedral, France, thirteenth century). According to church tradition, Charlemagne is a pious saint; however, like his father Pepin before him, he made the church submit to his rigid imperial regime.

dividing it into margravates and administrative units and creating his own "service nobility"; it retained the structure he gave it well into the Middle Ages. He established a uniform currency, church, and legal and judicial systems, which took into account the particular needs of the many peoples of the empire. His sponsorship of education and science, led by his court chapel and the scholars Alcuin and Einhard, was also a factor in his being seen as the "father of Europe."

DIVISION OF THE EMPIRE

Charlemagne's peace-loving son, Louis the Pious (778–840, emperor from 814), proved to be very indulgent toward the church and was in constant conflict with his sons, who were trying to acquire domains of their own. The Treaty of Verdun in 843 divided the empire among them. Lothair I (795–855) was given the title of emperor and the Middle Frankish Kingdom of Lotharingia, stretching from north Germany and the Netherlands across Burgundy and Lorraine (from Lotharingia) as far as Upper Italy; Louis the German (806–876) received the east Frankish kingdom, and Charles the Bald (823–877) the west Frankish kingdom. When Lothair's line died out in 875, Louis and Charles divided his kingdom up between them, thereby creating the borders of Germany (east Francia) and France (west Francia). The Carolingians ruled until they died out—in the eastern kingdom (Germany) until 911 and in the western kingdom (France) until 987.

Vikings: Normans and Varangians

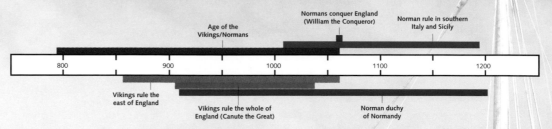

					Normans conquer England (William the Conqueror)		Norman rule in southern Italy and Sicily	

Age of the Vikings/Normans

800	900	1000	1100	1200

Vikings rule the east of England

Vikings rule the whole of England (Canute the Great)

Norman duchy of Normandy

It is principally the former coastal inhabitants of Denmark and Norway who are described as "Vikings." In the west and the south they are known as Normans, in the east as Varangians; for many years "to go viking" referred not only to the pillaging, but also the trading voyages of the Norsemen.

WAY OF LIFE AND SOCIETY

The Age of the Vikings (probably from the Old Norse *vikingr*: sea warriors) is seen as being the period between around 520, but increasingly from 793 (attack on Lindisfarne in northeast England), and the conquest of England in 1066 (*see p. 166*) by the Normans.

They lived in small settlements from agriculture, raising livestock, fishing, and trading, and like other Germanic peoples, were divided into nobles, freemen (warriors), and unfree (servants); prisoners of war and those captured in raids had to work as slaves. Family groups and the exchange of gifts were crucial in determining social prestige. The area's warrior kings relied on a personal following, and functional state institutions such as tax collection only became widely established at a relatively late stage.

Reconstruction of Leif Ericson's Viking ship (circa 970–1020); the son of Eric the Red sailed to North America in around 1000 and was probably the first European to set foot on that continent.

Norse navigation

With their feared longships that had both oars and sails, the Vikings were true masters of navigation and on their raids they carried out a mixture of plundering and bartering. Their leaders in the early days were "sea kings" with no land but with a personal following; there were also groups of young warriors who took up plundering and coastal scavenging and were sometimes seen as criminals even in their own countries. The boats held on average between 20 and 25 warriors, who also rowed, and formed (generally fairly small) fighting units—on large raids there could be as many as 250 ships. The comrades (*felagar*) formed a special fighting and trading community, dividing the booty and traded goods. Swedish Vikings began to secure their access to the east coast as early as the seventh century; there they subjugated the native Slavic/Finnish population and established their own trading stations (such as Grobina near Liepāja in Latvia).

Pillaging and raiding

In 799 the Norsemen began to carry out raids into France and in the ninth century they posed a threat to the whole of western Europe, sailing up the rivers and burning down

the towns, which were mainly built of wood. In this way they destroyed Seville in 844 and Hamburg in 845, plundered Paris several times from 845 onward, and sacked Bremen in 850 and 858. The Vikings' merciless method of fighting with their battle axes was particularly feared. They even plundered Christian churches and monasteries. Some regions tried to keep themselves safe from plundering by paying tribute. It was only when the Norsemen settled in England and France that these devastating attacks largely ceased. The town of Haithabu (present day Hedeby on the German/Danish border) became the leading trading center for North Sea trade from the ninth century.

The Vikings' lightning attacks and raids were a plague for many European cities. This illustration (from 1884) shows an attack on Paris in 885 by the Normans under their leader Rollo. In 911, the king of the western Franks, Charles, made Rollo the first Duke of Normandy, thereby pacifying the wild hordes.

THE BATTLES FOR ENGLAND

The Norsemen not only settled in Iceland and Greenland, but also sought to find a footing in England. The year 793, with the attack on the abbey at Lindisfarne (abandoned in 875 after renewed attacks), saw the beginning of a period of Norse attempts at occupying and settling new lands using a new type of ship, the knorr. From 865, Viking communities established themselves in Mercia and present-day East Anglia (on the east coast of England), captured York and levied danegeld (regular tribute as insurance against plundering) from other areas. When attempting to expand into Wessex, they were engaged in battle on several occasions by King Alfred the Great (871–899); in 878, Alfred and Danish King Guthrum (circa 874–890) divided England between them in the Treaty of Wedmore. Alfred induced Guthrum to accept Christianity and baptism. Gradually, a more peaceful exchange took place between the Vikings in eastern England (Danelaw) and the Anglo-Saxons; however, from 994 Danish King Sweyn Forkbeard (986–1014) made numerous ambitious attempts at invading and conquering the whole of England and exacted an increased level of danegeld, which the Vikings used to pay their warriors (*see also box, p. 167*).

THE NORMANS—NORSEMEN IN FRANCE

Groups of Vikings started invading West Francia with plundering raids as early as the 840s. In 911, the king of the western Franks, Charles III, the Simple (893/898–923), gave the fiefdom of territories in northwestern France to Norwegian Count (*Jarl*) Rollo and made him the first Duke of Normandy (911–927)—with the task of keeping other bands of Norsemen out of France. Rollo's successors allied themselves with the royal family and from the time of Duke Richard I, the Fearless (942–996), played a decisive role in French politics. Richard's great-grandson, William the Conqueror (1027–87), Duke of Normandy from 1035, laid claim to the English throne on the death of his uncle Edward the Confessor (1066), landed with a mighty army on the south coast of England, and won the English throne at the Battle of Hastings in October

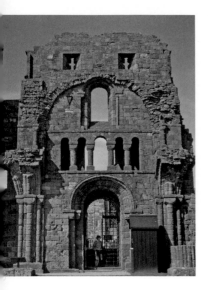

Above: Ruins of the abbey at Lindisfarne, Northumbria (northeast England); the abbey was first attacked and plundered by the Vikings in 793.

Below: A scene from the Bayeux Tapestry (circa 1080) that depicts William the Conqueror's crossing to England and his victory at the Battle of Hastings in 1066.

1066. He allotted the largest landholdings in England to his Norman relations—which led to ongoing conflicts with the Anglo-Saxons— and in 1086 completed the "Domesday Book," a land register for England, that declared the king's peace and transformed the danegeld into a fixed land tax. Normandy was ruled from England by William's heirs until 1204.

Lindisfarne Castle in Northumbria (northeast England); the coastal inhabitants were not always able to find safety behind walls from the attacks of the Vikings and the Normans.

> ▶ **CANUTE THE GREAT**
> **Sweyn Forkbeard's son Canute the Great (995–1035) had seized control over the whole of England by 1016; in 1018 he was also crowned king of Denmark (including the south coast of Sweden), and in 1028 he conquered Norway and converted it to Christianity. In this way he became ruler of a north European empire and controlled North Sea trade. His sons Harold and Harthacanute inherited the empire, but in 1042 England regained its independence under Edward the Confessor (1042–66), a stepson of Canute the Great.**

" Hedeby is a large town at the end of the ocean. In the center of the town there are freshwater fountains. Apart from a few Christians, who have their own church, the people there worship Sirius. In honor of their god they hold an eating and drinking feast. When a man kills a sacrificial animal, be it an ox, a ram, a billy goat, or a hog, he hangs it on a post outside his house so that passers-by know that he has made a sacrifice to the deity. **"**

From the chronicle of the Arab trader al-Tartushi, tenth century

The octagonal Castel del Monte, near Andria (southern Italy), constructed after 1240 by Hohenstaufen Emperor Frederick II (1194–1250); with their fusion of Norman, Arabic, and Byzantine culture and architecture, the Hohenstaufen Dynasty took up the legacy of the Normans in the south.

NORMANS IN ITALY AND SICILY: THE HAUTEVILLE FAMILY

Restlessness and the urge for further adventures overseas spurred the Normans onward, even after they had settled in Normandy. In the eleventh century, the Norman valvassor (noble) Tancred de Hauteville therefore advised his 12 sons to seek fame and acquire lands for

The Cathedral of Palermo in Sicily was built in 1184/85 under Norman King William II, the Good (1166–89).

themselves; thereupon, eight of them joined Norman expeditions to southern Italy. Under the leadership of the eldest, William of the Iron Arm (1043–45), Drogo (1045–51), and Humphrey (1051–57), they conquered the county of Melfi and, with the blessing of the Pope, extended their territories in Lower Italy (at the expense of the Byzantines).

ROBERT GUISCARD AND ROGER I

The younger brothers Robert Guiscard ("the Cunning" 1015–85) and Roger I (1031–1101) had in the meantime also arrived in the south. As leader of the Apulian Normans (Count of Apulia and Duke of Benevento), Robert conquered Calabria in 1058 and Sicily from 1060; in 1072 he captured Palermo. A cunning tactician and resourceful power strategist, he became a vassal of the Pope, and during the Investiture Controversy he drove Emperor Henry IV out of Rome in 1084, hoping, among other things, to appropriate imperial territories in Italy. His restless spirit also caused him to move against Byzantium, presumably with the aim of seizing the Byzantine imperial crown himself. His brother Roger I had distinguished himself in driving the Arabs out of Sicily and had since 1071 borne the title of Count of Sicily, but he nonetheless took large numbers of Muslims into his service. This resulted in a unique mixture of Norman, Arab, and Italian culture developing on the island.

THE NORMAN KINGDOM OF SICILY

The well-educated son Roger II (1095–1154), Count of Sicily from 1105, took the title of king in 1130. He spoke Greek and Arabic and made his tolerant court in Palermo (at which Arab scholars also lived) into an intercultural meeting place, which his successors, who reigned until 1194, continued to develop. Many buildings there, such as the royal chapel in Palermo, still show clear Byzantine and Arab influences. The Hohenstaufen Dynasty, which conquered Sicily in 1194, carried this unique culture forward, particularly Emperor Frederick II (1194–1250), who because of his erudition was called *Stupor mundi* ("Wonder of the world").

The mosaic of Christ as Pantocrator in the royal chapel of the Cathedral of Palermo, begun in 1131, shows clear Byzantine influences both in the selection of motifs and in its execution.

▶ BOHEMOND OF ANTIOCH

The Norman Bohemond (1051/52–1111), eldest son of Robert Guiscard, was one of the most audacious adventurers of his time. He was Count of Taranto from 1085 and became one of the leaders of the First Crusade in 1097. After the conquest of Antioch (Syria) in 1098, he launched a lightning attack and seized for himself the city, which he and his successors then ruled until 1268. He was a tough combatant, whose giant stature, ferocity, and ruthlessness are described by Byzantine and Arab sources with a mixture of awe and loathing. His temporary capture by the Arabs prevented him from becoming king of Jerusalem in 1100.

Kingdoms and peoples in eastern Europe and Asia Minor

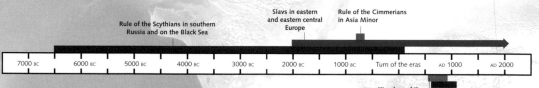

Rule of the Scythians in southern Russia and on the Black Sea

Slavs in eastern and eastern central Europe

Rule of the Cimmerians in Asia Minor

| 7000 BC | 6000 BC | 5000 BC | 4000 BC | 3000 BC | 2000 BC | 1000 BC | Turn of the eras | AD 1000 | AD 2000 |

Kingdom of the Avars in Pannonia

Kingdom of the Khazars in southern Russia (circa AD 800 conversion to Judaism)

First empire of the (proto-) Bulgarians in eastern Europe (adoption of Christianity in AD 864)

After the territories of eastern Europe and Asia Minor had been settled firstly by Scythians and Cimmerians, then also by steppe peoples of Eurasian origin—Avars, proto-Bulgarians, and Khazars—the culture of the Slavs finally gained ascendancy in eastern Europe.

DISTRIBUTION OF SLAV GROUPS

To this day, Slavs still inhabit eastern central, eastern, and southeastern Europe, divided into separate Indo-European linguistic and cultural communities. Although the early period is sparsely documented, the oldest traces of their culture can be dated back to circa 2000 BC. Authors in late antiquity named three closely related ethnic groups: the Veneti (Wends) on the Vistula, the Antes (Ants) between the Dniester and the Don, and the Slavs between the Vistula and the Danube. During the Migration Period, Slavs and Ants advanced from the Caspian and the Black Seas and across the Danube into eastern Roman territories; they were feared archers and spear-throwers.

From the fifth century AD, western Slavs colonized the Danube regions of Bohemia, Moravia, Slovakia, Hungary, and the east of

Background image: Satellite image of the Caspian Sea, the largest saltwater lake on Earth; along its coasts lies the original homeland of the Scythians and Cimmerians.

Above: The Apostles of the Slavs, Methodius (circa AD 815–885) and Cyril (AD 826/827–869), brought Christianity to the eastern Slavic peoples and developed the Cyrillic alphabet.

Austria, and after AD 600 pushed westward as far as the Elbe and the Baltic Sea. Their southern tribes later formed the kingdoms of Bohemia and Poland, while the northern tribes pushed into the areas of eastern Francia and the German Empire and from the time of King Henry I (919–936) were systematically colonized and christianized. Eastern Slavs settled in the Belarus and the Ukraine and pressed forward toward the northeast. Their most important political achievement was the Kievan Rus state in the ninth century and its legacy, the empire of the Russian Czars. Southern Slavs settled in the Balkans, in Pannonia, Thrace, Macedonia, and parts of Greece; they took over the Kingdom of the Avars (*see p. 174*) and the western provinces of Byzantium. A further reason for the division of the Slavic groups was the founding of states by Eurasian Turkic peoples in eastern Europe, by the Magyars in Hungary, and by the proto-Bulgarians, who later mixed with the Slavs. It was not until after their christianization that the Slavs (from 863) obtained their own script—first the Glagolitic and later the Cyrillic—from the "Apostles of the Slavs," Methodius (815–885) and Cyril (826/827–869).

SETTLEMENT AND WAY OF LIFE

The Slavs settled in small villages, though the nobility lived in fortified wooden castles. Their houses were shared by people and livestock and, like bridges and other buildings, were made of wood (only very little has therefore been preserved). Their social structure was characterized by clan and kinship groups with the extended family managing property jointly, and it is probable that their leaders were elected. The Slavs lived by growing cereals and produced pottery for everyday use; livestock farming and trade did not play a major role until later periods. They worshiped weather, star, and war deities, for example, Dazhbog the sun god. Their folktales also featured numerous spirits of nature and demonic beings, among them the witch Baba Yaga.

The Cyrillic alphabet—shown here on a panel of wood and bone (together with numerals and a carved bone as a pointer instrument)—formed the basis of the rich Slavic written culture.

Procession of Persian vassal peoples, presenting their tributes to the emperor; the top row shows Scythian dignitaries with pointed helmets (relief in Persepolis, sixth/fifth century BC).

THE SCYTHIANS: THE ARCHETYPAL HORSE-RIDING NOMADS

The Scythians, who belonged to the Indo-Germanic-Iranian language group, wandered the steppes of southern Russia and the Ukraine as far as the Black Sea from the seventh millennium BC. It is difficult to arrive at a precise definition of the Scythian tribes, which also included the Sacae, since some authors in antiquity referred to all the peoples of the Black Sea region or all steppe nomads as "Scythians." They were ruled by warrior-kings; their social status was based on the ownership of gold and livestock, especially horses. Using the feared weapon of all nomadic horsemen, the composite bow, and making forays in small and highly mobile groups, they plagued almost all the empires of antiquity and accumulated gold by exacting high tribute payments as protection from pillaging. By around 600 BC, they controlled the north of Iran and Armenia. The Scythians held on to their nomadic way of life and resisted all attempts at urbanization and later Hellenization. From the second century BC, they merged increasingly with the Sarmatians, a related Iranian horse-riding people.

KURGANS AND SCYTHIAN GOLD

Kurgans were a characteristic feature of the culture of the early steppe nomads; these were burial mounds, up to 66 ft. (20 m) high, containing burial chambers in which men and women of higher social status were buried with rich grave goods—some also with servants (slaves) and horses. In many cases, their "ice mummies," some of which were clothed in animal hides, have been well preserved by permafrost. So-called "Scythian gold"—jewelry, vessels, and bowls of gold and other precious metals that were adorned with finely worked, naturalistic representations of animals and people (animal style) and may have been used in cult rituals (in which animals and animal-like beings played a special role)—provide evidence of their material wealth and astonishing handicraft skills.

THE CIMMERIANS

The Cimmerians were another Indo-European horse-riding people, who originally lived between the Crimea and southern Russia, then on the "Cimmerian Bosphorus" (Strait of Kerch). They, too, built kurgans and developed their material culture probably even before the Scythians. In the ninth and eighth centuries BC, the migrations of the Scythians forced them to start moving, and they advanced very rapidly toward the southeast and the Caucasus. In the process, they defeated the Kingdoms of Urartu (714 BC) and Phrygia (696/695 BC), invaded the Assyrian Empire, as well as Lydia and the Greek cities, on several occasions, and occupied Sardes and large parts of Ionia. Some of them were killed in battle against the Assyrians in Cilicia, while others were defeated by Lydian King Alyattes (607–560 BC) in their sanctuary at Troas (Anatolia) in 575 BC. Their descendants were absorbed into the population there.

Above: This finely worked Scythian hand mirror with ornamentation on the back shows the artistic skills of the horse-riding people from the Caspian Sea (late seventh/early sixth century BC).

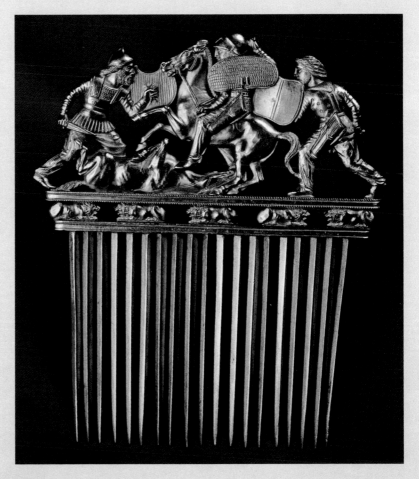

Right: The decoration on this gold comb from a Scythian grave depicts a battle scene and demonstrates the craftsmanship of the horse-riding people (circa 400 BC, present-day St. Petersburg, Russia).

HORSE-RIDING PEOPLES IN EUROPE: THE AVARS

In the wake of the Huns, horse-riding peoples from central Asia established themselves in eastern Europe. The Avars, possibly related to the Hunnic Hephthalites (*see p. 182*), first appeared in 463 on the Black Sea, migrated westward in 555 under pressure from Turkic peoples advancing behind them, and from 558 settled on Byzantine imperial territory as federates. In 567, together with the Lombards (*see p. 155*), they destroyed the Gepid Kingdom in Transylvania and ruled Pannonia and the Carpathian Basin, with offshoots to the north as far as the Volga and the Baltic. Under their Khagan Bayan (562–602) they rose to become the leading power between the Frankish and Byzantine Empires and demanded tribute payments from both neighbors. In order to lend force to his demands, Bayan plundered and occupied the Balkans and Dalmatia. In 598, he stood at the gates of Constantinople. After besieging Constantinople again in 626, uprisings by subjugated Slavs weakened the Avar Kingdom and caused the Bulgarian khaganate to enter into an alliance with Charlemagne (*see p. 162*), who had previously set up the Pannonian marches as protection

Stone castle wall fortifications of the Bulgarian Czars on the mountain ridge of Veliko Tarnovo (Bulgaria); from the twelfth century AD, Tarnovo developed into the Bulgarians' most powerful stronghold.

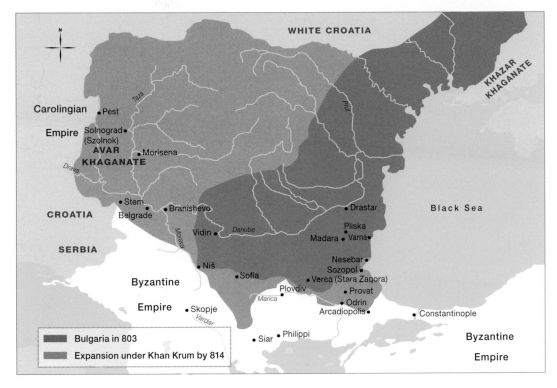

AVARS AND PROTO-BULGARIANS With tactical skill and merciless cruelty, Khan Krum (803–814) doubled the size of the Bulgarian kingdom on his campaigns of war, making it a major eastern European power that brought Byzantium to the brink of collapse.

against Avar invasions. Between 791 and 803, the Franks and the Bulgarians together destroyed the Kingdom of the Avars, the remnants of which were assimilated into the Slav population there.

THE KINGDOM OF THE BULGARIANS

The proto-Bulgarians (also called Hunno-Bulgarians) were a Turkic-speaking horse-riding people who had united with other Turkic peoples and migrated in circa 463 from Kazakhstan and western Siberia to eastern Europe, where they mixed with the remnants of Attila's returning Huns. From 567, they were forced westward by the dominant Avars, but detached themselves from the Avars in circa 635, initially under Byzantine protection, to found the first Great Bulgarian Empire. After 654 this split into several kingdoms, among which the Danube Bulgars (with their capital at Pliska) became dominant in

the area of present-day Bulgaria and the Balkans and expanded into Macedonia. They were soon waging war with Byzantium and conquering its territories. Under Khan Tervel (700–721) they became a leading power, and the feared Khan Krum (803–814) had at his disposal an empire stretching from the borders of Francia in the west to the walls of Constantinople in the east. There was a certain amount of pacification under Boris I (Michael) (852–889), who was baptized in 864. Under Simeon I, the Great (893–927), who—in opposition to Byzantium—proclaimed himself in 917 to be "Czar of all the Bulgarians and Romans [eastern Romans]" and elevated the Slavic language to be the language of state and church, Bulgaria became the center of the Christian Slavic world. In 1018, however, the Byzantines, having regained their strength, destroyed the first Great Bulgarian Empire.

"The very flower of Christianity perished . . . . This happened on July 26, [811]. Khan Krum had the head of Nicephorus cut off and had it put on a stake for many days to display to all the outsiders coming there, to our disgrace. After that he had it taken down, the skull cleaned, plated in silver, and ostentatiously offered it to the Slavic princes to drink from."

From the *Chronicles* of Theophanes, seventh/eighth century AD

THE MYSTERIOUS KHAZARS

There is much speculation about the origins of the Khazars, initially a nomadic Turkic people from central Asia. Because of their subsequent conversion to Judaism (*see below*), Jewish sources see them as a "lost tribe" of Israel. They initially lived in the Kingdom of the Göktürks (552–745) and probably migrated with the latter's western tribes, the Bulgars, toward Europe. In circa 670, they founded a khaganate reaching from the northern Caucasus to the coast of the Caspian Sea; by the ninth century it extended across southern Russia, between the Volga and the Dnieper, eastern Ukraine, Armenia and Georgia, and reached northward as far as Moscow. They were initially allies of Byzantium, were closely embroiled in Byzantine power struggles, and entered into marriage alliances with the imperial family. In 730, they gained a decisive victory over the Muslims at Ardabil, but later maintained good relations with the Abbasid caliphs.

SOCIETY AND TRADE

Like many Turkic peoples, the Khazars were probably originally subdivided into "white" Khazars (nobility and warrior caste) and "black" Khazars (traders and commoners). Their *khagan* or representative leader was flanked by a *bek* or military ruler, both of whom resided in Itil on the Volga. Their tributary peoples also had to provide them with soldiers for their armies. The kingdom acquired considerable wealth by controlling the western section of the Silk Road and thereby Asiatic trade with Byzantium and Europe. There were always Jews among the members of the powerful merchants' guilds (which probably facilitated the conversion). They exported wool, furs, cereals, honey, fish, ceramics, and glassware; Khazar silver coins have been found as far away as Arabia and Scandinavia. After 940, their economic power led to an alliance between Byzantium and Kievan Rus and to inroads being made by both powers into the Khazar Kingdom. With the capture of Itil by Kievan Rus in 969, the kingdom essentially collapsed.

THE THIRTEENTH TRIBE OF ISRAEL?

The Khazars were originally followers of shamanism, with a cult based on the sky god Tengri, but were always tolerant in matters of

religion. In around 800, under Khagan Bulan (Hebrew name Sabriel), they were converted to Judaism. It is considered likely that the reason behind this conversion was to underline their cultural and spiritual independence from the Christian Byzantines and the Muslim Arabs. There is disagreement as to whether just the elite or—as more recent grave finds suggest—broader sections of the population converted to Judaism, which probably became the state religion in around 830. The rulers continued to demonstrate their tolerance, corresponding with numerous scholars. The question of whether the Khazars were absorbed into the population following the decline of their kingdom or went on to become the forefathers of the eastern European Jews (Ashkenazim) is still unresolved today.

Above: The Khazars established a flourishing kingdom near Zelenchukskaya in the mountains of the Caucasus (Russia).

Below: The church of Tsminda Sameda in present-day Georgia; even after their conversion to Judaism, the Khazars were tolerant of different faiths.

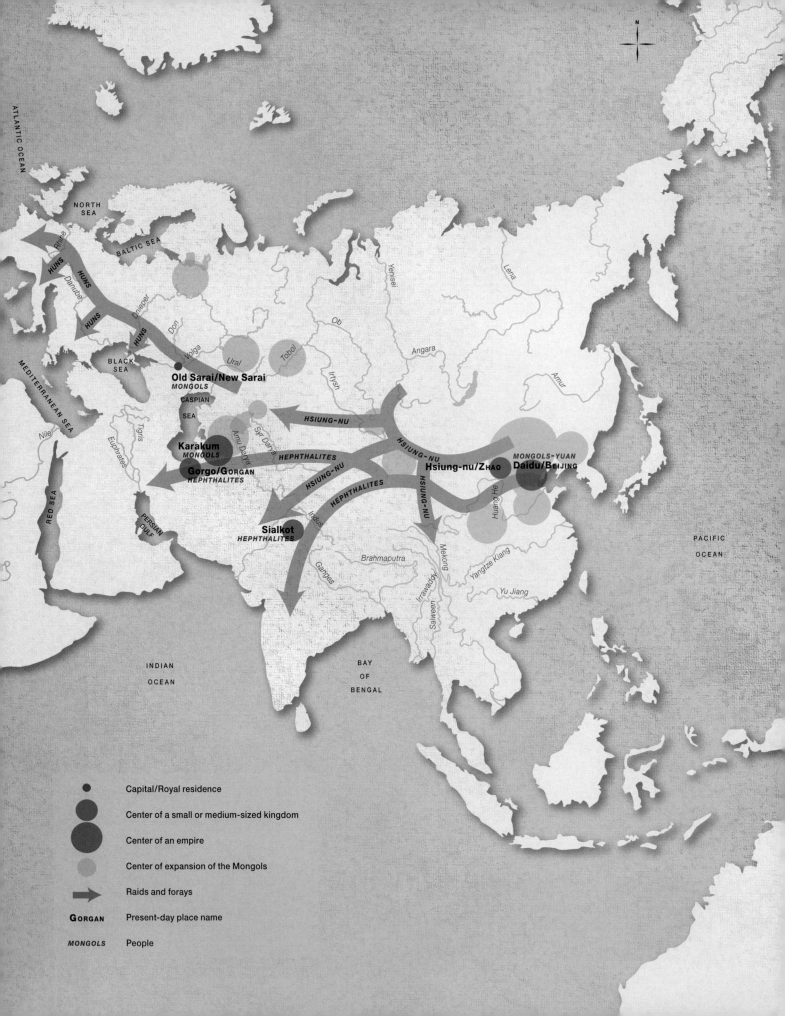

ATLANTIC OCEAN

NORTH SEA

BALTIC SEA

HUNS
HUNS
HUNS
HUNS

Rhine
Danube
Dnieper
Don
Volga
Ural
Tobol

BLACK SEA

MEDITERRANEAN SEA

Nile

Tigris
Euphrates

CASPIAN SEA

Old Sarai/New Sarai
MONGOLS

Karakum
MONGOLS

Gorgo/GORGAN
HEPHTHALITES

Amu Darya
Syr Darya

HSIUNG-NU

HEPHTHALITES

HSIUNG-NU

HSIUNG-NU

HEPHTHALITES

HSIUNG-NU

HSIUNG-NU

Sialkot
HEPHTHALITES

RED SEA

PERSIAN GULF

Indus

Ganges

Brahmaputra

Mekong

Salween

Irrawaddy

Yenisei

Ob

Irtysh

Angara

Lena

Amur

Huang He

Yangtze Kiang

Yu Jiang

Hsiung-nu/ZHAO

MONGOLS-YUAN
Daidu/BEIJING

INDIAN OCEAN

BAY OF BENGAL

PACIFIC OCEAN

N

● Capital/Royal residence

● Center of a small or medium-sized kingdom

● Center of an empire

● Center of expansion of the Mongols

→ Raids and forays

GORGAN Present-day place name

MONGOLS People

Mongols   Huns   Mongol ruler   Mongols   Attila,
                               Genghis Khan   King of the Huns

CENTRAL ASIA

The migrations of the nomadic horse-riding peoples from central Asia more than once brought fundamental changes, both political and cultural, to life in Asia and Europe; they also brought with them immense destruction, cruelty, and suffering for the populations affected. However, the conquerors were not mindless destroyers of culture. They adopted numerous elements from the cultures of the peoples they subjugated, and the synthesis of these with their own culture gave rise to completely new cultures.

At first, the central Asian Hsiung-nu migrated eastward and posed a major threat to China, but they were ultimately forced back toward the west. In the fourth and fifth centuries, the Black Huns, as they are known, (possibly descendants of the Hsiung-nu) triggered the great Migration Period in Europe and advanced, most notably under Attila, far into Europe. Later, confederations of White Huns, also called Hephthalites, threatened the Sassanid Empire in Persia and destroyed the Gupta Empire in India.

In the thirteenth century, the Mongols under Genghis Khan and his successors undertook strategically ambitious campaigns of conquest, firstly into northern China, and later the whole of the Chinese Empire, central Asia, the Islamic world (Persia in particular), and also Russia and the various eastern European states. Besides the Great Khanate in Karakorum, they established permanent dominions (khanates) in a number of areas, for example, that of the Golden Horde in Russia. However, the unity of all the Mongol tribes that Genghis Khan had sought very soon disintegrated into politically and religiously differing spheres of interest and tribal territories.

CENTRAL ASIA

The map shows the movements of the central Asian horse-riding peoples: the Hsiung-nu in China, the Hephthalites in India and Persia, and the Huns as far as western Europe, and also the westward migrations of the Mongols—from eastern China across Persia as far as eastern Europe.

Hsiung-nu, Huns, and Hephthalites

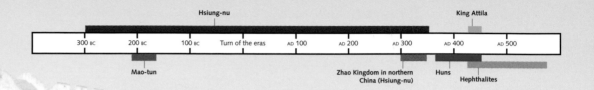

			Hsiung-nu						King Attila		
300 BC	200 BC	100 BC	Turn of the eras	AD 100	AD 200	AD 300	AD 400	AD 500			
	Mao-tun					Zhao Kingdom in northern China (Hsiung-nu)	Huns	Hephthalites			

Section of the Great Wall at Mutianyu, northeast of Beijing. All the early dynasties of China devoted themselves to extending this bulwark against the horse-riding peoples of Inner Asia. However, its psychological effect was greater than the actual impact: Hsiung-nu, Göktürks, and Mongols broke through the Great Wall on several occasions.

The central Asian Hsiung-nu (Xiongnu) were the first of the nomadic horse-riding peoples of the steppes to make large-scale, and often destructive, advances against the empires of the ancient world; in doing so, they triggered migrations of entire peoples. They are mentioned for the first time in Chinese sources in around 260 BC and probably emerged from a confederation of the various tribes of Mongolia and the Altai and Sayan mountains; they are believed to be, at least in part, forebears of the Huns, Hephthalites, and Göktürks, and they exploited the internal weaknesses (Eastern Zhou and Warring States, *see p. 207*) of China, whose early defensive installations prior to the Great Wall were unable to hold them back.

MAO-TUN, THE SCOURGE OF CHINA

The Hsiung-nu ruler Tou-man (240–209 BC) united the tribes for the first time into a loose state structure. His son Mao-tun (209–174 BC) killed him, eliminated all his rivals, and by means of merciless drilling, perfected the art of horseback archery to produce a powerful army consisting of a personally loyal following of soldiers (*ordu*); the entire cavalry of horse archers shot as one man in directions and at targets that the cavalry leaders pointed out with their arrows. After heavy defeats had been inflicted on the Chinese chariots by the maneuverable cavalry groups of the Hsiung-nu, Mao-tun lay siege to the Han emperor (*see p. 212*) in his capital Chang'an, thereby obtaining vast tribute payments and a Chinese princess for a wife, but

he established a firm legal order and a system of taxation. His son Jiyu (also Laoshang, 174–161 BC) gave the kingdom solid structures and a functioning tax system by apportioning power to the 24 leading clans, and took the title Kok Khan (Gök Khagan: divine ruler).

The late period

The final subjugation of the Yuezhi by the Hsiung-nu triggered their westward migration (to Bactria) after 160 BC; they were joined by the Scythian Sakas. After the reign of the last powerful central ruler Hu-han-yeh (58–31 BC), the Hsiung-nu disintegrated

continued his plundering raids, particularly in order to acquire Chinese silk. By 190 BC he had annexed eastern Mongolia and by 176 BC he had subdued the Indo-Germanic Yuezhi in the province of Gansu and the Tarim Basin (northern China) as well as the Wusun between Tien-Shan and Lake Balkhash (Kazakhstan). He confidently reported to the emperor that he had "made them all into Hsiung-nu" and "now united the peoples who draw a bow into a single family." Within this first Hun Kingdom

into five rival tribes and in AD 48 split into a northern and a southern kingdom. China had in the meantime learned from the warfare of the Hsiung-nu and in AD 158 drove out the northern groups toward eastern Turkistan. The southern Hsiung-nu established a powerful kingdom along the Chinese Wall (Han-Zhao Empire after 304) and defeated the Chinese Jin Kingdoms as well as gaining control over the Silk Road. In 352, however, they were annihilated.

THE "BLACK HUNS"

The name "Huns" (probably from the Tungusic *chun* meaning "strength and courage") was generally used in the ancient world to refer to all the central Asian horse-riding nomads (including the Scythians). The "Black Huns" of the Hunnic invasions and the Migration Period in Europe are linked to the forced displacement westward of the northern Hsiung-nu (*see p. 180*). The Huns crossed the Volga in 375, probably because of a shortage of food for such large groups and their herds; they occupied the Caucasus, defeating the Ostrogoths (whom they annexed to their bands of warriors), and drove the Visigoths and other Germanic peoples westward before them. In around 395, they initially turned southward and plundered the Roman and Persian territories between Antioch and Ctesiphon. Their groups combined under the leadership of the brothers Oktar (circa 425–430) and Rua (also Rugila, circa 425–434). Rua was already pursuing plans for an empire and exacting high gold tributes from the Eastern Roman Empire. In 432, Roman General Aetius came under his protection and with Rua's help became the *de facto* leader of the Western Roman Empire.

The pillaging of a Gallo-Roman villa by Attila's Huns. The Huns' search for gold and valuables was frequently accompanied by terrible destruction—a measure deliberately calculated by Attila to nip in the bud any resistance from those he defeated, by spreading fear and terror.

THE HUNNIC WARRIORS

In Europe, the wild, mercilessly pillaging Hun warriors were seen as creatures from hell. Their guerrilla-type combat tactics (small, seemingly uncoordinated parties of horsemen abruptly falling into combat formation with their composite bows and feigning retreats followed by sudden about-turns) threw the armies of Europe, which moved forward in an orderly fashion, into confusion. Like the Mongols who followed them, the Huns slept in the saddle and ate raw meat that they had ridden soft under the saddles. Their use of stirrups enabled them to use both hands when fighting on horseback.

THE HEPHTHALITES: "WHITE HUNS"

In around 425, groups of light-skinned ("White") Huns—probably originally Indo-Germanic or inhabitants of Junggar (north of the Chinese Wall)—established themselves in central Asia and penetrated far into the Persian Empire of the Sassanids (*see p. 62*). Following initial successes, they were pushed back by the Sassanids. After 500, small groups of Hephthalites invaded northern India, causing enormous destruction. During the fight against the Gupta Empire (*see p. 202*), their King Mihirakula (circa 515–542) ruled over a kingdom between Persia, central Asia, and the Ganges Plain. They caused extensive destruction and took over large parts of the Gupta Empire, but from 528 they were forced to retreat to Kashmir. As seminomads, the Hephthalites lived partly in permanent settlements; they had a distinct cult of the dead and in religious terms were close to Zoroastrianism (*see p. 58*) and later Buddhism. In 561/563 Persian King Chosrau 1 wiped out the Iranian Hephthalite tribes, while their Indian and Afghan counterparts were largely absorbed into the local populations in around 600 and 700, respectively.

Facing page: Illustration of the battles between Huns and Alans; in southern Russia, the Alans, who were of Iranian origin, were largely defeated and subdued by the Huns in 374.

Above: Attila on horseback, torch and sword in hand, burning down a town during his invasion of Upper Italy in 451/452 (wood engraving from the nineteenth century).

KING ATTILA: THE MILITARY CAMPAIGNS OF THE "SCOURGE OF GOD"

In 434, Rua's nephews Attila and Bleda inherited the Hun Kingdom. In 444/445, Attila had his brother Bleda murdered, and from then on proved to be the decisive power factor in Europe. Attila resided in a wooden fort on the Tisza between the Eastern Roman Empire and the Western Roman Empire. He was initially on good terms with the latter under the imperial General Aetius, who sent Attila to destroy the Germanic Kingdom of the Burgundians in 436. He exacted increased

Below: Hunnic warriors on horseback attacking the Romans and Visigoths in force during Attila's campaigns in Gaul; in 451, however, they were defeated at the Battle of the Catalaunian Fields.

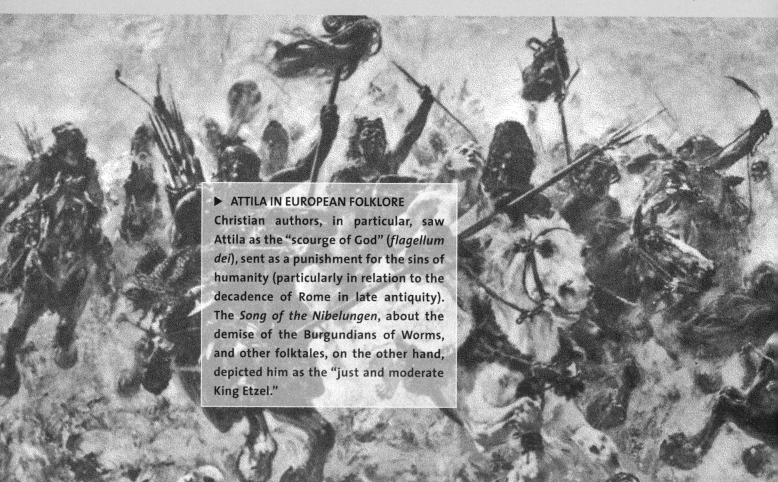

▶ ATTILA IN EUROPEAN FOLKLORE

Christian authors, in particular, saw Attila as the "scourge of God" (*flagellum dei*), sent as a punishment for the sins of humanity (particularly in relation to the decadence of Rome in late antiquity). The *Song of the Nibelungen*, about the demise of the Burgundians of Worms, and other folktales, on the other hand, depicted him as the "just and moderate King Etzel."

tributes from the Eastern Roman Empire and, when payments were delayed, he laid waste to the Balkans and parts of Greece. In 450 the Eastern Roman Emperor Marcian (450–457) refused to pay the tributes and forced the Huns back westward. Attila laid claim to the Western Roman throne with a plan to marry Honoria, the sister of Valentinian III, the emperor of the Western Roman Empire, and marched as far as Gaul. In 451, a battle took place on the Catalaunian Fields (near Troyes) between Attila's Huns and their allies, the Ostrogoths and the Gepids, on one side and the Romans under Aetius and their allies, the Visigoths and the Franks, on the other. Although Attila was initially defeated, the following year he advanced into Italy, burning down Aquileia and conquering Milan and Bergamo. His advance on Rome was brought to a halt principally by epidemics of disease in his army. In 453, after returning to the Tisza, Attila died of a hemorrhage on the night of his marriage to the Gothic princess Ildico. The empire collapsed immediately in a feud between his sons, and the Huns either withdrew to Asia or mixed with the Hungarians and Turkic peoples.

ATTILA'S RULE

Although Attila was for a long time viewed as merely a destroyer and plunderer, more recent research is striving for recognition of his achievements as a politician. Attila employed shrewd tactics to exploit the rivalry between the two parts of the Roman Empire and planned to establish a multinational empire. He distributed the enormous wealth gained from tributes to his warriors and to the Germanic peoples affiliated to his fighting forces, upon whose princes he bestowed high honors. The Huns utilized precious metals to manufacture, in particular, cauldrons and mirrors and they looked on gold jewelry as a status symbol. Attila saw himself as having been selected by the "lord of heaven" and was skilled at using propaganda to spread his fame.

Above: While churchmen particularly saw Attila as a "rod of God" for the sins of humanity, others presented him as a noble warrior prince and praised his bravery (idealized portrait of Attila, based on a sculpture by J. Chapman, 1810).

The Mongols

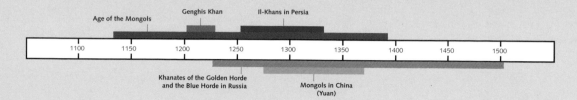

Age of the Mongols Genghis Khan Il-Khans in Persia

| 1100 | 1150 | 1200 | 1250 | 1300 | 1350 | 1400 | 1450 | 1500 |

Khanates of the Golden Horde
and the Blue Horde in Russia

Mongols in China
(Yuan)

Above: A stone dragon relief in the ruins of Har Balgas (Mongolia), the capital of the Mongolian Uyghur Khaganate (eighth century).

Like the Huns, the central Asian Mongols initially formed distinct tribal confederations that were united by Genghis Khan and his successors. The Mongols' campaigns of conquest induced terror among the conquered peoples in the same way that the Huns had done centuries earlier.

WAY OF LIFE AND THE KURULTAI

The Mongols (Tungusic *monggol*: the invincible ones) lived as nomadic shepherds (as some still do today) and were organized in clans. Strict exogamy (marriage outside one's own clan) secured alliances and friendships; tribal confederations, on the other hand, repeatedly lapsed into bloody feuds and rivalries. The

Mongols lived in the steppes in spacious tent dwellings called yurts (Turkic *yurt*: home). These consisted of a wooden frame that was quick to erect and dismantle, which was then covered with animal hides, woolen felt, or textiles and made weatherproof. Their austere and privation-filled way of life taught the Mongols to make use of all kinds of animal products such as *kumis* (fermented mare's milk). As young children, they learned to handle horses, and horse breeding determined the social prestige of the clan. The latter was (initially) grouped strictly hierarchically around the clan leaders

Below: Mongolian yurts in the Hulun Buir steppe in Inner Mongolia (today an autonomous region in northeast China).

and elders. The nobles or tribal leaders gathered in the kurultai, the people's assemblies, in which everyone was free to speak, adopted from the Göktürks; here wars were decided upon and leaders elected (as Genghis Khan was in 1206). The Mongols were devotees of shamanism and animal cults, but showed themselves to be both tolerant of other religions and eager to learn and most of them later adopted a Tibetan version of Buddhism (Lamaism) (which they continue to follow to the present day); some groups turned to Islam or Christianity.

THE MONGOLS' METHODS OF WARFARE

The Mongols perfected the methods of warfare of the horse-riding peoples (Scythians, Göktürks, Huns) with advanced riding techniques and reflex composite bows. Every soldier carried with him a quiver containing about thirty arrows, half of which were heavy, for long-range combat, the other half light and suitable for close combat; these were aimed primarily at their opponents' horses. The army, initially arranged by clan, fought in groups of 10, 100, 1,000, or 10,000 cavalry soldiers, which operated not in close formation but in maneuverable units; these

sometimes penetrated behind enemy lines, and moved into formation only in battle. The enemy was never completely encircled, but was always given an opportunity to escape, causing its troops to fall into disarray; they were then pursued by the Mongols, sometimes for days on end, and annihilated. The Mongols were masters of all forms of psychological warfare (spies, rumors, and propaganda), time after time committing atrocities on the civilian population as an example in order to demoralize the enemy. They also drove prisoners before them into battle as human shields.

Ao Bao, a Mongol stone stupa (shrine) in Mongolia; attached to the shrine are prayer flags, as used in Tibetan Buddhism, which is the religion of most Mongol tribes.

GENGHIS KHAN: YOUTH AND RISE TO POWER

Information about Temujin (1155–1227), who under the name Genghis Khan ("Oceanic Ruler") was to write world history, comes principally from the *Secret History of the Mongols* recorded after his death. Following the murder of his father by Tatars, at whose expense he had conquered a considerable territory, the boy initially led a danger-filled life on the run with his mother and brothers. His courage in battle and diplomatic skills allowed him gradually to unite several Mongol clans under his command and to take revenge on his father's murderers. Once he had subdued the steppe peoples of the Merkits and Keraits (in 1203/04), he was elected Great Khan of all the Mongols at a kurultai in 1206.

GENGHIS KHAN'S CAMPAIGNS OF CONQUEST

Genghis Khan conquered a global empire that extended from the Sea of Japan in the east to the Caspian Sea in the west. He initially turned eastward, subduing the Tanguts in western China in 1209, then invaded the Chinese Empire from the north with over 100,000 warriors in 1211, conquered Bejing in 1215, and advanced as far as the Shandong Peninsula on the east coast of China. In 1218, he conquered the steppe Kingdom of Kara-Khitai in Kazakhstan and in 1219 also made Korea a tributary. At first, a peace treaty existed with his western neighbor, the Islamic Kingdom of Khwarazm-Shah in Transoxania and Persia; however, when the Khwarazm-Shah Ala ad-Din Muhammed (1199–1220) authorized an attack on a Mongol trading caravan and refused to make reparation, from 1220 Genghis Khan proceeded to conquer this Islamic kingdom, the largest up until that time, and by 1231 it had collapsed completely. As early as 1220, Mongol units advanced farther westward, conquered southern Russia and the Caucasus, and advanced into the Ukraine. In August 1227, the Great Khan died on a punitive expedition against the Tanguts as a result of injuries sustained in a riding accident.

Mongol horsemen in traditional warrior clothing from the time of Genghis Khan. The picture shows festivities held in the Sergelen region (Mongolia) in 2006 to mark the 800th anniversary of his election as Khan of the Mongols in 1206.

WHAT DID GENGHIS KHAN WANT?

Even though the khan's campaigns were accompanied by destruction and cruelty, he proved to be a considerate ruler within his own empire. His aim was to unite all the Mongol tribes into a powerful nation (*mongol ulus*). In the army, he introduced a universal military service and the division of military formation into units comprising multiples of tens, hundreds, or thousands. The sole deciding factors for promotion were military skills and courage, not clan affiliation. As the supreme legislator, he enacted a kind of basic law (*yassa*) with rules governing how all the Mongols should live together. He promoted the sciences by learning constantly from the peoples he subjugated and, although he was himself illiterate, he commissioned the development of a Mongol script for administering the state. He recognized the significance of free trade, and so always left the Silk Road traders unmolested.

Below: Scene from Genghis Khan's camp, as represented at the festivities in honor of Genghis Khan held in the Sergelen region (Mongolia) in 2006.

Above: Bronze relief showing the facial features of Genghis Khan (1155–1227), the Mongol conqueror of the world (Tsenkher-Mandal, Mongolia).

Genghis Khan's successors

Genghis Khan had made arrangements for his succession and the division of the conquered territories at an early stage: his eldest son Jochi (who died before his father in 1227), and later Jochi's sons, received Uzbekistan and Kazakhstan (western khanate), his second son Chagatai (d. 1242), central Asia (*ulus chagatai*), and his fourth son Tolui (d. 1232), the homeland of the Mongols. The third son, Ögedei, who was seen as being level-headed, followed him in the role of Great Khan (1229–41). He gave the empire

The Mongol attack on Baghdad in 1258 under Hulagu Khan (1217–65), which left the ancient Islamic world in ruins (illustration from the chronicle Jami al Tawarikh of Rashid ad-Din, circa 1310, Bibliothèque Nationale, Paris, France).

a solid infrastructure by setting up an orderly system of taxation and a swift postal service (*ortoo*) with horse-relay stations and horse-breeding centers. These were also used by the khan's couriers, who had their own state seals (*paixas*). Karakorum (Mongolia), which was founded in 1220 by Genghis Khan, was developed by Ögedei into the royal capital. Goods of many kinds reached the Mongol Empire via the Silk Road. Ögedei's death in 1241 put an end to the westward movement of the Mongols, as all the Mongol leaders wanted to take part in the kurultai to determine the succession. Following a number of khanates under members of Ögedei's family, the Mongol leadership passed in 1251 to Tolui's line.

Möngke, Kublai, and Hulagu

With the aid of Batu Khan (*see p. 192*), Möngke (1209–59), the eldest son of Tolui, became Great Khan in 1251, having eliminated opposition from other princes, in some cases violently. He improved the taxation system by introducing various taxation categories based on wealth and lifestyle, developed Karakorum into a cultural center, and organized interreligious debates, in which the Franciscan William of Rubrouck (*see box, p. 191*), among others, took part. In 1253/54, he put his younger brothers in charge

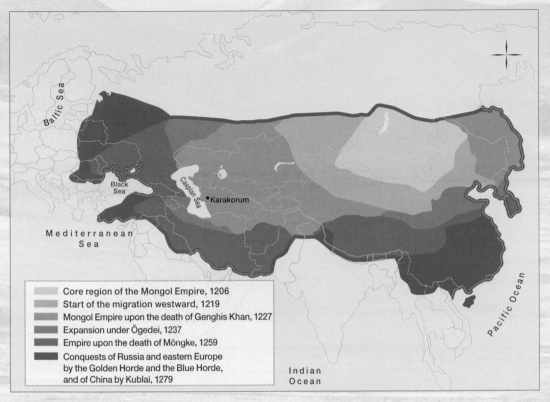

THE EXPANSION OF THE MONGOL EMPIRE
The map shows the expansion of the Mongol territories over the course of just three generations. After the conqueror of the world Genghis Khan, it was primarily his grandsons, the generation of Möngke, Kublai, Hulagu, Batu, and Berke, who successfully led Mongol armies into China and southeast Asia, Persia, and Mesopotamia, and Russia and eastern Europe.

Map legend:
- Core region of the Mongol Empire, 1206
- Start of the migration westward, 1219
- Mongol Empire upon the death of Genghis Khan, 1227
- Expansion under Ögedei, 1237
- Empire upon the death of Möngke, 1259
- Conquests of Russia and eastern Europe by the Golden Horde and the Blue Horde, and of China by Kublai, 1279

Map labels: Baltic Sea, Black Sea, Caspian Sea, Karakorum, Mediterranean Sea, Pacific Ocean, Indian Ocean

of the second wave of Mongol conquests. Kublai (1215–94) conquered China, where he installed the Yuan Dynasty in 1279 (*see p. 219*), and succeeded Möngke as Great Khan in 1260. Under the more urbane Khans Möngke and Kublai, the unity of the Mongols collapsed, as the central Asian tribes clung firmly to their old nomadic way of life. Their brother Hulagu (1217–65) conquered Persia in 1256 and in 1258, after the Caliph had refused to surrender, launched an attack on Baghdad in which the ancient Islamic world perished. He founded the dynastic rule of the Persian Il-Khans (1256–1335), who in 1295 adopted Islam. In 1260 Egyptian Mamluks halted Hulagu's westward advance, at the Battle of Ayn Jalut.

Mongol yurts in the Orkhon River valley (Mongolia), in which the excavated ruins of the capital Karakorum lie.

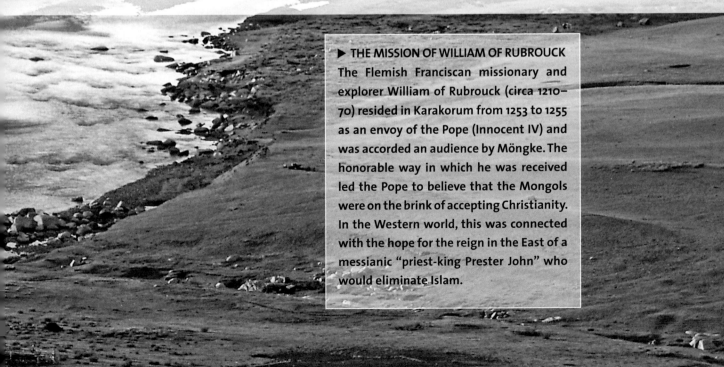

▶ **THE MISSION OF WILLIAM OF RUBROUCK**
The Flemish Franciscan missionary and explorer William of Rubrouck (circa 1210–70) resided in Karakorum from 1253 to 1255 as an envoy of the Pope (Innocent IV) and was accorded an audience by Möngke. The honorable way in which he was received led the Pope to believe that the Mongols were on the brink of accepting Christianity. In the Western world, this was connected with the hope for the reign in the East of a messianic "priest-king Prester John" who would eliminate Islam.

Batu Khan

In 1235, Ögedei charged his nephew Batu (1205–55), a son of Jochi, with the conquest of the west. Between 1236 and 1242, Batu subjugated virtually the whole of Russia in devastating military expeditions, burned down Moscow in 1237, occupied Kiev in 1240, and made the Russian princes pay tribute. In 1242, Old Sarai (from 1342 New Sarai, near Volgograd) became the capital of the western khanate, which was now called the "Golden Horde." In 1251, Batu turned down the position of Great Khan that he had been offered (see p. 190) and in 1252 installed Alexander Nevski as Grand Prince of Russia. In 1240 he advanced into eastern Europe, occupied Krakow and the whole of Hungary, and in 1241 destroyed a German/Polish army of knights at Liegnitz in Silesia. He pushed forward as far as the Adriatic and the outskirts of Vienna, and the whole of Europe appeared to be defenseless when he turned back to the east in order to intervene in the dispute over Ögedei's succession.

The hordes in Russia

The Golden Horde was divided into sub-hordes, of which the Blue Horde in the Sarai region, under the command of Batu's family, was the most important. Until 1357/59 it held supremacy over all the confederations of the Golden Horde. The others included the White Horde of Batu's brother Shibani (d. 1266) and the Orda Horde of the eldest brother Orda (d. 1280), which shared control of Siberia between the Ural and the Irtysh. In 1257, Berke (d. 1267), another of Batu's brothers, seized control of the Golden Horde and the Blue Horde; he had already converted to Islam in 1252, and started the process of islamization of the Russian and Uzbek hordes. Berke introduced the Mongol system of taxation into Russia, by means of which the khans acquired great wealth. Enraged by the attack of the Mongols, under the command of his cousin Hulagu, on Baghdad (see p. 191), Berke supported the Mamluks against Hulagu in the Battle of Ayn Jalut in 1260. This finally shattered the unity of the Mongols.

THE HISTORY OF THE GOLDEN HORDE

The Golden Horde, which was islamized in the fourteenth century, maintained its dominance over Russia until 1480, but had to repeatedly fight against uprisings by the tributary Christian princes. The khans, who engaged in lively trade with the Italian mercantile republics, particularly via the Crimea, attempted to establish a balance between the nomadic and the sedentary sections of the population; the mixing of Mongols and Russians led to the emergence of the Tatars. In 1346/47 they were severely decimated by the Black Death and in 1380 suffered their first heavy defeat against the Russians. Khan Toqtamish (1380–95) once again established the sovereignty of the Golden Horde over Russia, but after 1419 its rule disintegrated into rival khanates that were gradually conquered by the Russians. The latter vanquished the last Mongol khan of the Crimea in 1502.

Right: Batu Khan (1205–55), the Mongol conqueror of Russia and founder of the Golden and the Blue Hordes, captures the city of Kozelsk in 1238 (illustration, mid-sixteenth century).

Above: View of the south coast of the Crimean Peninsula; the last Mongol khanate of the Golden Horde survived here until 1502.

CASPIAN
SEA

Don
Volga
Ural
Tobol
Ob
Irtysh
Yenisei
Angara
Lena
Amur

Gorgo/**G**ORGAN
HEPHTHALITES

Syr Darya
Amu Darya
Indus

Harappa *INDUS*

Mohenjo-Daro *INDUS*

Kannauj
INDUS-HARSHA

Rajagriha/
Pataliputra/PATNA
INDUS-MAURYA/NANDA/
GUPTA

Brahmaputra
Ganges
Mekong

INDIAN

OCEAN

BAY

OF

BENGAL

Irrawaddy
Salween

Pagan *BURMANS*

Lamphun MON
Thaton MON

Hongsawatoi/
Pegu/BAGO MON

Hariharalaya
KHMER

Yasodharapura
KHMER

Angkor
KHMER

Yangtze Kiang
Huang He

Pyongyang
HAN-GOGURYEO

Kaesong
GOGURYEO

Fujiwara-kyo
JAPANESE-SOGA

Kamakura
JAPANESE-MINAMC

Daidu/BEIJING
MONGOLS-YÜAN

Anyang
CHINESE-XIA

Chang'an/XIAN
CHINESE-
QIN/HAN/SUI/TANG

Kaifeng
CHINESE-SONG

Ao
CHINESE-SHANG

Gyeongju
HAN-SILLA

Yoshino
JAPANESE-ASHIK

Nara
JAPANESE-FUJIWAF

Heian/KYOTO
JAPANESE-FUJIWARA/
ASHIKAGA

Gongju/
ONGJIN
HAN-BAEKJE

Sabi
HAN-BAEKJE

Yu Jiang

Sinhapura *CHAM*

Indrapura *CHAM*

Vijaya *CHAM*

PACIFIC

OCEAN

N

Legend:

City-state

Center of a small or medium-sized kingdom

Center of an empire

PATNA   Present-day place name

MONGOLS   People

YÜAN   Kingdom

Japanese   Champa   Chinese   Khmer   Indus

SOUTH AND EAST ASIA

The early Asiatic cultures, first and foremost those of China and India, are among humankind's oldest advanced civilizations. Here, the Indus civilization was followed by the invasion of the Aryans, who introduced the Vedic system of religion and established various kingdoms, with those of Maurya and Gupta growing to become the most important of the Indian kingdoms. The subcontinent underwent countless further political, religious, and ethnic upheavals during the course of its history.

By contrast, the development of China, Japan, and most of the southeast Asian peoples appears less disrupted. Although China did experience division of its empire on a number of occasions, it was also repeatedly unified under powerful and culturally influential dynasties that established efficient public administrations with trained bodies of officials. Here, as in Japan, the combination of ancient indigenous religions with Confucian state ideology and Buddhist humanism ensured relatively stable rule. In China and in the Khmer Empire, but most of all in Japan, the status of the ruler took on distinctive forms of sacred legitimization. In Japan, this led ultimately to the tenno (emperor) being assigned merely ritual functions, whereas rival noble clans secured the political power for themselves and established the military rule of the shoguns.

The historical kingdoms of the peoples of Burma (Myanmar), Vietnam, and Korea were strongly Hindu or Buddhist in character and frequently fell under the influence of Indian culture or were under the sovereignty of the dominant power in China. This was true in the case of the Khmer Empire in Cambodia, whose imposing temple complexes at Angkor remain to this day evidence of its former importance.

SOUTH AND EAST ASIA
The map shows the kingdoms of Asia: the states of the
Indian subcontinent, the empires of China and Japan, and
the kingdoms of the peoples of Burma, Thailand, Vietnam,
Cambodia (Khmer), and Korea.

India

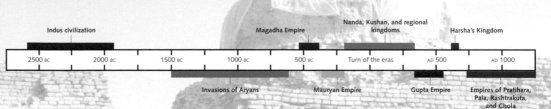

	Indus civilization				Magadha Empire	Nanda, Kushan, and regional kingdoms		Harsha's Kingdom

2500 BC	2000 BC	1500 BC	1000 BC	500 BC	Turn of the eras	AD 500	AD 1000

		Invasions of Aryans		Mauryan Empire		Gupta Empire	Empires of Pratihara, Pala, Rashtrakuta, and Chola

Since the settlement of Baluchistan (Mehrgarh) by village-dwelling arable farming peoples in circa 6500 BC, India has been one of the oldest and, over the course of its history, most diverse of humankind's advanced civilizations. Since the Aryan period, it has been strongly influenced (right into the modern era) by the caste system and the religious systems of the subcontinent.

THE INDUS CIVILIZATION: HARAPPA AND MOHENJO-DARO

The earliest advanced civilization of the indigenous peoples of India is believed to be the Indus civilization (circa 2600–1900 BC), with its fortified cities on rivers, first and foremost the Indus and its tributaries. It engaged intensively in agriculture, livestock farming, and trade, produced pottery and developed its own (as yet undeciphered) script of symbols, the Indus script. Its centers were the clay-brick cities of Harappa and Mohenjo-Daro (Pakistan), which, laid out in a chessboard pattern and defended by city walls and citadels, had granaries and extensive trading contacts and were possibly ruled by priest-kings with a cult based on the lord of the

Background image: The excavated ruins of Mohenjo-Daro (in present-day Pakistan), one of the most important centers of the Indus civilization and one of the earliest cities in history.

Above: Sculpture of a bearded man, often interpreted as being a "priest-king," from Mohenjo-Daro (circa 2500 BC; Museum of Karachi, Pakistan).

animals. Mohenjo-Daro, with over 600 wells and sewers, must have been one of the world's earliest highly developed cities. From 1900 BC, the Indus civilization fell into decline as a result of various factors (e.g. changing climate, drying up of rivers, clearing of forests, invasion of the Aryans), and knowledge of the script was lost, but their agricultural and water engineering practices were adopted by the Aryans.

The Dravidian cultural group

In early times, the Dravidian culture, which (like the Tamil) nowadays has its home principally in southern India, was widespread over large parts of India and Pakistan, and it is for this reason that Dravidian language enclaves are still to be found in the north today. The invading Aryans drove the Dravidian culture southward, and it subsequently became the stronghold of ancient Indian culture and religion. After adopting Vedic Hinduism, the Dravidian cultural group opposed first Buddhism in the north and then the triumphal march of Islam in northern and central India, sometimes using military force.

The invasion of the Aryans

Between 1500 BC and circa 600 BC, India suffered a succession of invasions by the originally nomadic Aryan peoples native to the steppes of central Asia, who also occupied Persia. This immigration from the northwest, which occurred over a long period of time, took place primarily without violence and was more akin to migration than invasion *per se*. However, the Aryans, with their military superiority as horse-riding warriors and charioteers, overcame resistance wherever they encountered it.

In the early Vedic period (circa 1300–1000 BC) they colonized the river valleys of the Indus, Ganges, and Yamuna and installed the oldest Vedic religion. The middle Vedic period (circa 1000–600 BC) saw urbanization and the formation of the first kingdoms that in the late Vedic period (circa 600–450 BC) ruled the whole of the north of India; in the northeast, Magadha (in the present-day federal state of Bihar) became particularly dominant (from circa 500 to 350 BC).

This ensemble of figures from Mohenjo-Daro shows a cart drawn by oxen and indicates the importance of cattle even in pre-Vedic Indus culture. It is possible that they already practiced a cattle cult.

Brama.

The creator god Brahma, whose four additional heads frequently symbolize the four holy Vedas or the compass directions.

focused initially on ritual purity and the correct prescribed forms for sacrificial ceremonies. Only gradually did a more ethical and philosophical focus of the religion develop, characterized by the reciprocal influence of religious and philosophical-cosmological questions about the origins of the world, ethical world order (*dharma* and *rita*), and human actions in the world; the West summarizes these under the term Hinduism. The Hindu teachings are laid down principally in the four holy Vedas (Rig Veda, Sama Veda, Yajur Veda, and Atharva Veda) as well as in a series of later supplementary writings, but the great epics of India (the *Mahabharata*, containing the "Song of God," the *Bhagavad Gita*, and the *Ramayana*) are also heavily infused with religion and philosophy. Among the main teachings (to this day) are the Brahman-Atman doctrine—according to which the soul of the individual (Atman) constantly strives to return to, and eventually enters, the

VEDIC RELIGION

The Aryans brought to India the Vedic religion that in the early stages was still heavily influenced by the Indo-Aryan cattle cult (its legacy is the sanctity of the cow in India) and

"A ruler are you, powerful and sublime,
A destroyer of enemies, matched by no one,
Vanquished and slain will never more be
He to whom you in mercy have bowed . . . .
Free us, Indra, from adversaries,
Drive the enemy fighters from the land,
And let him who threatens and persecutes us be
banished by you into deepest darkness."

From *Rig Veda*: song to Indra

Right: A statue of the Hindu god Vishnu as Narayana (eternal man, son of man)—a popular way of representing Vishnu as Lord of the Cosmos (Kathmandu, Nepal).

Universal Ground carrying it, the Brahman or all-soul—and the doctrine of karmic retribution. According to the latter, good or evil deeds during life (karma) result in the reincarnation of the individual soul in different life forms, seen as superior or inferior, with the aim—through morally good deeds and ritual purity—of breaking through the cycle of reincarnations (Samsara) that causes suffering, and ultimately entering into the all-soul Brahman. Buddhism has also adopted the principal Hindu doctrines.

THE CASTE SYSTEM

The system of castes introduced by the Aryans is seen as a characteristic feature of Indian culture and constitutes both a religious and a social stratification that has become the prevailing order. It defines the degree of ritual/religious purity in each case: specific people, animals, plants, precious stones, and colors belong to each caste; the member of a caste feels traditionally more closely connected to them than, say, to the people of a different caste. A distinction is made between spiritual/religious membership of, on the one hand, the four main castes (Sanskrit *varna*: status, color) and, on the other, the thousands of subcastes (*jatis*), which vary according to the clans and occupational affiliations that shape everyday life.

The four main castes of the *varna* order (whose origins can be traced back to the limbs of the dissected mythical universal male being, Purusha) are (1) Brahmins (priests and scholars), (2) Kshatriya (kings, princes, warriors, and administrators), (3) Vaishya (landowners, farmers, merchants, traders, and moneylenders), and (4) Shudra (artisans, tenant farmers, day laborers, and servants). The Dalit (untouchables), who in India even today lead a life of hardship and are socially despised, are viewed as standing beyond, that is, below, every caste.

The richly sculptured portal of the Vaikunthaperumal Temple in Kanchipuram (India, built AD 674–800), flanked on each side by the guarding figures of the primeval bull Nandi.

RELIGIOUS CHANGES

In the post-Vedic period, there were changes in the diverse Vedic pantheon; the previous supreme gods Indra and Mitra-Viruna gave way to the trinity (Trimurti) of Brahma the Creator, Vishnu the Preserver, and Shiva the Destroyer; together they symbolize the cycle of all living things, even though it is Vishnu and Shiva who have ultimately prevailed as supreme gods today. Over time, two significant reform movements also emerged that opposed Vedic animal sacrifice and the caste system, called for strictly ethical and peaceable forms of living, and ultimately became separate religions: Jainism, initiated by Mahavira (circa 599–527 BC), and Buddhism, introduced by Siddharta Gautama Buddha (563–483 BC). The rulers of India soon recognized the

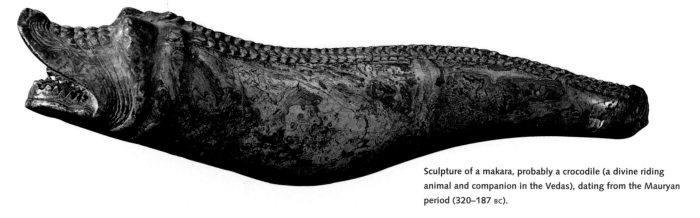

Sculpture of a makara, probably a crocodile (a divine riding
animal and companion in the Vedas), dating from the Mauryan
period (320–187 BC).

potential of both religions to promote peace in society and looked favorably in particular on Buddhism, which under the Mauryas became the leading religion of northern and central India.

THE MAURYAN EMPIRE

After Alexander the Great's Indian campaign (*see p. 110*), Chandragupta Maurya (321–297 BC) founded the first Indian empire, in emulation of Magadha. Through peace treaties with the Seleucids (*see p. 114*) and with the Graeco-Bactrian Empire (256–129 BC), founded by Alexander's Diadochi in Bactria and parts of Afghanistan, which had an Indo-Greek culture, he also secured for himself rule over Baluchistan and the Kabul region (Afghanistan). Chandragupta promoted Jainism and at an early stage gave the empire a rigid organization based on occupational status. According to the work Arthashastra (the book of statecraft) by his leading minister Kautilya, he was kept very much in the picture on everything that was happening in his empire by a system of informers and spies. His son Bindusara (297–268 BC) extended the empire as far as Kalinga (Orissa). The reign of Asoka (268–232 BC), who ruled over what was then the largest Indian empire in history, stretching as far as southern India, Pakistan, and Afghanistan, marked the cultural high point of the Mauryan Empire. After a rapid succession of different rulers, the empire then fell into ruin and was finally swept away in 180 BC.

EMPEROR ASOKA AND THE DHAMMA SYSTEM

The role played by Asoka in Buddhism was of similar importance to that played by Constantine the Great in Christianity. Shocked by the suffering of the population on his campaigns, he avowed himself a Buddhist and proclaimed in rock edicts and crowned pillars a doctrine in which the law, custom, and religious ethics (*dhamma*) are central. He introduced comprehensive social reforms,

sent missionaries to various courts and ended arbitrary taxation; he distributed government land to the poorer strata of the population and set up schools and hospitals (even for animals). He also prescribed the Dhamma: a moral and peaceful social order comprising respect for gods and fellow humans including ancestors and descendants; against opposition from traditionalists, he had the observance of Dhamma regulations monitored by state inspectors.

A stone relief depicting Buddha's footprints (which bring luck) and the wheel of law on a pillar of the Great Stupa of Sanchi, built by Emperor Asoka.

"All people are my children. Just as I desire for my children that they may attain in every respect well-being and happiness in this world and the next, so do I desire this also for all other people. However, you do not yet know to what extent this is my desire. One of you may well understand it, but even he will understand it only partially, not fully. Therefore, focus your attention on this . . . ."

Emperor Asoka: separate edict on impartial jurisdiction, third century BC

The Guptas: From the foundation of the empire to Chrandragupta II

Between 100 and 250, the Kushan Empire, originally a federation of nomadic Indo-European tribes who came from the east, was dominant in central Asia and northern India, but then disintegrated into a large number of smaller dominions. Chandragupta I (320–335) brought an end to this proliferation of small states and established the Gupta Empire in the Ganges region. His son Samudragupta (335–375) captured Magadha with its capital Pataliputra (present-day Patna), which he developed into a cultural and trading center, and ruled over the whole of central India. The most important Gupta ruler was Chandragupta II (375–414/415), who pursued a shrewd marriage policy, and under his rule the Gupta Empire flourished and prospered, with a well-functioning government administration and worldwide trade links; the merchants, artisans, and bankers who were organized in guilds, as well as the state itself, became so rich through trade that Chandragupta largely abolished taxes. He was strongly religious by nature, and so he also abolished the death penalty; at the same time, however, to counter one-sided domination by Buddhism, he attached renewed importance to the caste system, thereby paving the way for Hinduism to regain strength.

The Later Guptas

The emperors Kumaragupta (414/415–455), Skandagupta (455–467), and Buddhagupta (476–495), in a spirit of religious tolerance and piety, made use of a long period of peace to

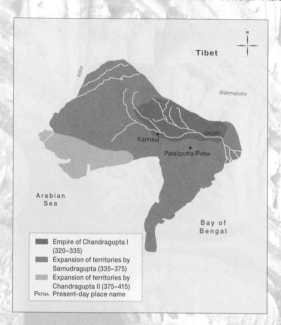

THE GUPTA EMPIRE
The map shows the last of the ancient empires of India, indicating its extent under the first rulers. The Gupta Empire later fell victim to invasions by the Hephthalites.

Tibet

Indus

Brahmaputra

Ganges

Kannauj

Pataliputra/PATNA

Arabian Sea

Bay of Bengal

■ Empire of Chandragupta I (320–335)
■ Expansion of territories by Samudragupta (335–375)
■ Expansion of territories by Chandragupta II (375–415)
PATNA Present-day place name

▶ THE STATUS OF THE BRAHMINS

▶ THE STATUS OF THE BRAHMINS

The reemergence of Hinduism established the privileged Brahmins in particular as the leading class and they often possessed large properties. As priests and members of the highest caste, many of them exploited their monopoly on interpretation of the Vedas to exert political influence and supplied their rulers with an ideological basis to legitimize decisions that also served their own interests.

endow and promote large numbers of Hindu, Buddhist, and Jain temples and monasteries; these were provided with immense land holdings and became virtually autonomous entities. The powerful army of the Guptas was still able to repel the first invasion of the Hephthalites (*see p. 182*) in 458, but after 495 the latter established themselves firmly in Kashmir and Punjab; from 515 onward, the Gupta rulers paid tribute to the Hephthalites, who fostered disputes between the Gupta pretenders to the throne and broke up the empire in around 550.

Left: View of the interior of the cave temple of Ajanta (India), which was a major center of Buddhism in India until the seventh century AD.

KING HARSHA

The last powerful ruler of northern India was King Harsha (Harshavardhana, 606–647), originally a Gupta general, who, from his base in Bengal, unified northern India into a modern-seeming centrally administered state. A ruler who also wrote plays, he promoted a synthesis of Hinduism and Buddhism and established numerous foundations for the poor and needy. However, though he was able to guarantee peace for 30 years, economic decline set in under his rule as India was cut off from its trade routes to the west and to the east by nomadic peoples.

The so-called Stupa No. 3 in Sanchi (India, constructed between the first century BC and the first century AD); the structure of the stupa is clearly seen as a (hemispherical) cosmic egg, crowned by a stone umbrella, with steps up to it and a circular terrace. In its interior, the structure of the world is represented around the cosmic Mount Meru. The path into the area around the stupa leads through a stone gateway.

> "The observance of one's own particular duty leads to heaven and to infinite bliss. If it were transgressed, then the whole world would perish completely as a result of the confusion of being confounded. For that reason the king must not allow beings to sin against their particular duties; for he who complies with his own norm for living will enjoy happiness after death and here in this life. If the world persists within the bounds on life of the Aryans, and follows the rules on castes and stages of life, protected by the Vedas, then it will surely rise up serenely and not fall."

Kautilya: *Book of Statecraft, Book 1: On education,* fourth/third century BC

Stone relief depicting gods and saints on a Hindu temple (mid-eleventh century).

THE INDIAN MIDDLE AGES: POLITICAL AND RELIGIOUS TURMOIL

The Islamic conqueror Mahmud of Ghazni (971–1030) receives envoys from the Hindu princes of India. He employed harsh measures to impose Islam upon the whole of northern India from 1001, and since then Islam has become a defining power on the Indian subcontinent (illustration from the chronicle of Rashid ad-Din, late fourteenth century).

Although King Harsha had argued for a balanced approach in religious policy, there was a significant reemergence of Hinduism in the period that followed, especially as Buddhism in India had been embedded almost exclusively among the upper classes. In addition, Buddhist monasteries were unpopular among the peasant population on account of the high levies that had to be paid to them. Eventually, Buddhism migrated farther to the east. The Indian Middle Ages, as they are called, saw the fragmentation of political power in the north among the kingdoms of the Rashtrakutas in central India (752–973), the Palas in Bengal (750–1151), and the Pratiharas (730–1036) in northeast India, which were a continuous threat to one another. Court culture became increasingly refined while the peasantry grew more and more impoverished and became wholly dependent on the large landowners. The fragmentation of power strengthened the autonomy of local princes and dynasties, whose influence the kings attempted to curtail, particularly in the tenth/eleventh centuries, through increasing gifts of land to the Brahmins (*see box, p. 203*).

THE CHOLA EMPIRE OF THE SOUTH

South India alone had remained true to Hinduism (Brahmanism) in the preceding centuries. It was chiefly with the rise of the southern Indian Tamil Empire of the Cholas after 850 that it regained its position as the leading religion of India. King Rajaraya I (985–1014) extended the influence of the empire to Sri Lanka and Kalinga (northeast India), and his son Rajendra I (1014–44) expanded the Chola Empire as far as the Ganges and Bengal. The kings conducted long-distance and maritime trading as far as China, promoted Indian national literature and art, and strengthened the cult of Shiva. Right to the end of their dynasty in 1279, the Cholas, whose final golden age occurred under Kulottunga I (1070–1120), put up fierce resistance to the advance of Islam. The dynasties that succeeded them also adhered to Hinduism and ancient Indian culture.

THE INVASION OF ISLAM

After the Hephthalites, the north of India came under pressure from a new power with a dynamic religion: Arab-Islamic armies had advanced into Pakistan (Sind) for the first time as far back as 711, but it was Mahmud of Ghazni (971–1030), one of the greatest of Islam's conquerors, who advanced into India from Afghanistan in 17 campaigns between 1001 and 1024 and conquered the north, destroying Hindu temples and images of the gods as he did so. Hindus' image-rich polytheism was viewed by the strictly monotheistic Muslims as "idolatry." From 1206, dynasties of Turkish military rulers established themselves in central India and founded the Delhi Sultanate, which after 1526 became the basis of the Moghuls' global empire. Only gradually did the Islamic conquerors come to understand and broadly tolerate the advanced ancient Indian culture.

The Shri-Minakshi-Sundareshvara Temple in Madurai in south India, profusely adorned with scenes and sculptures, attracts large numbers of Hindu pilgrims.

China

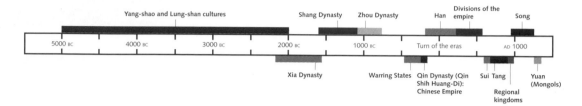

Yang-shao and Lung-shan cultures   Shang Dynasty   Zhou Dynasty   Han   Divisions of the empire   Song

5000 BC   4000 BC   3000 BC   2000 BC   1000 BC   Turn of the eras   AD 1000

Xia Dynasty   Warring States   Qin Dynasty (Qin Shih Huang-Di): Chinese Empire   Sui Tang   Regional kingdoms   Yuan (Mongols)

China has been permanently settled since the time of Peking Man (*Sinanthropus pekinensis*) in around 280,000 BC; people came together to form permanent village settlements practicing slash-and-burn agriculture and pottery production there from the time of the Yang-shao culture (circa 5000–3000 BC) and the Lung-shan culture (3000–2000 BC); numerous local cultures and centers emerged in this period. According to Chinese tradition, the establishment of major states by various emperors (Fuxi, Shennong, the Yellow Emperor Huang-Di, Yao, Shun, and Yu the Great), who are considered cultural heroes of agriculture and water management, began as early as 2200 BC.

THE KINGDOMS OF THE XIA AND THE SHANG

According to a tradition that is in part mythical

A richly decorated bronze vessel from the Warring States period (476–221 BC), an extremely fertile period in cultural, artistic, and intellectual terms.

and has in part been confirmed by archaeological finds, Yu the Great founded the Xia Dynasty (circa 2200–1570 BC), the first Chinese dynasty of a centralized state in the lower reaches of the Yellow River (Huang He). The dynasty is renowned for its dam-building and the working of bronze. It was followed by the far better-documented Shang Dynasty (circa 1570–1066 BC), which had its capital in the fortified city of Ao (northern Henan) and developed this into a commercial center covering 1.23 sq miles (3.2 sq km). The Shang already had an advanced civilization with highly developed agriculture, sericulture, and silk weaving, as well as copper and bronze working and the use of spoked wheels. With between 2,000 and 3,000 characters, it had already developed the foundations of the Chinese pictographic and character script still used today. Early Chinese religion practiced the bone oracle or turtle shell oracle, in which the cracks that emerged in the objects when they were heated were interpreted as written characters and messages.

THE ZHOU PERIOD

The Zhou, originally vassals of the Shang in western China, rebelled against them, seized power in circa 1066 BC and made Hao, in the west, the new capital. From their central base, the early Western Zhou (circa 1066–771 BC)

Above: A bronze mask, possibly used for ritual purposes, dating from the period of the Shang Dynasty (circa 1570–1066 BC).

imposed firm rule over the entire northwest region and expanded southward. They laid the foundations of the future Chinese feudal state by distributing large landholdings as fiefdoms to family members, allied clans, and former Shang vassals, who were thus bound to the new rulers but in their own territories acted with increasing autonomy. The peasants and liegemen of their territories increasingly became serfs of the landowners, a process that subsequently

intensified and repeatedly led to peasant uprisings. The cities, too, were organized in highly hierarchical fashion, with nobles and simple people to all intents and purposes living in two separate areas of a divided city. The independence and strength of the liege princes meant that the later Eastern Zhou (771–256 BC) were rulers in the capital city Lo-yang only in a formal sense and were restricted to ritual functions.

The Great Wall (the section shown here is near to Beijing) is the work of many generations and imperial dynasties of China. At several points, it has undergone repeated and thorough restoration.

A stone sculpture (from the period of the Song Dynasty, AD 960–1279) of the (probably mythical) sage Lao Tzu in Quanzhou (China). His work *Tao Te Ching* (*The Book of the Way and the Power*) is one of China's seminal philosophical writings, and he is seen as the founder of Taoism.

RELIGION AND PHILOSOPHY: THE WARRING STATES AND THE HUNDRED SCHOOLS OF THOUGHT

The period of the Warring States (476–221 BC) marks the rise of regional rulers and warlords from the class of liege princes who had become independent and who waged bitter wars against one another for supremacy. In the end, seven kingdoms rose to prominence. Because these also vied with one another culturally, this period turned out to be China's most intellectually fertile period. Wandering philosophers and teachers of wisdom offered their services to the new lords, so that it is also termed the "Period of the Hundred Schools of Thought," to emphasize its intellectual diversity. The doctrines of Confucianism (*see p. 213*) and of the more emphatically religious Taoism, which later came to dominate, emerged at this time. In his work, *Tao Te Ching* (*The Book of the Way and the Power*), the (probably mythical)

founder of Taoism, Lao Tzu, promulgated a peaceable, withdrawn life in harmony with nature and an ethic of nonaction (Chinese *wu-wei*) and of letting things happen and observing things. Further influential teachings included the Mohism of Mo Di (Mozi) (circa 490–381 BC), who preached an almost socialist universal love of humankind and condemnation of war, and the Agriculture School (*nong jia*), which demanded of rulers a knowledge and encouragement of agriculture and water engineering.

UNIVERSISM

The new doctrines were based on the ancient Chinese ideas of harmony that took as their starting point a cosmic correlation between heaven, earth, and humankind. The laws of harmony that heaven (*tien*) prescribed were relived on earth by people. According to these, all development is ultimately due to the interplay of two antagonistic forces, the male-light, active, warm, and dry Yang and the female-dark, receptive, cold, and moist Yin, the unification of which sets in motion the elements as well as winds and world developments. The ancient Chinese *I Ching* (*Book of Changes*) contains 64 combinatorial hexagrams, which are interpreted for oracular purposes. In China, astronomy, astrology, and natural sciences developed very early on, initially as a combination of divinatory practices and observations of nature and the sky, which later flourished.

The Tai-Chi, symbol of the principles of Yang (white, sun) and Yin (black, shade), is considered by many teachings to be the highest principle of the cosmos and symbol of the origin of all life.

▶ THE MANDATE OF HEAVEN

In China, the status of the ruler—later of the emperor—was enshrined both politically and cosmologically; as communicator of the will of heaven to the people and as the son of heaven, he was always assigned ritual tasks such as determining the calendar. However, an unjust action or the violation of a ritual duty could lead to the "Mandate of Heaven" being withdrawn from an emperor or dynasty and transferred to a different ruler or dynasty. The Zhou justified their overthrow of the Shang by declaring that the latter had lost the Mandate of Heaven.

" It is better to leave a vessel unfilled than to attempt to carry it when it is full.
If you keep feeling a point that has been sharpened, the point cannot long preserve its sharpness.
When gold and jade fill the hall, their possessor cannot keep them safe.
When wealth and honors lead to arrogance, this brings its evil on itself.
When the work is done, and one's name is becoming distinguished, to withdraw into obscurity is the way of Heaven. "

Lao Tzu: *Tao Te Ching, Part 1: The Meaning,* Chapter 9

A set of narrow stone steps leading to a Taoist temple on the northern peak of Hua Shan, one of the five sacred mountains of China. In China, Taoist shrines were frequently erected on mountains.

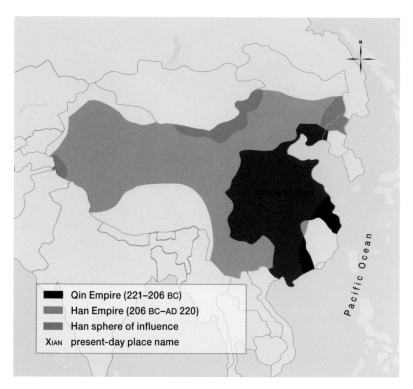

China, as well as the legal system. Violations of his laws led to forced labor or the death penalty for about two million Chinese; he used hundreds of thousands of forced laborers to regulate the flow of rivers, to lay about 4,225 miles (6,800 km) of roads and to construct the beginnings of the Great Wall against the Barbarians (nomadic horsemen) of Inner Asia, as well as his immense tomb (*see box, p. 211*). He monitored works in the provinces personally on countless tours of inspection. His desire to permit only "useful" books and books on technical/medical subjects led in 213 BC to the burning of a large proportion of the ancient Chinese philosophical writings; he had 480 Confucians who protested against this buried alive.

LEGALISM

Qin Shih Huang-Di made the Legalists or School of Law (*fa jia*) that had already made

THE QIN AND HAN EMPIRES (221 BC–AD 220) The map shows the empire under the first two formative ruling dynasties that encompassed the whole of China, the Qin (unifier of the empire, Qin Shih Huang-Di) and the Han (created the government structures).

QIN SHIH HUANG-DI: CHINA'S FIRST EMPEROR

The Qin military state (in the present-day province of Shaanxi), with its drilled army, emerged as the most powerful of the seven remaining Warring States. King Zheng (259–210 BC), who became ruler in 247 BC, honed the fighting force of his army and from 230 BC defeated the other six kingdoms in rapid succession and with great cruelty. In 221 BC he declared himself the first emperor of a centrally controlled China and adopted the title Qin Shih Huang-Di (First Supreme God-Emperor of Qin).

EFFICIENCY AND BRUTALITY

In the 11 years of his rule—despite his countless victims—the emperor achieved astonishing things. He eliminated the local vassal princes and made the new pillars of his rule an imperial bureaucracy (loyal to him) and a powerful army, providing a model for the dynasties to come. He standardized writing, money, weights and measures, clothes, hairstyles, and even the track widths between the wheels of carts throughout

Head of an ivory sculpture of the Kuan Yin—a Chinese Bodhisattva (enlightenment being) of limitless compassion (from the period of the Qing, AD 1644–1912).

Qin the leading state among the Warring States into the state ideology. This doctrine, which had been propagated by the state theoretician Shang Yang (d. 338 BC) and Shih Huang-Di's Chancellor Li-Ssu (circa 280–208 BC), was based upon strict centralism, an aggressive military policy, and rule by means of extremely harsh laws and strict education. They considered that people were intrinsically bad, egotistical, and lazy and had to be kept in order and made to work for the state through the fear of draconian punishments.

▶ THE TERRACOTTA ARMY

In 1974, farmers northeast of Xian (capital of Shaanxi province) accidentally stumbled on the tomb of Qin Shih Huang-Di, measuring over 6,500 by 2,950 ft. (2,000 by 900 m), on a site that covers 21½ sq miles (56 sq km) in total, and on the construction of which over 700,000 workers were employed. More than 7,200 life-size terracotta warriors were excavated, arranged in battle formation and each having individual features, together with bronze carts, and a complex of metal rivers on whose banks stood thousands of bronze birds. To date, only a section of the site has been excavated, which does not include the central burial chambers.

Statues of the terracotta warriors from the tomb of the first Chinese Emperor Qin Shih Huang-Di (221–210 BC); the site, which was discovered northeast of Xian and has since been only partially excavated, conceals numerous surprising finds including thousands of life-size, individually crafted warrior figures arranged in rank and file by branch of service. The figures were originally painted.

The first Han Emperor Kao-tsu (206–195 BC) with his retinue, journeying through a mountainous landscape (detail from *The First Emperor of the Han Dynasty Enters Kuang Tung* by Chao Po-chu, circa AD 1119–63).

THE HAN: INITIAL CONSOLIDATION OF THE STATE

In 207/206 BC, the Qin Dynasty collapsed in the face of peasant uprisings. Liu Chi, leader of the revolting peasants, founded the Han Dynasty in 206 BC and posthumously was given the emperor's name of Kao-tsu (206–195 BC). The Han emperors consolidated centralized rule and expanded the empire to its greatest extent by annexing Korea in the north and Vietnam in the south. However, they were constantly involved in defensive battles against the Hsiung-nu nomadic horsemen of central Asia (*see p. 180*). The Han, after whom the largest Chinese ethnic group to date is named (*Han-zú*: the Han people), based their rule on a standardized bureaucracy, on armies loyal to the emperor, and on the land owning upper class who were bound to the throne through their advancement to high state offices and had their estates managed by tenants. The originally despised eunuchs rose under the Han from being servants of the rulers to being (often secret) cabinet rulers who, by the end of the empire (in AD 1911), in many cases pulled the strings.

> "The Prince Ding asked how a prince should treat his officials and how the officials should serve their prince. Master Kung replied 'The prince should treat his officials as custom requires and the official should serve the prince as his conscience demands.'"
>
> Confucius: *Analects—Lun Yü, Book 3, 19*, sixth/fifth century BC

Cultural revival

The stable rule of the Han over a long period ensured flourishing trade along the routes of the Silk Road, particularly with India, Persia, and the Mediterranean region. During the Han period in China, paper was invented, the techniques of silk weaving were refined, the first suspension bridges were constructed, and holistic Chinese medicine was developed. The new service gentry emulated the fine lifestyle of the old feudal aristocracy. Legal texts were added on such a massive scale that the legal code had grown by the start of the third century AD to 960 volumes comprising 26,272 paragraphs and over 17 million words.

Confucianism: The state ideology

The most prominent Han emperor, Wu-Di (141–87 BC), replaced strict Legalism with more people-friendly Confucianism as the state doctrine. The teaching of Confucius (Kong-Zi, 551–479 BC) leaves the existence of the gods uncertain but stresses the importance of observing traditional rites, especially ancestor worship, for maintaining political stability. Cooperation between people is characterized by respect, politeness, and a lifelong willingness

to learn and is tied to the ideal of humaneness (*ren*). Ideal humans are the noble people (*junzi*) who uphold the values of family and loyalty, are proficient in the fine arts and all the sciences, and in contrast to the ideal of Taoism, devote their life to the service of the community and of the state. Noble people do not themselves strive for dominance, but serve the ruler as a loyal advisor in political and ethical matters. Emperor Wu-Di recognized the power of Confucianism in supporting the state and made knowledge of it compulsory for the state qualifying examination for imperial civil servants. The doctrine was able to maintain this leading position uninterruptedly until the empire came to an end.

Bronze statue of Confucius (551–479 BC) in front of the Confucius Temple in Nanjing (China). From the time of the Han Dynasty, Confucianism was the official state doctrine of the Chinese Empire and determined the structure of intellectual life, of the civil service, and of morals for over 2,000 years.

A vessel with a bird on the lid that was used for ritual purposes (from the Han period, 206 BC–AD 220).

according to this system are (1) father and son, (2) husband and wife, (3) older and younger brother, as well as, according to this model, (4) friend and friend, and (5) ruler and subject. Later Confucian state thinkers placed greater emphasis on subordination, particularly on that of children to parents, that of the wife to the husband and master of the house, and that of subjects to the emperor, and ignored the demands of Mencius for reciprocity. In China, this system of uncritical reverence for superiors in many cases led to the country's fossilization in rites and ceremonies and the paralyzation of innovative forces, which nonetheless did erupt violently from time to time.

Above: Stone relief of "The loving son," carrying his elderly, frail parents, in the caves of Dazu (China, circa 1127–1279).

Below: In accordance with Chinese court ceremonial, the emperor and senior officials (mandarins) were carried on litters, while people standing on the roadside had to prostrate themselves or bow (from a travel book by Giulio Ferrari, circa 1820).

CONFUCIAN IMAGE OF THE FAMILY

The establishment of Confucianism, which later arrived at a coexistence with Taoism and Buddhism, laid the foundation of the patriarchal and conservative social structure of China. The second great Confucian thinker, Mencius (Meng Zi, 372–289 BC), in particular, had developed a system of two-way human relationships in which the leading partner assumed the protective and leadership functions while the "weaker" partner was characterized by obedience and filial veneration. The five basic relationships

THE GREAT WALL

The symbol of the cultural demarcation of China from the nomadic horsemen of Inner Asia, who were seen as barbarians, is the Great or Chinese Wall, 4,163 miles (6,700 km) in total length and between 16 and 33 ft. (5 and 10 m) in height, built mainly of fired bricks cemented together with mortar. The first wall installations were erected as early as the seventh century BC by the regional kingdoms of northern China; however, it was only under Qin Shih Huang-Di and the

Han emperors that these were systematically enlarged to form the Great Wall, which later dynasties steadily continued and added to. It extends from Heilongjiang in the northeast via Xinjiang in the west as far as Hunan province in the south and is equipped with outwardly facing parapets, shooting platforms, watch towers, weapons stores, and signaling beacons. Its width of between 16 and 26 ft. (5 and 8 m) ensured that entire contingents of troops with carts could move along it. At intersections with the trade routes, guarded tunnels and gates were set into it. The Great Wall fell into disrepair in the seventeenth century and part of it was even removed as material for other buildings, but sections have subsequently been restored.

► **THE MIDDLE KINGDOM**
Since the early times of folklore, China has seen itself as the Middle Kingdom (*zhongguo*) and center of all civilization, surrounded by barbarians and foreigners. Over the course of its history, this led to a kind of cultural and political self-sufficiency that gave it internal strength, but from the fourteenth century onward also brought about a self-imposed isolation. In the nineteenth century this made the empire vulnerable to the military and commercial superiority of the expanding European powers, against which it could offer no defense save ossified traditions.

The Chinese Wall at Mutianyu: although it was unable to hold back horse-riding peoples from the north and west, the wall nonetheless demonstrated effectively the empire's capacity to defend itself, as well as its tendency to cut itself off culturally.

TROUBLED TIMES: THE DIVISION OF THE EMPIRE

The cost of defending the country against the Hsiung-nu and of Emperor Wu-Di's wars of conquest against Korea and Vietnam, together with the luxury with which the court of the Han emperor and the new aristocracy surrounded themselves, led to the impoverishment of the peasants. By the year AD 8, the Han lost the throne for the first time and had to cede to the socialist rule of Wang Mang, the leader of the revolutionary peasants' alliance, the "Red Eyebrows." Wang Mang made himself emperor (9–23). The Han returned to the throne in 25, but were finally driven out in 220 by the peasant and military revolts of the revolutionary "Yellow Turbans" that began in the provinces in 184. China was now divided into three kingdoms (until 265); the western Jin Kingdom, which acquired dominance (until 317, in the east until 420), restored temporary imperial unity. Nomadic Hunnic (Hsiung-nu) peoples made use of the internal power struggles to invade and set up their own Zhao

Above: Terracotta figures of civil servants in official attire from the period of the Sui (581–618) or early Tang (618–650).

Left: Buddhism found a place as a state religion in China alongside Confucianism and Taoism; this colossal Buddha statue stands in Leshan (China).

Kingdom in northern China (304–352); other peoples of Mongolian, Tibetan, and Göktürk origins did the same. In the end, there were four southern (420–589) and five northern (386–581) kingdoms competing with one another. During this period, Buddhism advanced from India across all of China and established itself as a third spiritual doctrine alongside Confucianism and Taoism.

THE SUI DYNASTY

A military reunification of the empire occurred under General Yang Jian, who as Emperor Wen-Di (581–604) founded the Sui Dynasty (581–618). An energetic ruler, he made Xian once again the royal capital, reintroduced the Confucian civil service examinations, simplified the laws, and commenced construction of the Grand Canal as a trading and shipping link between northern and southern China. However, the dynasty was overthrown during the reign of his son Yang-Di (604–618).

THE TANG KINGDOM

General Li Yuan removed the Sui and as Emperor Gaozu (618–626) established the Tang Dynasty on the throne (618–907). He succeeded in pacifying China internally—through aid measures to alleviate famines as well as by officially abolishing serfdom and distributing leased land to the peasants. His restructuring of the imperial administration—into a state council and hierarchically arranged ministries, chancelleries, secretariats, and civil service ranks—shaped the organization of the state until the end of the empire. The Tang rulers, who included Empress Wu Zhao (690–705), feared for her cunning and unscrupulousness, relied on economic prosperity achieved by exporting tea, silk, and Chinese porcelain, which was invented in around 700. During this period, the block printing of books, the newspaper, and the water clock were invented. Following the final persecutions of Buddhists (Buddhism was originally seen by Confucians as alien and against the interests of the state), and after confiscating monastic property to cover the treasury's requirements, the Tang emperors promoted the peaceful coexistence of Confucianism, Taoism, and Buddhism.

Mural of the seated Buddha, surrounded by Bodhisattvas, from the Dunhunag cave (China, painted in 585).

Marco Polo, his father, and his uncle being granted an audience with Kublai Khan (1215–94); miniature from Sir John Mandeville's book of his travels (undated).

"Since childhood, I have despised luxury, which makes people merely weak and vain. I find it repugnant when I see the upper classes bothering with such frivolities and sacrificing masses of money to it, which they should better use to alleviate poverty. Let them bring me wise and able men who grasp the importance of improving the well-being of the people and the standing of the empire, these are jewels to my liking, the others I despise."

Yuan Emperor Yön Tsung, fourteenth century

THE SONG DYNASTY

After the fall of the Tang in 907, China disintegrated once again into regional domination by five dynasties and ten kingdoms, the remnants of which remained until 979. However, by 960 General Zhao Kuangyin, famed for his combat skills, had largely conquered the north and, as Emperor Taizu (960–976), established the rule of the Song Dynasty (960–1279), which was divided into the Northern Song, with its capital at Kaifeng (960–1126), and the Southern Song, with its capital at Hangzhou (1126–1279).

Taizu broke the power of the military governors and in 963 placed the army directly under imperial civil administration, thereby ending the separation of the two sectors. The Song founded numerous schools and universities that led to a flourishing of scholarly and intellectual life. They also built state hospitals and homes for the elderly and altered

View of the Yuantong Temple in the park of Kunming (China), one of the most important Buddhist shrines in China (built in the thirteenth/fourteenth centuries).

the civil service examinations to meet practical administrative requirements. Manufacturing sites employing several thousand workers developed in the rapidly growing cities, but these were kept under control by government monopolies on trade goods. The emperors tried to meet the immense and growing expenditure on the military (up to 25 percent of the state budget) by minting more coins; however, galloping inflation led to renewed impoverishment of the peasants. From 1211 onward, China came under increasing pressure from the Mongols under Genghis Khan and his successors (*see p. 188*), and finally succumbed to the troops of Kublai Khan.

THE DYNASTY OF THE MONGOLS: YUAN

Kublai Khan (*see p. 190*), who was an avowed Buddhist, had already conquered the north of China and made Beijing (Peking) his capital by between 1264 and 1271. In 1279, he removed the last Song emperor, founded the Mongol Yuan Dynasty (1279–1368), and extended his rule to the whole of China. He took over the Song Dynasty's state administration, but installed Mongols in the senior posts. Some of these, like Kublai himself, very soon adopted a Chinese way of life in terms of clothing and education and becoming sedentary (sinoization), while others held firmly to the Mongol lifestyle of nomadic clans and repeatedly rebelled against the emperor and Great Khan. Kublai made China into an economically rich and cosmopolitan country with trading contacts worldwide and promoted astronomy and other sciences. His weak successors, however, found themselves increasingly faced with uprisings by the Chinese under the leadership of Buddhist monks. The last Yuan emperor fled to Mongolia in 1368, making way for the Chinese Ming Dynasty (1368–1644) and thus for absolute monarchy.

This landscape in snow, a popular motif in the genre of Chinese painting, is by the major landscape painter of the Song period, Fan Kuan (who worked from circa 990 to 1020).

▶ **THE TRAVELS OF MARCO POLO**
Between 1275 and 1292, Marco Polo (1254–1324), the son of a Venetian merchant, together with his father and uncle, stayed in the empire at the court of Kublai Khan. He rapidly won the trust of the ruler and was even appointed by him as a governor and sent on scientific and diplomatic missions. Following his return to his home country, he wrote down his fascinating travel adventures, which, however, many of his contemporaries were scarcely willing to believe.

Japan

				Kofun period			Kemmu	
	Jomon culture		Yayoi period		Nara period		Restoration	

| 10,000 BC | 500 BC | Turn of the eras | AD 500 | AD 1500 |

Asuka period   Heian   Kamakura   Ashikaga
period   shogunate   shogunate
(Minamoto
and Hojo)

People have lived on the Japanese islands since about 100,000 BC. Since the New Stone Age, Japan has been colonized by various groups of peoples from Korea, such as, for example, the bearded Ainu, whose last descendants still live on Hokkaido, Karafuto (present-day Russian Sakhalin), and the Kurils. The island location has favored the relatively uninterrupted development of culture along specifically Japanese lines.

THE EARLY CULTURES

In the second half of the Jomon period (circa 10,000–300 BC), named after its characteristic cord ceramics, people became sedentary dwellers and formed small agricultural village communities. In the Yayoi period (circa 300 BC– AD 300), with its higher-grade ceramics, larger communities based on bronze and iron working and wet-field rice cultivation emerged, as well as the first state entities with trading contacts; foremost among these was the Yamatai Kingdom in Kyushu or Honshu.

More accurate information is available about the Kofun period (AD 300–710), characterized by its mounded graves in the shape of keyholes (*kofun*), during which close contacts existed with Korea and China, in some cases involving

Background image: The sun goddess Amaterasu fleeing from her brother, the storm god Susanowo (from the Japanese picture cycle "Mirror of Famous Events," 1882).

Above: Shinto priests in a religious ceremony, the "Tsukinamisai," at the Grand Shrine of Ise; the priests are asking for a good harvest in the fall.

tributary payments, and the Chinese script and Buddhism reached Japan. The first unified state to emerge was the kingdom of Yamato (from approximately 250) that featured an imperial court culture, a rich class of nobles and rule by rival leading clans. Korea and China tried on several occasions to intervene politically in Japan, but succeeded mainly in bringing house-building techniques, medical knowledge, and Buddhist literature to Japan.

SHINTO: JAPAN'S INDIGENOUS RELIGION

Shinto (The Way of the Gods) is the Japanese natural religion involving the worship of a growing number of divine beings (kami) and extraordinary natural phenomena (mountains, springs). Its rituals, which are practiced predominantly at shrines (the paramount shrine today remains the shrine to the sun goddess in Ise), are connected with strict rules of purity and tend to be pragmatic in their orientation: gods and ancestors are believed to be helpful beings to whom people turn with requests and thanks. The two oldest national chronicles, *Kojiki* (recorded in 712) and *Nihongi* (recorded in 720), pass down the rich mythology of Japanese gods. Heading the pantheon is the sun goddess Amaterasu, who sent her grandson Ninigi no Mikoto down to earth as a cultural hero. His great-grandson is believed to be the legendary first Emperor Jimmu Tenno, whose rule is said to have begun in 660 BC. The emperors of Japan (tenno) are considered to be the direct descendants in an unbroken line of succession of Jimmu and thus of the sun goddess, which determined their untouchable position as "living kami," that is, god-emperors (which was not abandoned officially until 1946). Unlike the emperor in China, the *tenno* could not therefore lose the "mandate of heaven" (*see box, p. 209*) and to this day he performs numerous ritual duties and rites.

Clay statuette of a Haniwa warrior (sixth century AD); since time immemorial, the military tradition of sword fighting has played an important role in the life of the Japanese warrior nobility.

Asuka period: Prince Shotoku and the Seventeen Articles

The later Kofun period, after changes made to the structure of the state, is also referred to as the Asuka period (552–710). This period coincided with the triumph of Buddhism. In 593, Empress Suiko (592–628) appointed her son-in-law Prince Shotoku (574–622) as regent of the empire. In 594, this energetic regent, who also achieved prominence as a writer of historical works, elevated Buddhism, which had been brought over from Korea in 552, to the status of state religion; in 604, he gave Japan its first ethical/political constitution in the shape of his "seventeen articles," which prescribed harmony between the various classes and abolished the forced labor of peasants. The cultural system of China became the universal model, and in the period that followed, Shinto merged with Buddhism and Confucianism (*see p. 213*)—a process that was not always without conflict—to form the Japanese state ideology.

Taika Reforms and clan rule

After 622, the powerful Soga clan seized control and installed for the first time the Uji-Kabane system that was to serve as a model for the future: a widely connected noble clan (*uji*) filled all the key positions in the state administration, the military, and the economy with its patrons and made their ranks hereditary (*kabane*). In 645/646, the Soga were ousted by the rival Nakatomi clan, and with the Taika reforms a new state administration was set up.

An offering of oranges in front of the colossal bronze statue of the "Great Buddha of Kamakura" (Japan, erected in AD 1252); in Japan, Buddhism has taken on a very distinct form.

State government, taxes, the law, and land distribution were reorganized centrally in line with the Chinese model. The tenno was (at least officially) the owner and administrator of all property and distributed this at his discretion. The new capital cities of Asuka-kyo and for a time Fujiwara-kyo were administrative centers with a trained and loyally devoted bureaucracy that used land surveys and population censuses to divide and control the empire; the "Taiho code" (701/702) set out the new order definitively.

The rule of the leading clan remained, however. From the time of the conqueror of the Soga and founder of the dynasty Nakatomi no Kamatari (614–669), architect of the Taika Reforms, until 1238, the Fujiwara clan officially exercised the hereditary regency over Japan, even though it was at times considerably weakened and from 1160 onward was deprived of any real power.

Gatehouse of the Buddhist Temple of Horyu-ji (Temple of the Flourishing Law) in Ikaruga, near Nara (Honshu, Japan, built in 587–607 by Prince Shotoku).

THE NARA PERIOD

In 710, Empress Gemmei (707–715) finally made Nara into an imperial capital with a carefully planned layout, in which approximately 200,000 people lived. In the Nara period (710–794), the peasants in the countryside were once again forced to supply corvée labor and provide the army's soldiers, who had to feed and equip themselves. This brought about a mass rural exodus into the cities. Ambitious Buddhist monks and the rich monasteries, in rivalry with the Fujiwara clan, repeatedly intervened in politics. In 794, in order to regain more room for maneuver between rival groups, Emperor Kammu (781–806) moved the capital to Heian (Kyoto).

A Bodhisattva (enlightened being) in the posture of the Buddha of the future, Buddha Maitreya (Ausuka period, circa 552–645).

IMPERIAL RULE IN HEIAN

Emperor Kammu (*see p. 223*), Japan's most energetic ruling figure, restored imperial central power in Heian (Kyoto), which in 818 already had 500,000 inhabitants, through a complicated system of court ranks and a refined court culture. However, during the culturally glittering Heian period (974–1185), his successors and the Fujiwara, who were now related to the imperial family by marriage, increasingly cut themselves off in their luxurious court world and lost touch with the rest of the country. In the provinces, leading clans of the warrior nobility that were entrusted with fighting there, for example, against the Ainu in the north, became increasingly powerful and in many cases made themselves, in effect, independent. In 1028, the Taira clan, hereditary military governors in the area close to present-day Tokyo, ventured an uprising for the first time. The Fujiwara, who had themselves become courtiers, entrusted their militarily powerful allies, the Minamoto clan, with the suppression of the uprising.

The emperors exploited the weakness of the Fujiwara to establish a new system of indirect

Above: The fox-woman Tamamo no Mae (Jewel Maiden) with foxes, clothed according to the fashion in the Heian period (794–1185)—a motif from Japanese mythology (painting from 1858).

Below: The Phoenix Hall of the Byodo-in Temple in Uji, one of the most famous temple buildings in Japan, completed in 1053.

rule (*insei*). Emperor Go-Sanjo (1068–72) and some of his successors abdicated in favor of weak child emperors from their family and officially entered cloisters as monks, but then exercised *de facto* rule from there, protected by their status as monks, often over decades. Finally, Emperor Go-Shirakawa ruled, from 1155 to 1158, as the official emperor and then until 1192 as the cloistered emperor.

MURDEROUS POWER STRUGGLES

The power struggle of cloistered Emperor Go-Shirakawa against the Fujiwara and other members of the imperial house helped the newly powerful military clans to achieve dominance. After the Fujiwara had been eliminated in 1160, the Taira and the Minamoto took on one another. The initially victorious Taira, who were growing in power, spared the leaders of their opponents; the surviving Minamoto then began to support the emperor, and under the leadership of brothers Yoritomo (1147–99) and Yoshitsune (1159–89), launched the extremely bloody Gempei War (1180–85), which ended in the complete victory of the Minamoto in the naval battle of Dan-no-ura.

> ▶ **THE SAMURAI—RISE OF THE WARRIOR NOBILITY**
> While the *insei* system broke the power of the Fujiwara, it failed to bring the cloistered emperors the hoped-for gains in terms of control. Victors in the power struggle were the battle-hardened military clans from the provinces, who were considered coarse and ignoble but without whose help neither side could manage. From the escorts (*saburai*) who originally served these military princes rose the warrior nobility of the samurai, sword fighters who were unconditionally loyal followers of the warrior-princes and were ready to go to their death for them. Soon, they also ruled the imperial court as bodyguards and protectors.

Statue of the samurai leader Kusunoki Masashige (1294–1336) in the garden of the Imperial Palace of Tokyo; this folk and war hero, who remains popular even today, fell in battle fighting for Emperor Go-Daigo against the Ashikaga clan in 1336.

Minamoto no Yoritomo (1147–99), Japan's first shogun, releases cranes on the beach near his castle in Kamakura—seen in Buddhism as a worthy deed (from the picture cycle "Mirror of Famous Events," 1876).

The Kamakura shogunate

In 1185, Minamoto Yoritomo was the undisputed ruler of Japan; after eliminating his brother Yoshitsune, the real hero of the war against the Taira, he had himself appointed (hereditary) shogun for life in 1192 by cloistered Emperor Go-Shirakawa. The title of "shogun"—originally bestowed upon army commanders—subsequently designated the supreme military ruler and *de facto* regent of the empire, who directed policy from his headquarters or his residence (*bakufu*: tent government). The emperor, who was restricted to his ritual functions, and the old court nobility lived in a kind of golden cage. Kamakura, from 1180 residence of the Minamotos, became the actual political and cultural capital and gave the Kamakura shogunate (1185–1333) its name. The period of the hereditary shogunate in several leading families, which lasted until the restitution of imperial power in the Meji era (1868–1912), was characterized by the rise of the samurai (*see box, p. 225*), recognizable by the pair of swords (*daisho*) they carried, to become the leading class in society, with their own chivalrous code of honor (*bushido*). The original distinction between coarse warrior nobility and cultivated court nobility increasingly faded. The educated samurai also learned to appreciate poetry, painting, and tea ceremonies, whereas in contrast the samurai ideals of loyalty unto death, of honor to be defended at all costs, and of harsh self-discipline became the ideals of the nobility in general.

The Hojo Regency and the Kemmu Restoration

The Minamoto soon succumbed to the attractions of court life themselves and lost real power to their allied military clan, the Hojos, who acted on their behalf as regents of the shogunate (1203–1333) and brought Japan a period of internal stability. They were able to avert two Chinese/Mongol invasion attempts by Kublai Khan's fleet (*see p. 219*), in 1274

Representation of Buddhist ideas of paradise (detail from *Yamagoshi Raigo with Heaven and Hell*, Kamakura period, thirteenth century).

" Governing a country is like when a good doctor heals illnesses. He first finds out the cause of the suffering and then has to prescribe the right medicine . . . . What the world is suffering from today is greed. And this greed will lead to a wide variety of ills. It is the great suffering of the world. Healing this greed is the most important thing, everything else will then come right of its own accord."

Myoe Shoni, twelfth/thirteenth century

and 1281; in both cases, the Japanese were aided by typhoons (*kamikaze*: divine wind) that destroyed the fleets.

In 1333, Emperor Go-Daigo (1318–39), helped by the Ashikaga military clan, overturned the rule of the Hojo and Minamoto and attempted, in the Kemmu Restoration, to restore former direct imperial rule by strengthening the court nobility. However, in 1336, the Ashikaga clan itself sought to seize power. Go-Daigo fled from Kyoto, where the Ashikaga now installed a new emperor and took over the real power as shoguns (1336–1573), to Yoshino in the south. Until the resignation of his successors in 1392 there were now two imperial courts, one in the north and one in the south. The Ashikaga then assumed overall control until 1573, when the period of the Three Great Unifiers began. However, central power drained away increasingly, benefiting the Daimyo, the powerful military and civilian rulers in the provinces, who, with their enormous samurai followings dictated their own policies as autonomous local rulers.

Statue of a temple guard from Japan (made in 1215); the often terrifying temple guards were intended to ward off evil spirits, but protect believers.

The kingdoms in South and East Asia

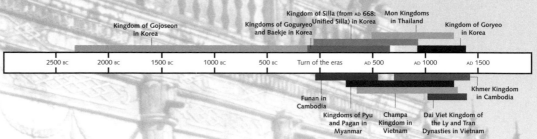

| 2500 BC | 2000 BC | 1500 BC | 1000 BC | 500 BC | Turn of the eras | AD 500 | AD 1000 | AD 1500 |

Kingdom of Gojoseon in Korea

Kingdoms of Goguryeo and Baekje in Korea

Kingdom of Silla (from AD 668: Unified Silla) in Korea

Mon Kingdoms in Thailand

Kingdom of Goryeo in Korea

Funan in Cambodia

Kingdoms of Pyu and Pagan in Myanmar

Champa Kingdom in Vietnam

Dai Viet Kingdom of the Ly and Tran Dynasties in Vietnam

Khmer Kingdom in Cambodia

Of the many ancient kingdoms of southeast Asia, only a few can be described here. All of them are characterized by magnificent buildings of Hindu and Buddhist provenance. The most significant of these are the world-famous temples of Angkor Wat.

BURMA AND THAILAND: THE KINGDOMS OF THE PYU AND PAGAN

The area to the south of the Chinese Empire as far as the Bay of Bengal has been colonized by peoples who migrated there from China and Tibet since about 3000 BC. The early advanced civilization of the Pyu in Burma (Myanmar) had developed along the trade routes between China and India by the turn of the eras at the latest, and by circa AD 240 was organized into 18 city-states. The Burmans started immigrating from about AD 800 onward, and founded the Kingdom of Pagan in the Irrawaddy Valley. In AD 1058, their King Anawratha (1044–77) conquered the Mon center of Thaton and achieved dominance over the entire region. The rulers were fervent patrons of Buddhism, but reduced state revenues by making tax-free donations of land to the monasteries. King Narapatisithu (1173–1211) therefore compelled Buddhism to revert to its original ideal of poverty and confiscated land holdings for the crown. Between 1277 and 1287, Kublai Khan's (*see p. 219*) Chinese/Mongol troops sacked Pagan, after the king of the Burmese had in 1273 authorized the execution of a delegation sent by Kublai to demand tribute payments. The subjugated Mon thereupon reestablished their independence.

Background image: Sculpture of a guarding figure—lion or dog—in front of the Ananda Temple in Pagan (Myanmar, circa eleventh century).

Above: A key symbol of Buddhism, which also appears in Hinduism, is the wheel of doctrine or wheel of law (seventh/eighth century).

THE KINGDOMS OF THE MON

The Mon, originally immigrants from the Indian/ Burmese region, settled in eastern Burma (Myanmar) and central and northern Thailand. Their culture, styles of architecture, and structure of government exhibited marked Indian influences. The state religion was Hinduism, together with Buddhism from the fifth/sixth centuries AD onward. The leading Mon Kingdom between the sixth and the eleventh century AD was the state of Dvaravati in Thailand, the oldest Buddhist kingdom in southeast Asia, which grew prosperous through trade with India. Evidence of this prosperity is provided by impressive cities with highly developed irrigation systems, as well as numerous stone temples, Buddha statues, and free standing sculptures, particularly those of the wheel of law, a symbol of Buddhism. The state was probably a confederation of autonomous principalities that were connected through marriage and trade.

In 573, another Mon Kingdom arose with its center at Hongsawatoi (later Pegu, Burma), which likewise profited from trade with India and also introduced the first writing system in Thailand. From the tenth century onward, the Mon Kingdoms were pushed back to the north or occupied by Pagan and the Khmer (*see p. 232*). The Mon used the destruction of Pagan to secure the kingdom's independence from Pegu, achieving a renewed blossoming of their culture lasting into the eighteenth century. The Mon living in northern Thailand, with a kingdom centered around Lamphun that was founded in about 660, were defeated by Thai King Mangrai the Great (1259–1317) in 1283 and incorporated into his new empire of Lanna in Laos and Thailand.

Entrance gate, crowned with a stone face, leading to the site of Angkor Thom (present-day Siem Reap, Cambodia), the palace complex of the last great Khmer builder, Jayavarman VII (1181–circa 1220).

Temples at My Son (Da Nang, Vietnam); most of these temples were constructed by the kings of the Cham—in honor of the gods, but also as their own burial sites.

VIETNAM: THE STATE OF DAI VIET

The Kingdom of Au Lac, established in circa 210 BC, was the first state in Vietnam, but from the second century AD it fell under the control of China and was administered as the "province" of Giau Chi. It was not until 960 that Vietnam was able to detach itself from China; in 1009, King Ly Cong Uan (Ly Thai To, 1009–28) founded the Kingdom of Dai Viet under the Ly Dynasty in northern Vietnam. His successor, Ly Phat Ma (Ly Thai Tong, 1028–54), established a hierarchical monarchy with an annual oath of allegiance to the ruler and in 1042 issued the first comprehensive legal code, the Minh-dao ("clear way"). He maintained close relations with China and sought to expand his kingdom southward at the expense of the Cham. Under Ly Nhat Ton (1054–72) and Ly Can Duc (1072–1127) Dai Viet even expanded to the

Relief of Hindu deities on the towers of Po Nagar (Nha Trang, Vietnam).

north into southern China. However, strong centralized power declined rapidly after 1127. Between 1225 and 1400, the Ly Dynasty was followed by that of the Tran, who, together with the Cham, warded off the invasion attempts of Kublai Khan (*see p. 219*). They endeavored to prevent struggles over succession to the throne by deciding that members of the royal family should always marry only among themselves. After 1407, however, the north of Vietnam fell once again under Chinese domination, and following the example of China, Confucianism became the state ideology.

THE KINGDOM OF CHAMPA IN SOUTHERN VIETNAM

Champa, the kingdom of the Chams, central and southern Vietnamese rice farmers, emerged in the second/third centuries AD as an Indian trading colony and made itself independent in the fourth century as an autonomous Hindu kingdom. King Indravarman II (875–896) founded Indrapura as the new capital, but its place was taken in 982 by Vijaya. The Cham kings developed a complicated court ritual that effectively shielded the ruler, and on the death of a ruler, most royal widows practiced self-immolation. Champa was in constant dispute with the Khmers (*see p. 232*) and was occupied by the latter in the tenth century and by the kingdom of Dai Viet in the eleventh century. However, in 1167, with Chinese help, Champa not only regained its independence but in 1177 even occupied Angkor, the capital of the Khmer Kingdom. Their joint resistance to the armies of Kublai Khan led to a rapprochement of the two Vietnamese Kingdoms, but in 1312 Champa was occupied by Dai Viet. The Champa culture left behind numerous stone relics, above all royal tombs, Hindu temples, towers, and shrines dating from the seventh to the thirteenth centuries. Here, Hinduism forged links with indigenous ideas of divinity. Marco Polo, who visited the Cham on behalf of Kublai (*see p. 219*), described their way of life and customs.

This charming stone sculpture dating from the time of the Cham kings can today be found in the garden of the Ana Mandara Complex in the coastal city of Nha Trang (Vietnam).

SOUTHEAST ASIA IN
CIRCA 1100
The kingdoms and peoples
were constantly engaged
in power struggles and
frequently intervened in the
internal affairs of neighbors;
overall, the region was
dominated chiefly by
the Khmer Empire from
Cambodia.

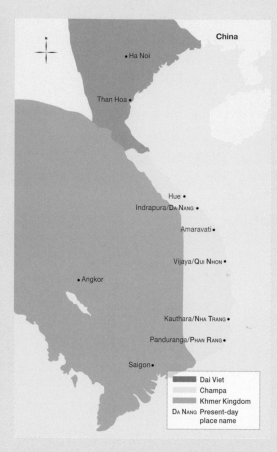

China

• Ha Noi

Than Hoa •

Hue •
Indrapura/DA NANG •

Amaravati •

Vijaya/QUI NHON •

• Angkor

Kauthara/NHA TRANG •

Panduranga/PHAN RANG •

Saigon •

	Dai Viet
	Champa
	Khmer Kingdom
DA NANG	Present-day place name

Below: Row of sculptures depicting the "Churning of the ocean of milk" from Hindu mythology; balustrade of the Khmer residence of Angkor Thom (circa 1200).

CAMBODIA: FROM THE FUNAN KINGDOM TO THE INDEPENDENCE OF THE KHMER

The Mekong Delta was colonized as long ago as circa 4000 BC. In the first century BC, the merger of city-states gave rise to the Kingdom of Funan with its capital of Vyadharapura (which remains undiscovered to this day). Its inhabitants, who lived by growing rice and farming alluvial land, were related to the Mon people (*see p. 229*). In the third century AD, Funan controlled with its fleet the coasts of Thailand and part of Burma. In the fifth century AD it made Hinduism (cult of Shiva) the state religion. In circa 550 Funan was absorbed by the Thai Kingdom of Chenla. The Cambodian Khmers in the Angkor region (*angkor*: city) were able to gain their independence in 707.

THE POWERFUL STATE OF ANGKOR

The Angkor Kingdom of the Khmer was one of the most important kingdoms in the whole of Asia, and not only because of its world-famous and unique temples. In 802, King Jayavarman II (790/802–850) proclaimed himself in the capital city of Hariharalaya to be *deva-raja* (god-king,

king of kings) and with his successors established the divine link of the Khmer kings; they were considered to be earthly incarnations of Hindu gods, although a number of the later kings were adherents of Buddhism. Indravarman I (877–889) became the actual founder of the kingdom, enlarging not by means of war, but rather through trade and diplomacy, and commencing the construction of vast irrigation facilities, canals, and temples. Yasovarman I (889–910) relocated the capital to Yasodharapura in the region of present-day Angkor. With the extensive building projects under Rajendravarman II (944–968) and Jayavarman V (968–1001), the state of the god-kings became prosperous through rice cultivation and trade with the whole of Asia. Suryavarman I (1002–49) began the expansion into southeast Asia, conquered territories in Thailand, put pressure on the kingdom of Champa, and brought several Malay states under his suzerainty. This policy was continued by Suryavarman II, the builder of Angkor Wat (see p. 235). However, in 1177 Angkor was plundered by the Champa.

Jayavarman VII and Angkor Thom

Jayavarman VII (1181–circa 1220) once again made the Khmer the leading kingdom in southeast Asia; not only did he drive back the Champa, but in turn occupied a large part of their kingdom in campaigns that continued up to 1203. As an ardent follower of the popular Mahayana Buddhism, he erected a monument to the Bodhisattva Avalokiteshvara, revered as the enlightenment being of compassion, in the vast temple complex of Angkor Thom (*angkor thom*: large city). The main temple of Bayon is crowned by 49 towers, and the walls are adorned by the transfigured and serenely smiling stone face of the Bodhisattva. Jayavarman VII also constructed numerous canals and reservoirs and crisscrossed his kingdom with a network of roads along which 121 large guest houses were built for officials, traders, and pilgrims, as well as 102 hospitals that were dedicated to the medicine buddha.

The Bayon of Angkor Thom with its spiritually refined and serenely smiling stone faces, constructed by Jayavarman VII (1181–circa 1220).

" XIX. It seemed to the king over the whole world, which he had conquered with his unmatched power, as if he were playing on the slopes of Meru with the sun as it leaves the mountain.
XX. On the proud head of the kings of China, of Champa, and of Yavadvipa, his medal shone like a faultless crown, like a garland of jasmine . . . .
XXIII. His glory, which continues unceasingly to radiate across the world, seems almost to be playing a game with the sun and the moon, which shine their light alternately. "

From the inscription of the guru Sivasoma in honor of King Indravarman I, ninth century AD

Suryavarman II and the temple in honor of Vishnu

Suryavarman II (1113–50) conquered the Mon Kingdom from the north of Thailand down to the south of present-day Laos, as well as parts of the Pagan Kingdom in Burma, the Dai Viet in Vietnam, and the Malay Peninsula, thereby making the Khmer Empire the leading power in Southeast Asia. Suryavarman established good relations with China. In contrast to his predecessors, who were devotees of Shiva, he worshiped the Hindu god Vishnu; it is to Vishnu that he dedicated his buildings in Angkor Wat (*wat*: pagoda, temple). In the murals, the life of Vishnu merges with that of the ruler, and in the southern gallery Suryavarman is shown after his death. Surrounded by dignitaries, he proceeds into the kingdom of the dead in order to be deified there as Vishnu. Since the temple faces west—the kingdom of the god of the dead, Yama—many researchers suspect that Angkor Wat was also the site of Suryavarman's tomb. He was posthumously given the name Paramavishnuloka, the king who entered Vishnu's heavenly dwelling place.

Angkor Wat: Liturgy in stone

The temple, which was constructed between 1122 and 1150, is probably the world's largest sacred building ever built. The rectangle, measuring 4,921 ft. (1,500 m) from west to east by 4,265 ft. (1,300 m) from north to south, surrounded by a 623-ft. (190-m)-wide moat, represents the geometrically idealized universe of Hinduism surrounded by the primeval ocean. Five towers in the shape of lotus buds (*prasat*) surround the main temple that symbolizes the world-mountain Meru. The exterior of the temple is encircled by a 2,624-ft. (800-m)-long bas-relief containing scenes from the Hindu *Rāmāyana* epic and the life of the helper of the gods Krishna, who is believed to be an incarnation of Vishnu. The sandstone buildings are almost entirely covered with ornamentation and more than ¾ sq mile

Stone relief from Angkor Wat containing scenes from the life of its builder Suryavarman II (1113–50), who fused his life with that of the Hindu god Vishnu.

(2 sq km) of reliefs, among which the individually worked figures of dancing girls or asparas—half-divine and half-human nymphlike beings—are particularly remarkable. The preservation of many of the buildings in the temples of Angkor is today threatened by weathering influences, by destruction wrought at various times by humankind, and by the overgrowth of the temples by trees and their roots, which creates bizarre effects.

Decline

After the death of Jayavarman VII in circa 1220, the kingdom found itself in decline. The conquests in Champa were lost again, and a Hindu backlash within the kingdom led to the destruction of the building works of Buddhist rulers. King Jayavarman VIII (1243–95) succeeded only with difficulty in averting defeat by Kublai Khan (*see p. 219*) by making high tribute payments. After 1350, the Khmer faced large-scale setbacks at the hands of the Thai rulers of Ayutthaya, who conquered Angkor in 1431 and annexed their kingdom.

Facing page: Angkor Wat, the largest temple in the world, was constructed as a rectangle surrounded by water and thus represents the ideal form of the Hindu universe.

> "A palace was built for the two sacred children at the foot of Namsan [southern mountain] and they were raised there . . . . When the two divinities were thirteen years old, in the year of the rat [57 BC], the boy was enthroned as king, and the girl became his wife. He ruled the country for sixty-one years, then he ascended to heaven. Seven days later, his mortal remains fell to earth. Then, so the story goes, his wife also died. The inhabitants of the country wanted to bury them together, but an enormous snake hindered their plan."

From the foundation myth of the Kingdom of Silla

THE KINGDOMS OF GOGURYEO, BAEKJE, AND SILLA IN THE FIFTH CENTURY
The boundaries of the three rival ancient kingdoms of Korea shifted several times. Goguryeo was later absorbed into the Kingdom of Unified Silla and the southern Kingdom of Gaya was annexed by Silla only after lengthy disputes.

KOREA: THE KINGDOMS OF GOJOSEON, GOGURYEO, AND BAEKJE

Siberian/Mongolian nomads colonized the Korean Peninsula as long ago as 16,000 BC and in the Bronze Age became a branch of the Han people (see p. 212). The first Kingdom of Gojoseon that existed until 108 BC, was according to legend founded in 2333 BC and was influenced culturally by China. The subsequent Three Kingdoms period was dominated initially by Goguryeo, which was founded in 108 BC and from the first century AD expanded into China and later even controlled Manchuria. It embraced Buddhism as the state religion in AD 372. In 427, King Jangsu (413–490), who ruled over three-quarters of Korea, made present-day Pyongyang the capital. The expansion northward led to continued attacks by the Chinese, who conquered Goguryeo in 668.

The Kingdom of Baekje in the southeast was founded in 18 BC and expanded steadily, but after 475 lost its northern territories to Goguryeo and entered into an alliance with the Kingdom of Silla (see below). King Seong (523–554) led the kingdom to a golden age of Buddhist culture, which then spread from here to Japan (see p. 222). In 660, Baekje was conquered by its dominant neighbor Silla.

SILLA AND UNIFIED SILLA

The southern state of Silla, which was founded in 57 BC, first became a powerful kingdom under King Naemul (AD 356–402). To counter the pressure from Goguryeo and Baekje, it allied itself with China. After King Muyeol (654–661) had broken the power of the nobility in favor of a central monarchy and had conquered Baekje, his successor Mummu (661–681) also acquired from the Chinese control over Goguryeo and in 668 unified the peninsula to form the Kingdom of Unified Silla. The capital Gyeongju had over a million inhabitants and became a center of East Asian culture, and the militarily powerful state was administered strictly in accordance with the principles of Buddhism (which became the state religion in 528) and Confucianism, and was subdivided into provinces having local autonomy. Evidence of its prosperity can be seen today in the numerous temples and pagodas as well as in the magnificent tombs of the rulers and of the nobility. After 780, power struggles and peasant revolts weakened the kingdom, which in 936 was conquered by Goryeo.

CHINA

Goguryeo

Pyongyang

Hanseong/SEOUL

Gongju/UNGJIN
Sabi

Silla

Gyeongju

Baekje Gaya

JAPAN

GORYEO

In 892, the Kingdom of Baekje regained its autonomy and was taken over in 918 by General Wang Geon (918–943), who conquered Silla in 936 and reunified Korea (until 1392) in the Kingdom of Goryeo, with its capital at Kaesong. The kingdom initially achieved some stability through the building of protective walls in the north. Goryeo evolved a Buddhist culture and at the end of the twelfth century invented book printing using movable type; this made it possible for the Tripitaka Koreana, the Buddhist canon, to be printed in Korean in 6,000 volumes in 1236–51. The Mongols launched attacks from 1231 onward, and in 1259 Goryeo became a Mongol vassal state until the Yi Dynasty liberated it in 1392 and established the Choson Kingdom, which endured until 1910.

Above: Model of the Sokkuram grotto in Kyongju (South Korea), which was constructed during the period of the Kingdom of Unified Silla (668–936).

Below: Detail of the wooden Temple of Naksan (east coast of South Korea); this famous shrine, dating from 676, was last destroyed in the Korean War (1950–53) and subsequently suffered further heavy damage in a fire in 2005.

ARCTIC OCEAN

BERING
SEA

LABRADOR SEA

HUDSON
BAY

Colville

Yukon

Tanana

Peace

Athabasca

Churchill

Columbia

Snake

Missouri

IROQUOIS

IROQUOIS

IROQUOIS

HOPEWELL

Mississippi

Ohio

Arkansas

Colorado

Folsom
FOLSOM

Clovis *CLOVIS*

APACHE

APACHE

Rio Grande

Mississippi

ATLANTIC

OCEAN

HUASTECS

San Lorenzo Tenochtitlán
AZTECS

Tollan/Tula *TOLTECS*

Tenochtitlán/Tlatelolco/
Mexico City *AZTECS*

Tilantongo *MIXTECS*

Monte Albán
OLMECS/ZAPOTECS

Aztlán
AZTECS

La Venta
OLMECS

ZAPOTECS

Palenque
MAYA

Yaxchilán
MAYA

Chichén Itzá
MAYA/TOLTECS

Calakmul *MAYA*
Cuello *MAYA*

Tikal *MAYA*

Copán *MAYA*

CARIBBEAN
SEA

PACIFIC

OCEAN

Magdalena

Orinoco

Rio Branco

ARAWAKS

Vaupés

Rio Negro

Japurá

Içá

Amazon

Amazon

Madeira

Tapajós

Xingú

Tocantins

Marañón

Ucayali

Purús

Juruá

Teles Pires

Araguaia

Tocantins

São Francisco

Cajamarca *INCA*

Chavín de Huántar
CHAVÍN

Machu Picchu *INCA*

Caral *CARAL*

MOCHE

Cuzco *INCA*

PARACAS

Guaporé

Paraguay

Brasília

Paranaíba

Rio Grande

NAZCA

Sucre

Paraná

Paraná

Paraná

Colorado

- ⬤ Center/Capital city/Royal residence
- ⬤ City-state
- ⬤ Center of an empire
- ⬤ Center of expansion
- ➡ Raids and forays

Mexico City Present-day place name

AZTECS People

Olmecs   Aztecs   Aztecs   Sioux   Inca

NORTH, CENTRAL, AND SOUTH AMERICA

The indigenous peoples of North America—referred to by Europeans as Indians—and those of Central and South America—called Indios in Europe—are made up of an immense variety of tribes and cultural and linguistic groups. After 1800, the tribes of North America were all severely oppressed and forced into reservations as a result of the expansion of white settlers and their governments. The differing climatic and economic conditions under which they lived meant that they developed different ways of life and forms of society—as nomads, as seminomads, or as sedentary dwellers.

The peoples of Central and South America, by contrast, established mainly sedentary farming cultures that tended to be based around towns and which were generally organized in city-states or alliances of towns and cities. Their highly developed division of labor and political administration led, particularly in the cases of the advanced civilizations of the Maya, Aztecs, and Inca, to the creation of true states that had a hierarchical social structure and exerted dominance over neighboring peoples, from whom tributes were exacted. Most notably, the Inca state in Peru operated strict control over the organization of the administration and the work that was performed, and thus exhibited key features of a developing empire.

In the sixteenth century, the peoples of Latin America were conquered by the Spanish and forcibly christianized; however, numerous elements of their cultures have survived into the present day. For example, their organizational structures were absorbed into the way of life and into the ways in which housing and labor was organized in the Reductions (mission stations) of the Jesuit state in Paraguay (1604–1767).

The map shows the areas of distribution of the Indians of North America and the movements of the seminomadic Apache tribes; it also shows the major city-states and cultural centers of the early peoples of Central and South America (focusing principally on Mexico and Peru) and the Empires of the Maya, Aztecs, and Inca.

The Indians of North America

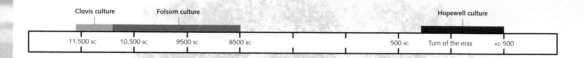

Clovis culture		Folsom culture					Hopewell culture		
11,500 BC	10,500 BC	9500 BC	8500 BC			500 BC	Turn of the eras	AD 500

The image conjured up by the indigenous peoples of North America, termed "Indians" by Europeans, is one of enormous diversity. The several hundred tribes and numerous cultural groups exhibit (sometimes vast) differences in terms of their way of life and forms of organization.

ORIGIN AND TRIBAL ORGANIZATION

Humans have permanently inhabited the North American continent since about 18,000 BC; they probably migrated there either as seafarers or from east Asia across the Bering Strait (there are numerous other theories concerning their origin). The oldest identifiable Indian culture is considered to be the Clovis culture (circa 11,600–10,700 BC) of big-game hunters and gatherers, which was named after the crafted spear points found near Clovis in the present-day state of New Mexico; it was followed by the Folsom culture (circa 10,700–8500 BC), with flint spear points. Of the regional cultures that emerged subsequently, the Hopewell culture (circa 300 BC–AD 500), with its burial mounds and ceramics in the Ohio and Mississippi Valleys, is the most notable.

The Indians of North America are subdivided into different cultural groups and numerous linguistic groups, all exhibiting distinct characteristic features, but none standing out particularly from the others. They were mostly organized in tribes or family groupings, and although there were alliances between the tribal groupings, no form of superordinate state or empire existed; some tribes were permanent enemies, which the white colonizers were later able to exploit for their own benefit.

THE CULTURAL GROUPS

The Indians' living environment determined to a large extent their ways of life and livelihoods (see p. 242). The tribes of the north, northeast, and northwest lived in well-wooded areas with a wide range of food; the tribes of the cold subarctic regions, on the other hand, lived from fishing and hunting along the lakes and rivers. In the southwest, the steppes and deserts meant that little if any soil cultivation was possible, in contrast to the southeast, with its mixed woodlands. The tribes of the semidesert plateau regions and those on the grass-rich prairies lived as semisedentary hunters and gatherers and in the nineteenth century found themselves under particular pressure from the westward expansion of the United States.

Background image: Burial mounds of the Hopewell culture, much of which is still a mystery today, in Hopewell culture National Historic Park (Ohio, U.S.).

Facing page: Little Big Mouth, a medicine man of the Arapaho (who form part of the Algonquian language family), in front of his teepee at Fort Sill (Oklahoma, U.S.; photo from about 1900)

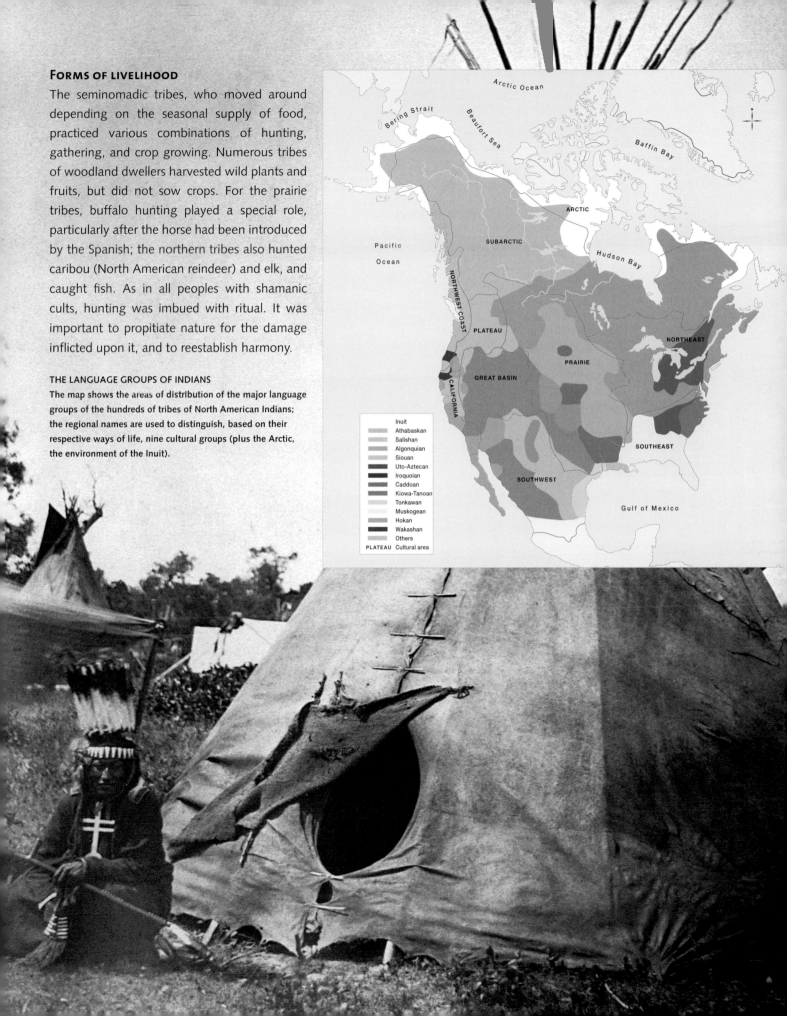

FORMS OF LIVELIHOOD

The seminomadic tribes, who moved around depending on the seasonal supply of food, practiced various combinations of hunting, gathering, and crop growing. Numerous tribes of woodland dwellers harvested wild plants and fruits, but did not sow crops. For the prairie tribes, buffalo hunting played a special role, particularly after the horse had been introduced by the Spanish; the northern tribes also hunted caribou (North American reindeer) and elk, and caught fish. As in all peoples with shamanic cults, hunting was imbued with ritual. It was important to propitiate nature for the damage inflicted upon it, and to reestablish harmony.

THE LANGUAGE GROUPS OF INDIANS
The map shows the areas of distribution of the major language groups of the hundreds of tribes of North American Indians; the regional names are used to distinguish, based on their respective ways of life, nine cultural groups (plus the Arctic, the environment of the Inuit).

Arctic Ocean
Bering Strait
Beaufort Sea
Baffin Bay
ARCTIC
Pacific Ocean
SUBARCTIC
Hudson Bay
NORTHWEST COAST
PLATEAU
NORTHEAST
PRAIRIE
CALIFORNIA
GREAT BASIN
SOUTHEAST
SOUTHWEST
Gulf of Mexico

Inuit
Athabaskan
Salishan
Algonquian
Siouan
Uto-Aztecan
Iroquoian
Caddoan
Kiowa-Tanoan
Tonkawan
Muskogean
Hokan
Wakashan
Others
PLATEAU Cultural area

*"*When a vision comes from the thunder beings of the West, it comes with terror like a thunderstorm, but when the storm of vision has passed, the world is greener and happier; for wherever the truth of vision comes upon the world, it is like rain. The world, you see, is happier after the terror of the storm.*"*

Black Elk, medicine man of the Oglala Lakota Indians, nineteenth/twentieth century

CHIEFS AND SHAMANS

The status of tribal leaders differed from tribe to tribe—it ranged from virtual monarchical leadership to membership of democratic councils with majority decision making. The tribal leaders, often referred to by the whites as "chiefs," represented the tribe and enjoyed special prestige, not only as brave warriors and arbitrators of disputes, but also on account of their wisdom and level-headedness, or eloquence as speakers.

The shaman or "medicine man"—the word is a corruption of the Chippewa word *Medewiwin*—was not only a healer and herb expert but also the guardian of tribal traditions and myths (which he passed on exclusively orally), advisor, priest, dream reader, and prophesier (consulter of oracles). By means of trance and certain ecstasy techniques—that chiefly involved drum rhythms and dances but could also include drugs—he established contact with the "other world" of the ancestors and tribal spirits. Certain illnesses and states of rapture signaled the acquisition of shamanic abilities.

TYPES OF DWELLING

Through the nomadic plains Indians (Lakota, Blackfeet, Crow), in particular, we are familiar with the teepee—the conical pole-frame tent that had a (usually painted) leather or canvas cover stretched over it and had a smoke hole for the fire—and the more comfortable wigwam of the Algonquian tribes—a dome covered with hides and bark. Other tribes lived in dome-shaped earth-covered houses sunk into the ground or in bowerlike chick huts (structures on stilts, without walls), in grass huts covered

The teepee (pole tent), covered with painted animal hides, of a chief of the plains-dwelling Assiniboine (painting by Karl Bodmer, nineteenth century).

in woven grass mats, or in a *hogan*—a domed hut made of logs laid across one another. The Iroquois tribes erected longhouses of up to 164 ft. (50 m) in length with divided living areas, whereas the tribes of the northwest also built houses from planks with a pitched roof. The Pueblo Indians of the south lived in villages with permanent clay or stone houses.

WEAPONRY

The Indian tribes used weapons for a combination of hunting, warfare, and defense. From early times, they used spears and bows and arrows as long-range weapons, and clubs with heads made of wood or stone, later also iron, as close-range weapons. Not until the battles against white settlers, was the throwing ax (*tomahawk* in the Algonquian language) converted from a tool to a weapon; its blade was originally made of stone, later of forged iron. In the eighteenth century, arrow-tomahawks, a combination of a hollow-handled tomahawk and an arrowhead, appeared, but these were used only for ritual purposes and as a status symbol. Lances, which were used not only as throwing weapons but also as stabbing weapons, also played a role in

dances and ritual ceremonies. Some tribes used throwing-sticks and blowpipes (Iroquois, Cherokee) or slingshots for hunting, and for defense some used handy small leather shields and breastplates made of long bones.

A Sioux chief (1904) from the series *The North American Indian* (1907) by Edward Curtis (1868–1952); he photographed Indians in their traditional way of life.

A tomahawk from the eastern woodlands of the U.S. with engravings on the blade, used principally for ceremonial and representative purposes.

formed a confederacy of six nations, which gave itself a liberal democratic constitution in the shape of the Great Law of Peace; this is also said to have been the force behind the United States Constitution. The Iroquois lived in fortified villages and longhouses and subsisted primarily by growing corn; they established trading contact with white settlers as long ago as the seventeenth century. In the eighteenth century they formed secret ritual societies—the medicine societies, which took the form of false face societies or totem animal societies.

THE SIOUX

The language family of the Sioux formed three main groups (Dakota, Lakota, Nakota) and lived as nomadic hunter-gatherers, primarily in teepees in the prairies of the mid-United States. The Sioux put up the greatest resistance to the expansion of white settlement; under the leadership of their imposing chiefs Sitting Bull, Crazy Horse, Spotted Elk, and Gall, in June 1876 they defeated the Seventh U.S. Cavalry Regiment under Lieutenant Colonel George A. Custer in the famous Battle of the Little Bighorn (Montana), but in December 1890 were massacred by U.S. troops at Wounded Knee (South Dakota) or were forced into reservations.

APACHES AND COMANCHES

The Apaches, made famous by the Winnetou novels of the German author Karl May (1842–1912), formed six main groups, among them the Kiowa, and lived largely as seminomadic hunter-gatherers in the southwest of the present-day U.S. and in northern Mexico. The tribes provided themselves with supplies by carrying out raids and forays against neighboring peoples. Apache society was generally centered around influential men or women who radiated a special power (*diyah*: prestige) and also often functioned as shamans (*diyin*).

In Oklahoma and eastern Texas, there were frequent wars between the Apaches and the

Greg Red Elk, a member of the Assiniboine tribe near Fort Pack (Montana, U.S.), in traditional warrior clothing with a headdress of eagle feathers.

THE IROQUOIS CONFEDERACY

Only a very small number of the literally hundreds of Indian tribes can be described here. In around 1570, the originally warring Iroquois tribes, who mainly inhabited the area of the present-day states of Ohio and New York, as well as on Lake Ontario (Canada),

▶ THE TOTEM OR HERALDIC POLE

Freestanding poles, decorated with carved animals or faces and painted, that originally functioned as the central supporting pillars in huts, first appeared in the eighteenth century in British Columbia (Canada); to be correct they are "heraldic poles" as they represent not a totem animal, but rather the heraldic animal of a clan or family. Such poles were also erected in honor of a tribal elder or ancestor and may recount unusual incidents, in the form of scenically represented stories that are read from bottom to top.

Comanches, who belonged to the Uto-Aztecan language family of Shoshone; in around 1650, the latter had fought the Spanish on their territory and had learned from them the art of horsemanship, which they subsequently used to diminish the influence of the Apache tribes.

Indian totem or heraldic poles in Stanley Park, Vancouver (British Columbia, Canada).

Sioux and Apache chiefs at a meeting (photo circa 1900); regular meetings of tribal leaders were held to resolve disputes or conclude alliances, as well as to reach decisions in favor of war or peace.

Early cultures of Central and South America

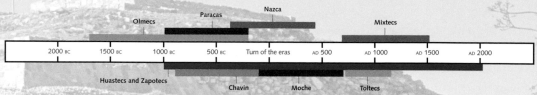

2000 BC	1500 BC	1000 BC	500 BC	Turn of the eras	AD 500	AD 1000	AD 1500	AD 2000

Olmecs · Paracas · Nazca · Mixtecs

Huastecs and Zapotecs · Chavin · Moche · Toltecs

Large numbers of indigenous peoples also lived in Central and South America; ultimately, these all became sedentary and are characterized as arable farmers chiefly by their cultivation of corn, and as advanced civilizations by their urban centers with stone buildings, their burial sites, and their production of artifacts, especially gold jewelry and pottery.

THE OLMECS

Central America was settled by circa 10,000 BC at the latest, probably via North America. The Olmecs in the tropical jungle of eastern Mexico are considered to be the oldest advanced Mesoamerican civilization (circa 1700–200 BC); they influenced all those that followed. Several of their cultural centers have so far been discovered, the most important of which are

Background image: Ruins of a temple in Monte Albán (Mexico); the city was a center of the Olmecs and later of the Zapotecs (between the sixth century BC and the eighth century AD).

Above: Stone warrior statues of the Toltecs in central Mexico (tenth century AD); the Toltec priest-king Quetzalcoatl later became a god of the Aztecs.

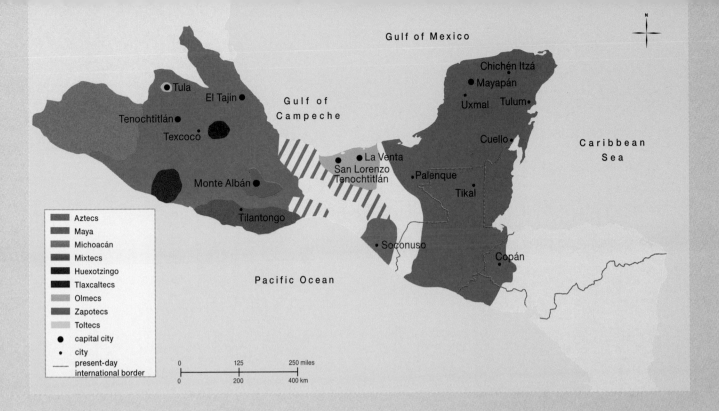

Aztecs
Maya
Michoacán
Mixtecs
Huexotzingo
Tlaxcaltecs
Olmecs
Zapotecs
Toltecs
capital city
city
present-day
international border

San Lorenzo Tenochtitlán (circa 1200–900 BC) and La Venta (circa 900–300 BC). The two centers, where altars and the characteristic colossal heads made of basalt—probably portraits of priest-kings—are to be found, had been abandoned and largely destroyed. As early as 900 BC, the Olmecs developed a glyphic script, a precursor to the Aztec and Mayan scripts, as well as knowledge of numbers. A mixed being, half-human and half-jaguar, played a key role in their religion. The climate in the environment in which they lived allowed farmers to harvest crops twice a year. Their artifacts are particularly characterized by works in jade.

OTHER CULTURES OF CENTRAL AMERICA

In around 1000 BC, the Olmecs were joined in northern Mexico by the warlike Huastec people, who were later subjugated, though not entirely, by the Aztecs (see p. 256) and the Spanish; they left behind only a few circular temples and palaces. In the south of Mexico, the Zapotecs established themselves from about 1000 BC as sedentary city dwellers with a developed form of agriculture. They took the Olmec city of Monte Albán as their capital in

around 500 BC. Large numbers of stone slabs carrying representations, and tombs containing rich finds have been found, dating from the golden age of the Zapotecs (circa AD 150–400). After AD 1000, they were driven off by the Mixtecs to the Mitla area (their new capital), where they built palace complexes and lived under Aztec sovereignty. The Mixtecs, who founded their capital, Tilantongo in southern Mexico, in 692, reached their heyday in around 900–1200, displacing the Zapotecs and erecting pyramids and magnificent tombs; they were also highly proficient at the art of goldsmithing. From 1519 they were conquered by the Spanish. The Toltecs (circa 720–1150) used military force to rule central Mexico. They did not create a uniform empire, but at Tollan (Tula) constructed a capital city with large temple complexes. Their ceramics are typified by cylindrical vessels decorated with scenes. Their priest-king Quetzalcoatl (circa 947–1000) achieved particular significance; he led his people into Mixtec and Maya regions, was driven away, and vanished over the sea, but it was said he would return as ruler. Later, he was elevated by the Aztecs to the status of chief god and founder-hero.

ADVANCED MESOAMERICAN CIVILIZATIONS
The map shows the centers and city-states of the early advanced civilizations of Mesoamerica and the territories controlled by them.

Skeletons of members of his retinue, together with urns and artifacts, in the richly adorned tomb of the "Lord of Sipán" (Peru), dating from the second century AD; the tomb was discovered in 1987 by grave robbers and plundered of its gold treasures, but the skeletons and a large proportion of the tomb furnishings remained intact.

INITIAL SOUTH AMERICAN CULTURAL DEVELOPMENT

Once again, it is possible to describe here only a few of the innumerable peoples of South America. South America was probably settled by peoples arriving by sea from about 14,000 BC. Stone tools, blades, cave paintings, and evidence of agriculture have been found dating from the period around 8000 BC. The oldest city, discovered in 1996, is Caral in Peru; a pyramid there has been dated to the year 2627 BC. Between 1000 and 500 BC, the Arawak people settled the Orinoco, living by hunting and cultivating corn, beans, and sweet potatoes.

CHAVÍN AND MOCHE

The Chavín civilization (circa 900–100 BC), named after its center of Chavín de Huántar in northern Peru, is seen as South America's earliest advanced civilization; during this period, numerous religious buildings, pyramids, and temples with stone sculptures were erected, and advanced goldworking skills developed. It was followed by the Moche or Mochica culture on the coast of Peru (circa 100 BC–AD 700), whose people caught fish and other sea creatures and used the rivers of the region to feed advanced irrigation systems, enabling agriculture and crop cultivation to flourish. Llama breeding and cotton cultivation also helped their communities to prosper. Their relative prosperity created the conditions for rapid population growth, as a result of which the Moche expanded, through alliances of larger communities (city-states), farther and farther into the country. Their society probably had a pronounced social hierarchy, as is evidenced by the tomb of a nobleman—the Lord of Sipán—discovered in

1987, as well as by other grave finds. The ruler's mummy, adorned with turquoise plates and a gold crown, was accompanied into the tomb by thousands of gold and ceramic artifacts as well as other mummies.

PARACAS AND NAZCA

Distinctive features of the Paracas culture in southern Peru (circa 1000–200 BC) include tomb complexes with bottle-shaped shaft tombs and finely worked ceramics. Hundreds of mummies, bound together in "mummy bundles," were buried in separate necropoles, some of which fell victim to grave robbers. The clothing of the mummies (mantles, tunics, ponchos, cloths, and headbands with rich pictorial motifs) demonstrate the highly developed textile art of the Paracas culture. They also, as long ago as 400 BC, performed skull trepanation (circular or square holes) for medical or religious purposes, with most of the patients surviving. The Paracas was followed by the Nazca culture on the south coast of Peru (circa 370 BC–AD 450); their tomb complexes yielded tattooed mummies showing the artificial skull deformation (flattening of skull parts) typical of numerous ancient American cultures. The Nazca lived in fairly large settlements around cult centers; they collected the skulls of

Part of a mantle from a tomb of the Paracas culture (south coast of Peru), decorated with a design representing two hummingbirds (circa 600–200 BC).

their enemies for use in their ceremonies. The Nazca culture became known principally for its creation of enormous geoglyphs that were carved into the ground of the pampa (desert) as lines or in the shape of animals or humans; their meaning remains a matter of dispute.

Geoglyphs in the shape of a candelabra, dating from the Nazca culture (circa 370 BC–AD 450) in the desert of Paracas (Peru); the meaning of the lines drawn in the earth has not been fully resolved.

The Maya

Preclassic period				Classic period	Postclassic period	Conquest by the Spanish
3000 BC	2000 BC	1000 BC	Turn of the eras	AD 1000		AD 2000

The Mayan-language-speaking tribes formed the longest-lasting advanced civilization in Latin America, the area in which they lived covering present-day southern Mexico, Belize, Guatemala, Honduras, and El Salvador. Descendants of the Maya still live there today.

CULTURAL ERAS

In many of their achievements, the Maya exhibit the influence of the Olmecs (*see p. 246*), who are viewed by many as their cultural forerunners. The Mayan periods are broken down into the following: the Preclassic (circa 3000 BC–AD 250) (which is itself subdivided still further), the Classic (circa 250–900), and the Postclassic (circa 900–1511). Evidence from Cuello (Belize, circa 2000 BC) and Copán (Honduras, circa 1100 BC) is seen as marking the beginnings of the culture. A characteristic feature is the rise and fall of individual city-states and cultural centers, the periodically occurring crises and declines being a particular focus of research interest. These are traced back either to environmental causes (growth of the population

Background image: A ceramic incense burner from the Classic period of the Maya (Palenque, Mexico, dating from circa AD 300–800).

Above: This fresco from a Mayan tomb shows a procession of musicians (Bonampak, Mexico, eighth century AD).

accompanied by deteriorating soil fertility, climatic changes, and natural disasters) or to other causes (invasion by Toltecs, dominance of Teotihuacán, epidemics).

ECONOMY AND FOOD SUPPLY

The Maya, like all the major advanced ancient civilizations of the Americas, were primarily crop-growing cultures; however, they had a wide-ranging supply of food and cultivated corn, beans, pumpkins, tomatoes, and tobacco, and in wetter areas also yucca, cocoa, chili, and cotton. The forests provided deer, peccaries (South American pigs), small game, and many types of timber for building, while the rivers, lakes, and coastal waters supplied all kinds of aquatic animals for eating. The large volcanic areas supplied tuff and obsidian, used principally for sacrificial knives; the northern areas contained limestone, used for building and for obtaining lime, mortar, and cement.

STRUCTURE OF SOCIETY AND WARS

The Maya were organized city-states that were rivals, but which also traded with one another and from time to time joined forces to form alliances. Mayan societies, which were made up predominantly of farmers and artisans, were headed either by hereditary sovereigns (*ajaws*), who could be women, or by oligarchic ruling families (as, for example, in the case of the Quiché Maya people). Wars among the Maya, but also against surrounding peoples, occurred frequently and had either political/economic causes, such as the struggle for dominance, control of trade, and demands for tribute, or religious causes, such as the capture of prisoners for sacrificial ceremonies (*see p. 255*). For weapons, the Maya used spear-throwers (*atlatl*) and blowpipes for long-range combat, and used striking and stabbing weapons (axes, clubs, and knives) for close combat. They generally avoided open-pitched battles, depending instead on lightning-fast attacks or the besieging of fortified cities.

"This is the account: All was at rest. Not a breath, not a sound. The world was motionless and silent. And the expanse of the sky was empty. This is the first account, the first word. There was not yet any man or animal. There were no birds, fishes, crabs, trees, stones, caves, or ravines. No grass. No forest. Only the sky was there. The face of the earth had not yet revealed itself. There was only the calm sea and the great expanse of the sky."

Popol Vuh—The Book of the Community (Sacred book of the Quiché Maya); Part 1: The Creation

Stone sculpture with human face, from the Mayan Classic period (Palenque, Mexico, seventh century AD).

The centers of Tikal and Yaxchilán

Of the numerous Mayan centers, only a few will be described here: Tikal, north of Guatemala, was settled in circa 900 BC, but did not rise to become an important city-state with a ruling dynasty until about AD 200. Its rulers frequently bore names that were combined with those of animals (e.g. jaguar or frog). They built strongholds against neighboring states, as well as large temple complexes, and pyramids adorned with hieroglyphic texts and tableaux of images recounting significant events and military expeditions. Tikal was in constant dispute with its rival neighboring state of Calakmul. It was defeated by the latter in 562, liberated itself again in 695, but fell into decline in around 880. With over 3,000 buildings, the city extended over 25 sq miles (64 sq km).

Yaxchilán, on the middle reaches of the Rio Usumacinta (Mexico), also had a powerful ruling dynasty after 320, and reached its artistic peak from around 680, reflected in representations of ritual scenes on temple buildings. The city rivaled Palenque; its rulers, whose succession is documented over a 500-

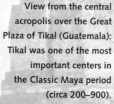

View from the central acropolis over the Great Plaza of Tikal (Guatemala); Tikal was one of the most important centers in the Classic Maya period (circa 200–900).

year period, also called themselves names such as "Shield Jaguar" or "Bird Jaguar." The last ruler died in 808.

Copán and Palenque

Tradition has it that the ruler Yäx-K'uk'-Mo' founded a dynasty in 426 at Copán (Honduras), immortalized in the numerous architectural structures in the city, which extends over 30 acres (12 ha), and is laid out in accordance with the Mayan cosmos. King "Smoke Jaguar Imix Monster" (628–695) had a 12-mile (20-km)-long chain of steles erected around Copán, and his successor "Smoke Squirrel" (749–763) built the famous "Temple 26," with its 55-step stone staircase, whose 2,200 hieroglyphic-covered stone blocks constitute the longest known Mayan inscription. The last inscription at Copán dates from the year 822.

Palenque, south of Mexico, whose first king is believed to have been born in 993 BC, also developed a rich architecture, most notably the palace complex, measuring 262 by 328 ft. (80 by 100 m), and the stone pyramid (temple of inscriptions). The city became important

from about 550 AD and experienced its heyday under King Pakal the Great (615–683)—whose tomb was found undisturbed—and under his son Chan Bahlam (also Kan Balam II, 684–702). After 780, Palenque's power declined rapidly.

CHICHÉN ITZÁ

In the Postclassic period, other peoples (Putun, Toltecs) advanced from the north (Mexico) toward the south and mixed with the Maya. Chichén Itzá, founded in circa AD 435, underwent a revival between 987 and 1240 as a Toltec trading and religious center. The dominant features here are the step pyramid of Kukulcán, the feathered snake god of the Maya, the Temple of the Warriors, and the largest of all Mayan ball-game courts—these have also been found in other centers. In the ritual game, the ball had to be conveyed through stone rings in a wall without being touched with the arm or leg (only the hip, chest, and shoulders were allowed to be used). It symbolized the passage of the sun. It is likely that the defeated team was routinely sacrificed.

Above: Stela N, erected in 761, at Copán (Honduras) shows "Smoke Squirrel" or "Smoke Shell," the fifteenth ruler of Copán (749–761/763).

The culture of the Maya: The calendar system

The importance of the priest caste (the Mayan scholarly class) lay above all in its knowledge of the ceremonial calendar. The Maya, who organized their lives according to time cycles, had two calendar systems: for everyday life, a sun calendar that was probably taken over from the Olmecs that comprised 365 days (*haab*) and which divided the year into 18 individually named sections (months) of 20 days each—the extra five "unlucky days" being appended at the end of the year. Alongside this, they used a ceremonial calendar for ritual and divinatory purposes (bean oracle), which comprised 260 days and was divided into 16 units of 20 days each. Every 52 years, or 18,980 days (i.e. equals 52 yearly cycles of 365 days or 73 divinatory cycles of 260 days), the two calendar systems shared a new start; this so-called "calendar round" (of 52 years) was for the Maya the highest unit in their cyclically interpreted calculation of time.

The Mayan script

The hieroglyphic script that was used in the lowlands but was not in the highlands employs for many concepts or names both logograms (symbols and pictographs) and syllabograms, which are divided into vowels and consonants and are combined, usually below one another,

Above: Relief of Shield Jaguar II, ruler of Yaxchilán (681–742); he is holding a ceremonial spear under which his sister-wife Xoc is offering a blood sacrifice.

Below: A French book with an illustration of Mayan hieroglyphs; the fact that they are composed of pictograms and syllabograms made deciphering the script difficult.

in such a way that a square hieroglyph is produced. The multiplicity of forms and possible combinations for representing certain words and names pose a particular difficulty.

RELIGION AND CULT OF SACRIFICE

The Mayan cosmos can be broken down into the sky (world of the gods), the earth (human world), and the underworld (realm of the dead). The Maya had a distinct funerary cult involving grave goods and worshiped a large number of gods, among whom the god of rain and vegetation, Chaac, and the god of wind and storm, Huracan (from whose name the word hurricane is derived), were prominent. The sun god Itzamná, who brought humans corn and cocoa and as "Lord of Knowledge" taught them the calendar and writing, was seen as the state god and cultural hero.

As was the case with most Mesoamerican peoples, blood and human sacrifice also played a role in maintaining the cosmic order and the well-being of gods and humans, although not to as great an extent as for the Aztecs. Priests and high-ranking figures drew blood from themselves by piercing their lip, tongue, or penis; there was also a ritual significance attached to the pain. Prisoners were sacrificed by being beheaded, being drowned in the cenotes (circular pools in each city), or by having their hearts cut out while they were still alive, on the platforms of the step pyramids.

DECLINE AND CONQUEST

From circa 1240, Mayan territories, particularly those in the north, disintegrated into a large number of communities engaged in extremely brutal warfare. In 1511, the first Spaniards landed in Yucatán, who, followed in 1519 by Hernán Cortés (see p. 261), from 1527, began the gradual conquest and subjugation of Mayan territories, which thus came under Spanish rule.

A reconstructed Mayan ceremonial scene from the burial site of Bonampak (Mexico, eighth century AD).

The Aztecs

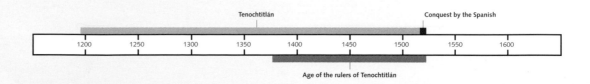

Representation of the sun calendar of the Aztecs; the calendar was used principally in the ceremonial calculation of harvest cycles and sacrifice times.

The Aztecs (from *aztecatl* in the Uto-Aztec language Nahuatl, signifying someone who comes from Aztlán) called themselves "Mexi'ca" (they gave their name to Mexico) and lived in the Basin of Mexico and in the Pueblo Valley. They initially formed a triple alliance of cities, of which Tenochtitlán took the lead, and created one of the most important Central American empires.

CLASS SOCIETY

Until Tenochtitlán became dominant after 1428, Aztec communities exhibited marked regional differences. The Tenochtitlán system was nonetheless prototypical of other Aztec cities. At its head stood the Great Speaker (*huey tlatoani*), who is frequently called the king and actually reigned as an absolute monarch in a system of male succession. Aztec society consisted of four classes: nobles (*tecuhtán*), who owned property with dependent peasant farmers and whose sons were trained to be army commanders, senior government officials, or priests; peasants (*macehualtin*), who made up the bulk of the population, were free, and also owned their own small parcels of land but had to perform military service; merchants (*pochteca*), who lived in separate city districts and joined forces to form guildlike associations; and finally, slaves (*tlatlacotin*), whose status was not hereditary and who generally entered slavery as convicted criminals or by becoming bonded laborers; they were allowed to own possessions and could also buy their liberty.

Economy and food

The Aztecs cultivated corn, beans, and pumpkins, and numerous grain and herb varieties in a fallow cropping system, as well as engaging in a form of artificial irrigation farming (*chinampas*) that allowed several harvests to be made in a year; the farmers joined together to form cooperatives and had to pay tribute to the ruler in the form rise to become nobles; outstanding warriors became members of the rival societies of eagle and jaguar warriors. These could be recognized by their magnificent plumes or by the jaguar skins they wore and were leaders in the so-called flower wars. In these, prisoners were captured for the sacrificial ceremonies, which were highly ritual in nature (*see p. 260*).

Below: View of the central sun temple in Teotihuacán, the capital of the Aztec Empire (north of present-day Mexico City, Mexico).

of produce. Aztec artisans were highly specialized—and the processing of gold, silver, and obsidian as well as textiles and bird feathers (primarily into clothing and ceremonial jewelry) conferred special status upon them. As long-distance travelers, traders had additional social importance as information carriers.

Warfare

The principal goal of wars against neighboring peoples was their economic exploitation and the exacting of tributes—they made the Aztec rulers rich. Refusals to pay tribute were followed by punitive expeditions, but the Aztecs never forced their culture and religion on dependent peoples. Peasants who showed particular prowess in war could

Left: Massive basalt statue of an Aztec warrior, which once supported the roof of the pyramid for the creator and sky god Quetzalcoatl in Teotihuacán (Mexico); the statues are armed with spears and carry the insignia of Quetzalcoatl.

away to found a new center. At a lake, they saw an eagle sitting on a prickly pear cactus and eating a snake—this image still adorns the emblem of Mexico today—and interpreted this as a sign to establish their new center, Tenochtitlán, there. It was long thought that the city had been founded between 1320 and 1350, but more recent finds point rather to the period between 1100 and 1200.

RISE TO BECOME CENTER OF THE EMPIRE

Tenochtitlán, which after 1473 was merged with Tlatelolco to form a dual city, was constructed on numerous interconnected islands on Lake Mexico and was connected to the mainland via causeways and bridges. In its heyday, up to 150,000 people lived here. The city consisted of four large (and several small) districts with their own temple complexes. In the middle of the dual city, traversed by straight roads and canals (which intersected one another at right angles), stood the two main temples in the form of two adjacent pyramids for the gods Tlaloc and Huitzilopochtli. Adjoining the temple district were the palaces of the rulers. In the outer districts, the *chinampas* (*see box, p. 259*) were located next to the housing settlements.

Portrait of the last Aztec ruler, Motecuzoma II, who died in July 1520 during an uprising against the Spanish or was murdered by the latter.

THE TENOCHTITLÁN EMPIRE: THE FOUNDATION MYTH

The Aztecs lived initially in Aztlán on Lake Texcoco in central Mexico, then, under the guidance of their god Huitzilopochtli, moved

" O our Lord, you have undertaken great exertions and have tired yourself. Now you have reached your own country. You have arrived in your city of Mexico. You have come here to sit on your throne, on your chair. They, your representatives who have already departed, the lords and kings Itzcóatl, Motecuzoma the Elder, Axayacatl, Tizoc, and Ahuitzotl, preserved it for you for a short while. They protected and preserved the city of Mexico in your name only for a short time. The people now stand under your government, under your protection. "

Welcome speech of Motecuzoma II to Hernán Cortés (1519), according to the Florentine Codex, sixteenth century

RISE OF THE AZTEC EMPIRE

Under their first rulers in Tenochtitlán, the Aztecs lived as tributary vassals of the mighty Tepanecs of Azcapotzalco (empire in the high valley of Mexico), but through military expeditions and marital alliances were able to increase their power. Their ruler Itzcoatl (1427–40) succeeded in breaking the Tepanecs' dominance militarily, establishing in 1428 the Aztec triple alliance of Tenochtitlán, Texcoco, and the new Tepanec center of Tlacopán, and securing the political leadership for his city. His nephew Motecuzoma I (1440–71) began the expansion of his empire into a major power. He conquered the region of Chalco (present-day Mexico City) and other territories as far as

► THE *CHINAMPAS*

The *chinampa*—the name means "fence of reeds"—was a unique Aztec method of cultivation; up to 656-ft. (200-m) -long rafts made of woven reeds were fastened to wooden stakes rammed into areas along the shores of the lakes to form floating areas for cultivation, which were then filled with fertile sludge from the lake bed and enabled up to four harvests to be made in a year. Corn, beans, tomatoes, sweet potatoes, avocados, and chilis as well as flowers were grown in this nutritious sludge.

the Gulf coast and exacted increased tributes deep into Mixtec territories, hoping in this way to overcome several famines and natural disasters. His successors consolidated this policy by conquering the neighboring state of Tlatelolco (1473).

Above: Aztecs creating a *chinampa*, a floating field on the lake shore (illustration from the sixteenth century).

Below: Model of the Aztec metropolis of Tenochtitlán with the double temple (Museo Nacional de Antropología, Mexico City, Mexico).

Right: A descendant of the Aztecs in traditional dress performing the Aztec fire dance; numerous elements of the ancient advanced culture are still alive today.

Below: Aztecs playing a board game in the presence of the god Xochipilli (illustration from the Codex Magliabechiano, mid-sixteenth century).

GODS, RELIGION, AND CULT OF SACRIFICE

The Aztecs adopted from the Toltecs various aspects of their culture, including their pantheon of gods. Special roles were played by the god of war and sun god Huitzilopochtli (Hummingbird of the South), considered to be the mythical ancestor of the people, the god Tlaloc, who sends rain as well as natural disasters and diseases, and the god of the wind and creator god Quetzalcoatl, whose myths tell of his rivalry with the god Tezcatlipoca, who represents the cold and the north but also acts as creator. Life-and-death struggles and blood sacrifices feature strongly in the myths of the gods.

Human sacrifices, the number of which was significantly higher than under the Maya (although reports by the Spanish did contain horror stories for propaganda purposes), were viewed as a way of settling debts to the gods

(*nextlaualli*). The Aztecs sacrificed not only prisoners of war, but also slaves and children and—like the Maya (*see p. 255*)—also engaged in practices such as the voluntary self-sacrifice of warriors and blood sacrifice by their rulers. Sacrificial victims had their hearts cut out on an altar on the platforms of the pyramids and their bodies were then thrown down the steep stone steps; in the case of certain prisoners, the body was even ritually consumed. One question preoccupying researchers is that of the extent to which the high number of human sacrifices was a phenomenon linked to the decline of Aztec culture in the face of natural disasters.

MOTECUZOMA II AND DEFEAT

Motecuzoma II (also known as Montezuma, 1502–20) waged prolonged wars in the mountains and tried to subdue the last independent people in southern Mexico, the Tlaxcaltecs. In 1515, he intervened in the allied city-state of Texcoco (member of the Triple Alliance) and placed his son on the throne there. Internally, he appointed noblemen to all important offices, thereby increasing the hierarchization of society.

When the Spanish conquistador Hernán Cortés (1485–1547) landed on the east coast in April 1519, Motecuzoma sent envoys to meet him. His consulting of the oracle beforehand had not provided any clear indication as to how the Aztecs should behave toward the Spanish. The king probably believed in the possibility of trading contacts. With their superior firearms, the Spanish initially subdued the Tlaxcaltec territories, reaching Tenochtitlán in November 1519. It is uncertain whether Motecuzoma offered his surrender; at all events, the Spanish took him prisoner during a meeting and then allowed him to continue ruling in accordance with their instructions. However, after he demanded the withdrawal of the Spanish in 1520, he was killed in July of that year during an uprising by the Aztecs led by his brother Cuitláuac—whether by the Spanish or by his own people also remains uncertain. With the aid of the Tlaxcaltecs, the Spanish conquerors then went on to complete the conquest of the Aztec Empire by August 1521, destroyed the images of the gods in Tenochtitlán, and in 1535 established the seat of the Spanish viceroy there; the city was renamed "Ciudad de México" (Mexico City).

An Aztec priest cuts out a prisoner's heart and offers it in sacrifice to the sun god (illustration from 1892). Bloody sacrificial rites like this were used by the Spaniards as justification for their forced christianization.

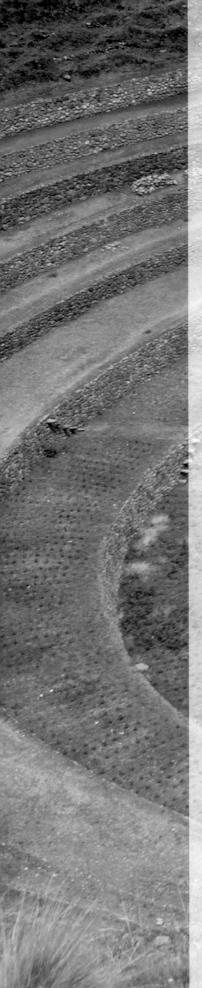

The Inca

Period of the great Inca rulers (Sapa Inca)

| 1200 | 1250 | 1300 | 1350 | 1400 | 1450 | 1500 | 1550 | 1600 |

Founding of Cuzco

Civil war Conquest by the Spanish

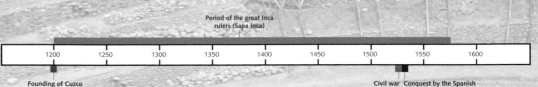

From its capital Cuzco, the advanced civilization of the Inca in Peru created an empire that is often referred to as the "Rome of South America" on account of its elaborate state structure and organization of labor. It is true to say that all the elements of modern state administration are found here.

ORIGIN

Myth and historical reality cannot be separated in the folk memory of the Quechua language group. The mythical first Inca (ruler) Manco Capac and his sister-wife Mama Ocllo are said to have come to earth as children of the creator god Viracocha on a sun island in Lake Titicaca and to have led their people to Cuzco; historians put the beginning of his rule at around 1200.

THE GREAT INCA AND HIS STATE

At the peak of his power, the Sapa Inca (Great or Unique Inca) had at his command a tightly organized bureaucratic state with structured administrative units, welfare and food distribution services, statistical surveys (by means of knotted strings (quipu) that mapped out numerical relations), and a comprehensively regulated infrastructure. The ruler, who was carried in a sedan chair and could be approached only with gestures

Background image: Terraces in the form of concentric circles at Cuzco (Peru); these were probably used by the Inca for experiments in plant breeding, as temperatures in individual terraced circles differed.

An Inca counting off the knots of a *quipu*, the traditional knot script (illustration dating from 1609).

of humility, was a sacred monarch with dynastic succession (but without the rule of primogeniture); he was considered to be the son of the sun god Inti, and he was married to his sister, the Coya.

Since the nobles were exempt from taxes, all their subjects, particularly the peasants, the backbone of the state, who cultivated corn, beans, tomatoes, manioc, potatoes, cocoa, and nuts on artificially irrigated terraced fields, had to give up one-third of their harvest to the sun god Inti (temple and cult) and a further third to the Sapa Inca and to provide for the nobility. They kept the last third for themselves and their families (work communities), but even from that further taxes were deducted to provide state social security for the elderly and the sick, widows and orphans, and the destitute and disabled.

THE ORGANIZATION OF LABOR

The Incas' system of labor is frequently referred to as a type of state socialism; the farmers did not own any land, but managed it as a family-based or neighborhood-based community (*ayllu*) with a strict obligation to provide mutual assistance and a general duty to work (*mitmak*). The activities themselves featured a marked division of labor and a high degree of specialization (*mitmakuma*) in the way they were organized. Farmers and artisans were in a permanent and tributary service and employment relationship (*camayo*) either directly to the ruler, the state administration, or to individual noblemen; specialists always worked in a profession that was inherited (*yanacona*), nonspecialists, by contrast, worked in different areas (*mitayo*). Members of vassal peoples, in particular, performed certain tasks by rota (*mita*). For the purposes of state integration, whole population groups were sometimes relocated—including vassal peoples. Lifelong forced labor was a more frequently imposed punishment than the death penalty.

" O Viracocha, who performs miracles
and things never seen!
Merciful Viracocha, great beyond measure,
Cause your people to multiply
and to bear children,
and let the fields and villages be free
from danger!
Those to whom you gave life, protect them
and hold them in your hand,
through the ages,
without end! "

Prayer for the people to multiply, recorded by
Cristóbal de Molina, circa 1572

An Inca *quipu* (made between 1430 and 1532). The position and number of knots provide information about population figures, quantities of food, or harvest yields.

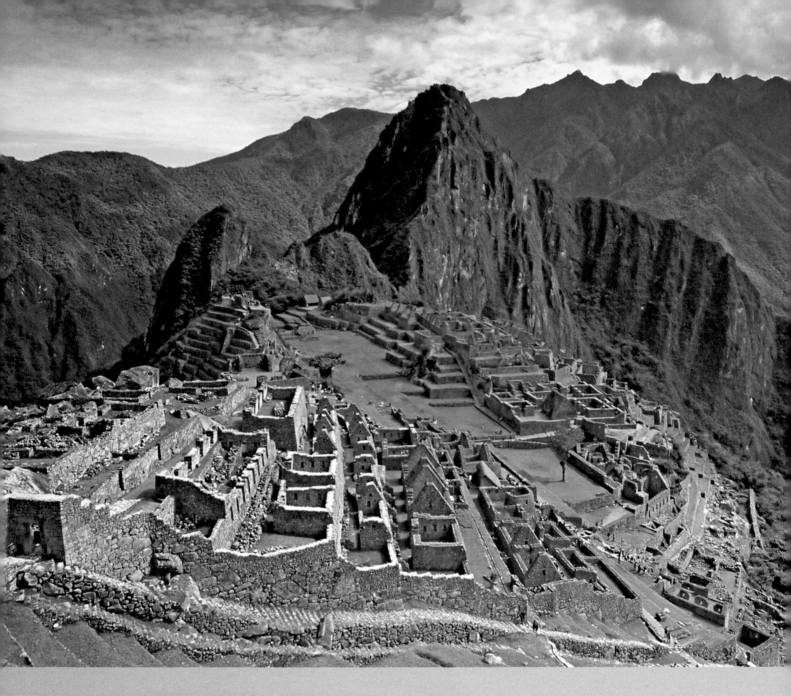

The ruins of the long-lost Inca city of Machu Picchu with its stone steps in the morning sun (Urubamba province, Peru).

ADMINISTRATION OF THE EMPIRE

The empire was divided into four main provinces (points of the compass), and bipartite and quadripartite division was practiced at almost all administrative levels. All important units were assigned dual leadership for reciprocal monitoring purposes. A relationship of strict reciprocity existed with the tributary vassal peoples. The tributes of vassals were matched by gifts and honorary titles from the Incas. Incas and vassals each built up large grain stocks and reserves and were obligated to provide for one another in the event of

shortages and emergencies. Evidence from skeletal remains suggests that the Inca did not experience food shortages.

SUN CULT AND ASTRONOMY

In their religion, the Inca borrowed from other Indio cultures and also incorporated the gods of vassal peoples. The pantheon of weather and celestial deities was headed by the sun god Inti, who was often equated with the creator god Viracocha. When the city of Cuzco was laid out, Pachacútec Yupanqui built a temple to Inti, with a golden statue;

▶ CUZCO AND MACHU PICCHU

Cuzco, in the Andean highlands of Peru, was a dual city which was divided into Upper Cuzco (Hanan Qusqu) and Lower Cuzco (Urin Qusqu). The first five rulers are said to have resided in the Lower City and subsequent rulers in the Upper City. Pachacútec Yupanqui started by laying out the famous Inca terraces around Cuzco—for corn cultivation. Above the city lies a fortified complex (Sacsayhuamán) with zigzag walls laid out in terraces. Another famous site is the water shrine at Tambo Machay, the Baths of the Inca, with its manufactured channels. Forty-six miles (75 km) northwest of Cuzco lies the "lost city" of Machu Picchu, with 216 stone structures which are connected to one another via stone steps. This most important Inca city for a long time remained undiscovered by the Spanish, and only entered public awareness upon its rediscovery in 1911.

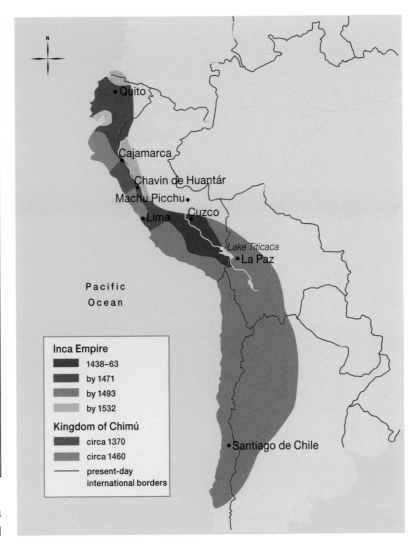

Inca Empire
- 1438–63
- by 1471
- by 1493
- by 1532

Kingdom of Chimú
- circa 1370
- circa 1460
- present-day international borders

the rituals that took place here employed a large number of people, comprising priests and temple maidens whose lives were determined by numerous taboos. The installation of sun idols and the establishment of central temples

and sacrificial squares throughout the empire served to disseminate the state cult and ritual celebrations, especially those safeguarding the weather and harvest cycles. It is probable that human sacrifices were made only when natural disasters or periods of drought occurred. The Incas practiced an extensive cult of the dead and of ancestors involving mummification and rich tomb offerings. They also calculated and read the star signs; astronomy and astrology were linked to divinatory practices and looking into the future. Their knowledge of medicine, particularly the use of medicinal plants, herbs, and wound care, was substantial.

A representation of successive Inca rulers, the "Great Incas," from the Peruvian School (circa 1780–99).

THE EXTENT OF THE INCA EMPIRE
The map shows the extent of the Inca Empire along the west coast of South America under the great conquerors Pachacútec Yupanqui (1438–71), Túpac Yupanqui (1471–93), Huayna Cápac (1493–1527), and the two warring brothers Huascár (1527–32) and Atahualpa (1527–33). The Kingdom of Chimú was assimilated into the Incan Empire in 1460.

The last Inca ruler Atahualpa (1502–33), who after 1527 was joint ruler, contributed decisively to the weakening and collapse of the Incan Empire by wiping out the nobility in the murderous civil war against his brother Huascár. In 1533 he was garroted by the Spanish.

History of the Inca

The Inca recorded for posterity the reign of thirteen or fourteen Sapa Incas, of whom only the last five can be placed historically. The early rulers subjugated the other tribes of Cuzco and established themselves through marital alliances and wars of conquest. Initially, they bore the title of "Sinchi"; only from the sixth ruler, Inca Roca (circa 1350), onward did they carry the title "Inca." The eighth Inca, Huiracocha (circa 1410), conquered extensive territories in the Urubamba Valley, and during an attack on the enemy Chanka in 1438, his son Pachacútec Yupanqui (1438–71) seized power, destroyed the Chanka, and extended his empire as far as Junín in central Peru. Called "He who remakes the world," he established the foundations of the Inca state internally by introducing technical innovations, and began recording the history of the people.

His son Túpac Yupanqui (1471–93), a patron of art and science, led the empire to its golden age and extended his rule as far as Chile and Ecuador. He made the peoples on the northern coast of Peru his tributaries and secured their loyalty to the empire by bringing their dignitaries to Cuzco and entrusting them with state duties. He had an army of 300,000 men at his disposal. His son Huayna Cápac (1493–1527) conquered parts of Colombia. In 1527, together with a large part of his army, he died of smallpox, which had been introduced by the Spanish and had spread from Central America. The power struggle between his sons

An Incan stone circle, probably used for ritual purposes, in Sacsayhuamán near Cuzco, Peru (circa 1475).

was a key contributory factor to the decline of the empire.

Civil war, defeat and decline of the Inca Empire

In 1527, Huayna Cápac divided his empire between two sons: Huascár (1527–32) received the central areas, with the royal seat of Cuzco, and his half-brother Atahualpa (1527–33) the northern regions, with the royal seat of Cajamarca. Immediately, a murderous civil war broke out, involving the brutal execution of captured nobles and warriors. In a decisive battle in 1532, Atahualpa was victorious. He had Huascár, who had been captured, executed, and systematically wiped out the entire nobility of Cuzco. In April of the same year, the Conquistador Francisco Pizarro (1478–1541) had landed on the Peruvian coast with 168 soldiers. Atahualpa received him outside the capital, but was captured by the Spanish, who with their superior firearms annihilated his noblemen. Atahualpa attempted to buy his liberty with a room full of gold and silver brought from all over the empire, but this merely inflamed the greed of the Spaniards. Pizarro's successor Diego de Almagro (1475–1538) had Atahualpa sentenced to death by burning on a charge of "fratricide, polygamy, and idolatry," and—after the Inca had been baptized—in 1533 "out of mercy" had him executed by garroting. The Spanish broke the resistance of the Inca and installed "by their grace" Atahualpa's half-brother Manco Cápac II (1533–44) as ruler. In 1536 he unleashed a revolt against the Spanish tyranny, which led to the final subjugation of the Inca. Manco Cápac was followed on the throne by three sons, the last of whom, Tupác Amaru (1570–72), was executed by the Spanish in 1572. Numerous elements of Inca culture have, however, survived to the present day, particularly in the areas of art and crafts and folk beliefs.

Facing page: The greatest battle between the Inca and the Spanish conquistadors took place in 1532 in this stone castle, which is shaped like a puma, in Cuzco (Peru).

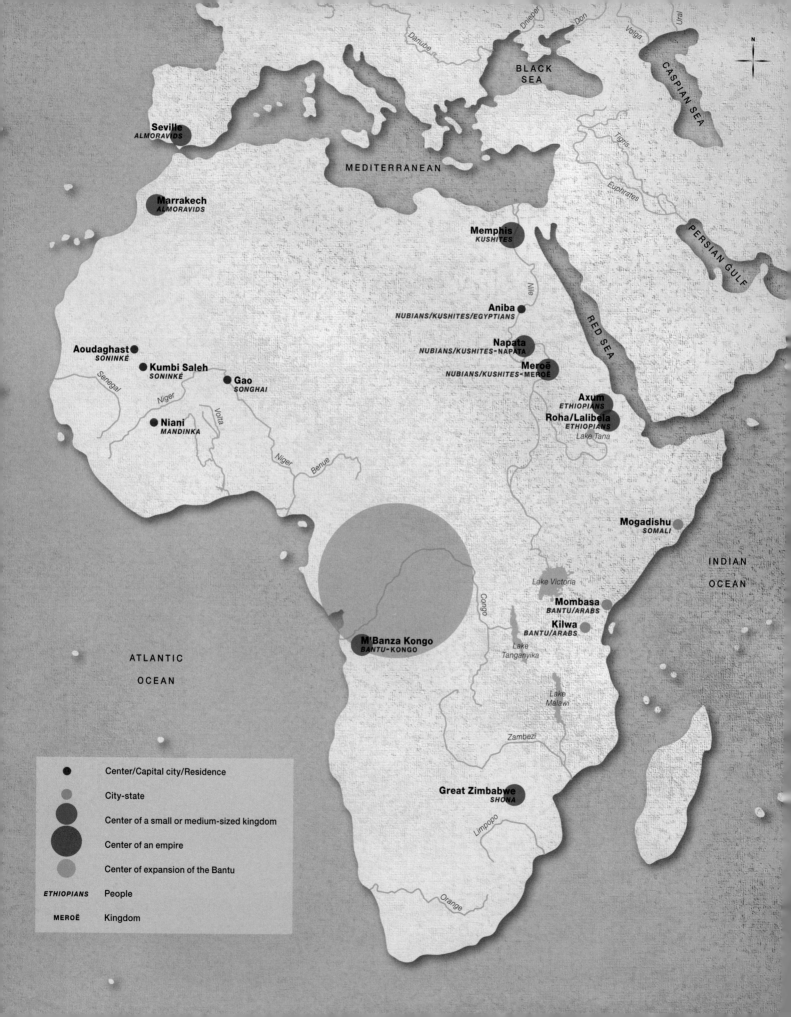

BLACK
SEA

CASPIAN
SEA

MEDITERRANEAN

PERSIAN GULF

Seville
ALMORAVIDS

Marrakech
ALMORAVIDS

Memphis
KUSHITES

Nile

RED SEA

Aniba
NUBIANS/KUSHITES/EGYPTIANS

Napata
NUBIANS/KUSHITES-NAPATA

Meroë
NUBIANS/KUSHITES-MEROË

Aoudaghast
SONINKÉ

Kumbi Saleh
SONINKÉ

Gao
SONGHAI

Axum
ETHIOPIANS

Roha/Lalibela
ETHIOPIANS

Lake Tana

Senegal

Niger

Volta

Niani
MANDINKA

Niger

Benue

Mogadishu
SOMALI

INDIAN

OCEAN

Lake Victoria

Congo

Mombasa
BANTU/ARABS

Kilwa
BANTU/ARABS

Lake
Tanganyika

ATLANTIC

OCEAN

M'Banza Kongo
BANTU-KONGO

Lake
Malawi

Zambezi

Great Zimbabwe
SHONA

Limpopo

Orange

Danube

Dnieper

Don

Volga

Ural

Tigris

Euphrates

Lake Tana

● Center/Capital city/Residence

● City-state

● Center of a small or medium-sized kingdom

● Center of an empire

● Center of expansion of the Bantu

ETHIOPIANS People

MEROË Kingdom

Shona   Kushite   Ethiopian   Songhai   Bantu

AFRICA

The spread and development of humankind started from the African continent. Here, an immense diversity of tribal communities and states developed, among which the kingdoms of the Kushites and of Ethiopia, which were Christian from early times, are notable for their distinctive and highly developed cultures.

In the western regions of sub-Saharan Africa, the kingdoms of Ghana (which is not identical with the modern state of Ghana), Mali, and the Songhai, as well as the Hausa and Banza states, established themselves; the latter soon fell under the influence of Islam as practiced by the Arabs and Berbers of Upper Africa. In central Africa, once the Bantu peoples had become sedentary, the empires of the Congo led the way in forming state structures; from about 1500, however, they fell under the sphere of influence of the Portuguese colonizers. The coastal towns of East Africa, mainly Islamic in character, profited from extensive maritime trading, becoming extraordinarily prosperous. Among the early kingdoms in the south of the continent, the most significant were Great Zimbabwe, to which puzzling stone structures still bear witness today, and Munhumutapa and the kingdoms that succeeded it. This region, starting with the coastal areas (Mozambique), also came under the influence of the Portuguese trading colonies from around 1500. There is no space here to do more than allude to the inhuman slave trade run by Arab and later European traders in collaboration with the indigenous elites; nonetheless, it has shaped the fate of many African peoples in a way that has been as distressing as it has been enduring.

AFRICA
The map shows the early kingdoms of West Africa (Ghana, Mali, the Kingdom of the Almoravids), the kingdoms of the Kushites and Ethiopians, and some of the East African coastal towns, as well as the more southerly kingdoms of the Congo and Great Zimbabwe.

The kingdoms of Kush and Ethiopia

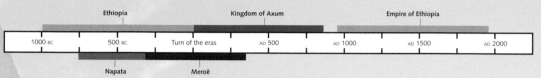

K ush, due to its close links with Egypt and Ethiopia, and due to its early and lasting christianization, occupies a special place among the early kingdoms of Upper Africa.

THE LAND OF THE KUSHITES

Nubia (present-day Sudan), called "Kush" by the Egyptians, was conquered by the pharaohs from approximately 2000 BC onward, but was able to liberate itself again during the period of the Hyksos (from circa 1650 to 1540 BC). In the New Kingdom, however (from circa 1540 to 1070 BC), Nubia as far as the fourth Nile cataract came under Egyptian administration headed by a viceroy residing in Aniba. The inhabitants of this Egyptian storehouse of gold and precious metals were highly valued as soldiers in the Egyptian army for their courage and physical strength, and rose to high military ranks there; large numbers of Nubians lived and worked in Egypt and were influenced by the culture there.

THE KINGDOM OF NAPATA

The Kushites exploited the weakness of Egyptian central authority after 1070 BC to set up their own kingdom in Napata (from approximately 750 to 270 BC). Its rulers made incursions into Egypt and, from the reign of King Piye (747–

716 BC) onward, also ruled over Egypt as the Twenty-Fifth Dynasty of "Black Pharaohs" until, under the reign of Taharqa (690–664 BC), they were driven out of the land on the Nile by the Assyrians after 671 BC (*see p. 79*). From 653 BC, they were again confined to Napata. The culture of Napata was strongly Egyptian in character, and here, too, the chief imperial god was Amun-Re. The royal capital was established

Background image: Pyramid tombs of the Kushite rulers in Meroë (present-day Sudan, 300 BC–AD 300); the Kushites built more pyramids than the Egyptians.

Above: Lifelike stone statue of a Kushite woman from the kingdom of Meroë (Khartoum Museum, Sudan).

on both sides of the Nile: west of the Nile stood the palaces and temple complexes and pyramids of El-Kurru and Barkal, and east of the river lay the town of Sanam for the ordinary people.

THE KINGDOM OF MEROË

Under King Ergamenes I (270–260 BC) a new dynasty came to power with its center located farther to the south at Meroë, where as many as 25,000 people lived. His reign also saw the start of the construction of numerous pyramids in which the Nubian rulers sought to immortalize themselves. The culture of the Kingdom of Meroë (circa 300 BC–AD 300), which experienced its golden age under King Natakamani at the turn of the eras, was far more independent in character, and in its numerous temple buildings exhibits elements drawn from a mixture of Egyptian and Nubian-African as well as Hellenistic styles. The population lived from agriculture and livestock farming, and the kingdom prospered from trade in gold and (from Taharqa's reign onward) iron—there appear to

have been separate centers of iron smelting—as well as in ivory, exotic animals, ostrich feathers, and black slaves. After 25 BC, a number of conflicts arose with the Romans in Egypt, who razed Napata in AD 279, but the battle-hardened ruling kings and queens, the latter carrying the title "Kandake," beat back the Romans and ultimately concluded trade agreements with them. In around AD 250, the rulers of Meroë were supplanted by the Blemmyes, a Nubian nomadic people, who advanced as far as Upper Egypt, but were repelled by the Romans; Meroë was destroyed in around 350.

This freestanding stone "kiosk" from the Meroitic era betrays Egyptian and—especially in the column capitals—Hellenistic influences; such buildings were used for temporarily storing relics during processions.

"He who is content with his city;
He who brings peace to his two lands; bull of his two lands;
Strong bull appearing in Napata; strong bull appearing in Thebes,
Unifier of the two lands, ruler of Egypt;
Whose kingship endures like Re's in heaven;
He who brings forth works of art;
Whose appearances are holy, whose might is powerful;
In whose sight everyone lives prostrated,
He who makes the bold (soldiers) numerous."

Titulary name of the Pharaoh Piye, eighth century BC

Ethiopia: The Kingdom of Axum

Ethiopia is one of the world's oldest states; the kingdom initially also covered Eritrea and parts of Sudan and Libya. The Ethiopians trace it back to Menelik I (circa 975–950 BC), who is deemed to have been the son of the biblical King Solomon and the Queen of Sheba and, according to myth, secretly brought the Ark of the Covenant of the Israelites to Ethiopia.

The kingdom, with its capital at Axum, emerged no later than the turn of the eras, and its rulers have been documented since about AD 50. The culture was heavily influenced by Saba in southern Arabia (*see p. 48*); only gradually did it develop its own language and script—Ge'ez. King Ezana (circa AD 325–355), who expanded the kingdom to the south and to the east as far as Arabia and who corresponded with Roman Emperor Constantius II, embraced Christianity, which had reached Ethiopia through Frumentius (called "Abuna our Father," circa AD 310–383), the first Bishop of Axum. The Ethiopian church was headed by the Patriarch of Alexandria and in AD 451 (Council of Chalcedon), together with the Copts, split away from the Orthodox Church to form a monophysitic church (monophysites believe that Christ had only a single, divine nature, and not also a human one). The Kingdom of Axum, which prospered through control of maritime trade in the Red Sea as well as through trading in gold, precious metals, ivory, and animal skins, with its numerous ecclesiastical buildings asserted its own independent Christianity; however, although relations were initially good during Mohammed's lifetime, it became increasingly isolated culturally during the course of the islamization of Upper Africa from the seventh century onward. Axum's power fell into decline, and the city was abandoned, having been destroyed in circa AD 842.

The empire—the Lion of Judah

Under the Zagwe Dynasty (916–1270), which can be traced back to Moses, Ethiopia's power

Above: Stone steles from the stele field of Tigray, a center of the ancient Ethiopian kingdom of Axum; the stele field is also associated with the semilegendary Jewish Queen Gudit, who is said to have destroyed the kingdom of Axum in circa AD 842.

Right: The rock Church of Bet Giorgys (St. George) in Lalibela (northern Ethiopia); the most important Zagwe emperor, Lalibela (1189–1229), in whose honor the capital Roha was renamed, had 11 rock churches hewn from the surrounding rock formations.

rose again in the new capital Roha (later Lalibela); until the reign of Haile Selassie (1930–74), the emperors bore the title "Negus Negest" (King of Kings). In 1270, Yekuno Amlak (Tasfa Jesus, 1270–85) reestablished the rule of the Solomonic Dynasty—its rulers were deemed to be descendants of the tribe of Juda—and detached the Ethiopian Church from Egypt under its own Abuna (Patriarch); it has remained independent to this day. Contacts with its Muslim neighbors alternated between exchanging commodities on the one hand and carrying out raids and military expeditions on the other. From the reign of David I, diplomatic contacts were established with European powers, notably with the Italian trading republics. To counter the threat of domination by the Muslims, after 1493 the emperors began to allow Portuguese into the country. They supported the Ethiopians militarily: Emperor Lebna Dengel (1508–40) fell in battle against the expanding Sultanate of Adal, whose advance his successor Claudius (1540–49) was able to halt only with Portuguese assistance. Rabid attempts at conversion to Catholicism by the Portuguese, however, led to their being expelled by Emperor Fasilidas (1632–67).

Ethiopian frescoes, which are reminiscent of icons, on the walls of the Debre Berhan Selassie Church in Gondar (Ethiopia); Emperor Fasilidas (1632–67) founded Gondar in 1636 as the new royal residence of the Ethiopian emperor (until 1855).

The kingdoms of sub-Saharan Africa

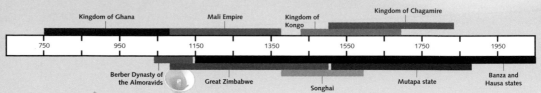

	Kingdom of Ghana		Mali Empire		Kingdom of Kongo		Kingdom of Chagamire		
750	950		1150	1350		1550	1750		1950
	Berber Dynasty of the Almoravids	Great Zimbabwe			Songhai		Mutapa state		Banza and Hausa states

In sub-Saharan Africa, kingdoms emerged in early times, which soon became targets for Islamic Arabs and Berbers and later the European colonial powers.

WEST AFRICA: THE KINGDOM OF GHANA

West Africa has been settled since the Stone Age and in circa 3000 BC developed the Kintampo culture. The first West African kingdom to emerge, in around AD 750, was Ghana, with centers at Aoudaghost and Kumbi Saleh (Mauritania), covering the present-day countries of Mali and Mauritania. Through trade in gold, ivory, and salt, the king of Ghana from the West African Soninké people became so powerful that the Arab traveler Ibn Haukal acclaimed him in 970 to be "the richest man in the world because of his gold," and the oasis of Aoudaghost became an important center of trade. At first, good trading relations existed with the Islamic powers of northwest Africa, until the fanatical Berber Dynasty of the Almoravids (1042–1147) from the coast of Senegal began a process of forced islamization; in 1054 they conquered Aoudaghost and in 1076 Kumbi Saleh. Between 1060 and 1147, the Almoravids also ruled over Morocco and Spain.

THE KINGDOMS OF MALI AND SONGHAI

When Ghana collapsed, the Mandinka tribes of Mali from whom Ghana had exacted tribute made themselves independent and established

The mausoleum of Askia Mohammed (circa 1442–1538), ruler of the Songhai Kingdom from 1493 to 1528, in Gao (Mali); Askia the Great eventually led his kingdom to Islam.

" The king adorns his neck and arms in women's jewelry. He puts on a tall pointed cap edged with gold and wrapped in a turban of very fine cotton. He holds audience and receives complaints under a domed roof. Around him wait ten horses with coats made of gold material. Behind him stand ten sons of nobles, carrying swords and shields of leather; they are splendidly dressed and wear their hair in plaits interlaced with gold thread. "

Abu Obeid Abdallah al-Bekri (d. 1094), from the chronicle of his journey to the King of Ghana

a kingdom of their own with Niani as its center. Its rulers were adherents of Islam and steadily expanded their territory. Besides producing food by means of arable and livestock farming, Mali also maintained extensive trading contacts. The founder of the kingdom, Sundiata Keita (1245–60), ascended to the title of "Mansa" (King of kings). A number of his successors undertook the pilgrimage to Mecca; Arab sources recount in particular the magnificent pilgrimage in 1324/25 of Mansa Musas (1312–37), who built Timbuktu into one of the most important trading centers in Africa. Mali was succeeded after about 1375 by the Kingdom of Songhai, with its center in Gao (Mali); the conqueror Sunni Ali (1464–93) occupied Djenné and Timbuktu, tamed the Tuareg nomads, and improved agriculture in his kingdom by installing irrigation systems. His successor Askia Mohammed (1493–

1528) put in place a strictly Islamic system of government with rich court ceremonial. In 1591, the kingdom was conquered by the Sultan of Morocco.

The Ribat of Sousse with its watchtower (Tunisia, ninth century AD); it was from such fortified Islamic monasteries, called *ribats*, that the Berber Almoravids subdued and islamized the West African kingdoms in the eleventh century.

THE HAUSA AND BANZA STATES

From origins shrouded in myth, the Hausa and Banza states emerged in the twelfth century in what is now Nigeria, Niger, and Chad. As major city-states, they wrestled with one another for superiority. They developed complex economic systems and traded in black slaves, who were also used as tribute payments to the kingdoms to the north in exchange for weapons and textiles. From the fourteenth century onward, the Hausa states, headed by the city-state of Kano, adopted Islam with which they had come into contact through Arab traders; the Banza states, by contrast, practiced a mixed form of Islam and indigenous traditional religion; there, the traditional sacral kingship found itself caught up in a power struggle with Islam.

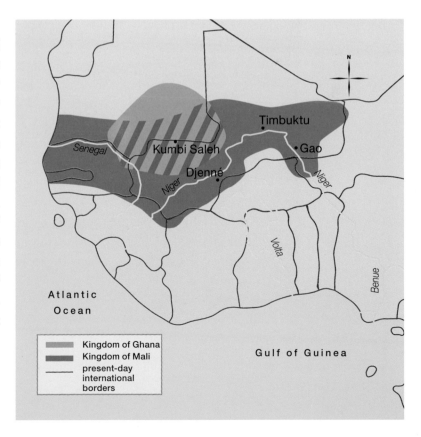

THE EARLY KINGDOMS OF GHANA AND MALI
The map shows the extent of the early Kingdoms of Ghana and Mali (Songhai) with their centers, which from the eleventh century were conquered by Muslim Berber peoples.

Kingdom of Ghana
Kingdom of Mali
present-day international borders

Mosques in the shape of a beehive are typical of Nubian and African architecture; shown here is the Kubbet al-Hawa mosque in Aswan (Egypt).

EAST AND CENTRAL AFRICA: THE CRADLE OF HUMANKIND

East Africa is nowadays considered to be the "cradle of humankind." Around four million years ago, it was inhabited by Australopithecines, forerunners of the hominids who spread to all the continents from here approximately 1.8 million years ago. At Kandar in Ethiopia, the remains were discovered in 1974 of "Lucy," an early form of hominid who lived approximately 3.2 million years ago.

THE BANTU PEOPLES

By 1000 BC at latest, the Bantu peoples began their migration from Cameroon and Nigeria to areas of central Africa, where by about AD 400 they settled in the areas in which they are found today. They were organized in tribes with religiously legitimized chieftains, some of which later established larger state structures.

THE KONGO KINGDOM

The Kongo Kingdom was established in 1390 in the area of the present-day states of the

A Bantu fetish figure from the Congo that was used for swearing oaths. It is believed to represent a deity or an ancestor.

Democratic Republic of Congo and Angola. We are familiar with descriptions of it primarily from Portuguese sources. It was rigidly subdivided into six provinces, and these in turn were subdivided into districts and villages. The center of the kingdom was M'Banza Kongo (in present-day Angola). Officials of the king who, together with the dignitaries of the court, formed the nobility (*mani*) acted as judges in the districts. At their head stood the "Mani Kongo" (Lord of the Kongo), the absolute monarch. Since there was no hereditary succession and the ruler was elected by a council of elders, all the royal princes formed factions; this repeatedly led to bloody family feuds.

In 1482, the Portuguese landed at the Congo estuary, made contact with the Mani Kongo and soon managed to establish themselves as permanent royal advisors. The fifth Mani Kongo, Nkuwu Nzinga (1470–1509), was the first ruler to be baptized (in 1491), taking the name João I in honour of Portugal's king at the time, João II. His son Nzinga Mbemba (1509–142/43), who took the Christian name Alfonso I, was acknowledged as an equal by the Portuguese king in 1512, and established schools and a state in accordance with the principles by which Portugal was governed. He led his kingdom to Catholicism, and in 1518 one of his sons was consecrated by the Pope as the first black bishop. Despite this, the Portuguese ran a large-scale slave trade from Kongo to the New World, which bled the kingdom dry and led to its collapse in 1665.

The overgrown ruins of a mosque in Gedi (Kenya) give a clear view through to the *mihrab* (prayer niche) that remains intact. The city of Gedi was ruled by Muslim Arabs between the eleventh and sixteenth centuries.

▶ THE COASTAL CITIES OF EAST AFRICA
Between 800 and 1500, the east coast of Africa between Somalia and Tanzania, which had been settled since around the turn of the eras, saw the rise of about forty significant and influential cities (city-states), including Mogadishu (Somalia), Mombasa (Kenya), and Kilwa (Tanzania), which prospered from maritime trade, principally with the Arab kingdoms, but also with India and China (porcelain finds). Some minted their own coins and from the twelfth century were chiefly under Islamic influence or the rule of Arab dynasties, to which mosque buildings still bear witness today. They traded in ceramics and metals (which they produced themselves), pearls, animal skins, and slaves.

> **"**In the middle of the plain, in the kingdom of Butua, among the ancient gold mines stands a fortress [Great Zimbabwe], four-sided, excellently constructed internally and externally of solid blocks. The stones the walls are made of, needing no lime compound for the joints, are of extraordinary size . . . . Even the inhabitants, who have no writing, have no information as to when and by whom these buildings were built. They merely say that they are a work of the devil, because people could not have managed it.**"**
>
> Carl Ritter, *Erdkunde* (Science of the Earth) Vol. 1, 1817

SOUTHERN AFRICA: GREAT ZIMBABWE

The center of early culture in southern Africa was located in what is now Zimbabwe and Mozambique; the name Zimbabwe means "great stone house" and indicates the residence of an important chief. The region had been populated since the second century AD by Shona pastoralist farmers who established permanent settlements from around AD 1000 and traded with one another. Old Zimbabwe with its stone constructions—the oldest south of the Sahara—is still something of an enigma today. As long ago as the tenth century, Arab sources tell of a kingdom with a significant trade in gold, which is borne out by traces of systematic exploitation of the region's rich copper mines and gold, iron, and tin mines. The walls of Great or Old Zimbabwe—located close to the town of Masvingo—were probably constructed between the eleventh and fifteenth centuries by forefathers of today's Shona peoples of Zimbabwe. They consist of unmortared granite blocks and principally form part of the ruins of a mountain fortress and of the elliptical wall enclosing an area that is thought to have been a temple precinct. The walls, with an overall length of 800 ft. (244 m), are up to 16 ft. (5 m) wide at the base and up to 30 ft. (9 m) high, were never roofed and enclosed huts and houses. For a long time, there was an ideologically motivated debate about whether putative white civilizations in early times had been the builders of the complex, especially as the Portuguese believed that in finding it they had discovered the residence of the Queen of Sheba; both ideas are today considered to be historically untenable.

THE MUNHUMUTAPA EMPIRE

In around 1430, a new empire emerged in the Zimbabwe region, whose ruler Nyatsimba Mutota (circa 1430–50) adopted the title

The tightly jointed outer walls of the stone complex of Great Zimbabwe, which were rediscovered in 1867 and have since been researched, have been the cause of much speculation.

A prehistoric cave drawing found near a farm in Rusape (Zimbabwe); numerous examples of these paintings from early human history, often several thousand years old, are to be found in southern Africa.

"Mwene Mutapa" (King Mutapa), from which the empire's name, Munhumutapa, is derived. His son Matope Nyanhehwe (circa 1450–80) became the actual founder of the empire by conquering all the lands between the Kalahari Desert and the Sofala region (Mozambique) on the Indian Ocean. He made numerous peoples tributary, intensified coastal trade, and arranged for the provinces to be administered by his sons and nephews. The empire exhibited a high degree of central organization, evidence of which is also provided by extensive irrigation systems in the Mazowe River valley.

The Changamire

Shortly after 1480 the Munhumutapa Empire disintegrated and was reduced to the Mutapa state of Karanga in the north. In the south, the Rozvi peoples split with the Tlokwa Dynasty, which in 1506 was overturned and replaced by Changa, a governor of the Munhumutapa Empire. The latter established the empire of Changamire, as it is called by the Arabs (from "Changa emirs"), which by engaging intensively in coastal trading in ivory and precious metals as far afield as Arabia, India, and China (as porcelain

finds testify) soon outstripped the Mutapa state. While Mutapa came under Portuguese influence after 1500 and was unimportant after 1629, Changamire remained a political power in southern Africa and a significant trading partner to the Arabs and Portuguese until 1834.

THE RUINS OF GREAT ZIMBABWE
The significance and function of this defensive complex, which served as a seat of government or cultural center, are still not entirely clear.

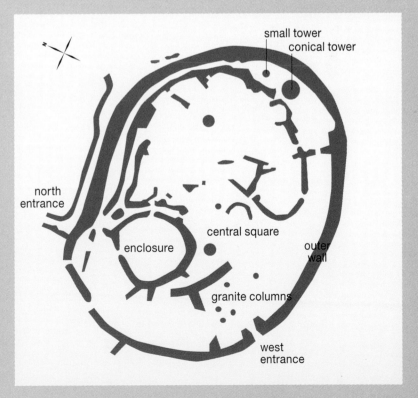

north entrance

small tower
conical tower

central square

enclosure

outer wall

granite columns

west entrance

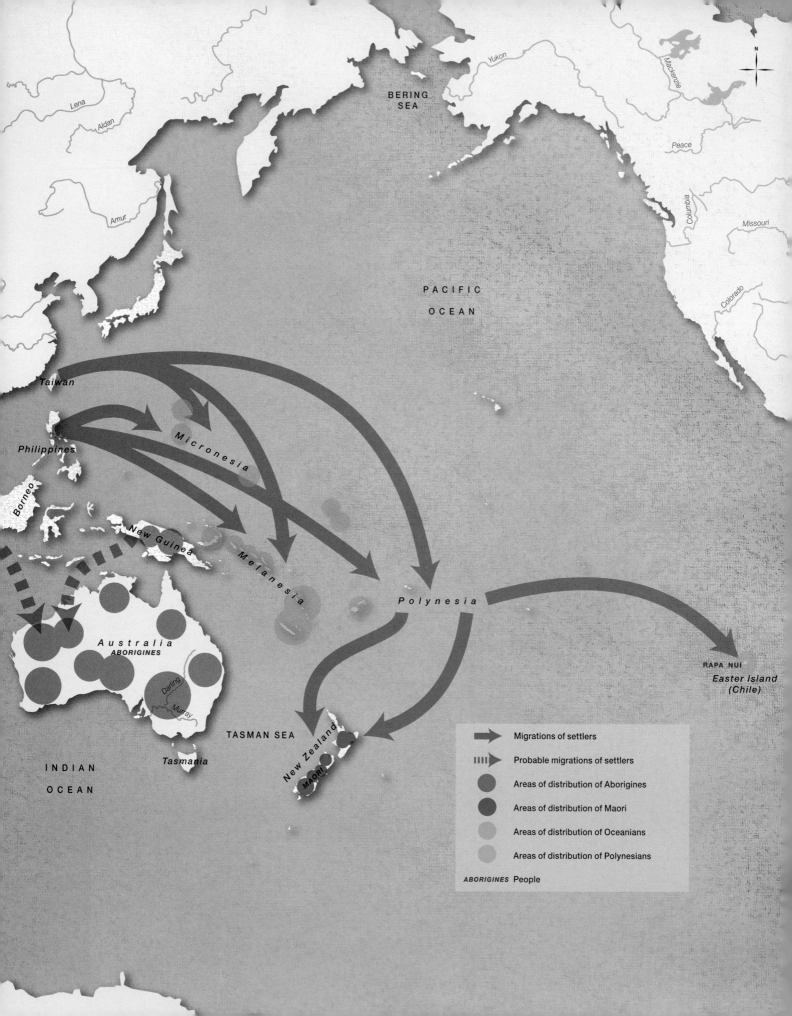

BERING
SEA

PACIFIC

OCEAN

Lena

Aldan

Amur

Yukon

Mackenzie

Peace

Columbia

Missouri

Colorado

Taiwan

Philippines

Borneo

Micronesia

New Guinea

Melanesia

Polynesia

RAPA NUI
*Easter Island
(Chile)*

Australia
ABORIGINES

Darling

Murray

TASMAN SEA

Tasmania

INDIAN

OCEAN

New Zealand
MAORI

→	Migrations of settlers
⇢	Probable migrations of settlers
●	Areas of distribution of Aborigines
●	Areas of distribution of Maori
●	Areas of distribution of Oceanians
●	Areas of distribution of Polynesians

ABORIGINES People

Polynesians (Samoa)   Polynesians (Fiji)   Maoris   Aborigines   Rapa Nui

AUSTRALIA AND OCEANIA

Across the whole of the South Sea (Pacific) region, Europeans in the eighteenth century encountered independent tribal and clan societies living in primitive conditions; they initially believed that in these they had found the primordial societies of human history.

Until the arrival of white settlers, the tribes of Aborigines in Australia had preserved relatively unchanged over thousands of years their clan system and their way of life, which were based upon extended family relations. Their close attachment to their ancestors and to the bringers of their culture in early times (dreamtime), as well as to the nature surrounding them, demonstrated a high degree of cultural self-sufficiency.

In contrast, the peoples of the Oceanic island world of Polynesia, Melanesia, and Micronesia, which in cultural terms include the Maoris of New Zealand as well as the inhabitants of Easter Island, were characterized by rigidly hierarchically structured societies, some of them warlike, led by chiefs and nobles. In these, a decisive role was played by genealogies and knowledge of boatbuilding and of navigation, as well as by the ritual connections of the spiritual force, *mana*, and the strict avoidance rules of the tabu. The cultural peculiarities of Easter Island (Rapa Nui)—such as the ancestor colossi of the *moai*, the Rongorongo script, and the birdman cult—have made this civilization a popular research subject even today, but also a subject of esoteric speculation. While the Aborigines of Australia and the Maoris of New Zealand had to suffer centuries of oppression, the island societies of Oceania were on the whole able to stand up more confidently to colonization by the whites.

AUSTRALIA AND OCEANIA
The map shows the movements of settlers to the island groups of Polynesia (including Easter Island), Melanesia, and Micronesia, as well as of the Maoris of New Zealand from the west, and the probable migration movements of the Aborigines of Australia.

Australia and New Zealand

Settlement of Australia by Aborigines

Settlement of New Zealand by Polynesian island inhabitants

| 60,000 BC | 50,000 BC | 40,000 BC | 30,000 BC | 20,000 BC | 10,000 BC | Turn of the eras | AD 1000 | AD 2000 |

Abel Tasman discovers New Zealand   James Cook lands in Australia

The continent of Australia was settled from across the sea between approximately 60,000 and 32,000 BC. However, it did have a land bridge to New Guinea, which was flooded only about 6,000 years ago. Seafaring peoples made landfall on Australia's coast on several occasions, notably the Dutch in the north from 1606 onward. In 1770, James Cook (1728–79) took "possession" of Australia for the British.

Above: A member of an Aboriginal tribe in the traditional costume of the inhabitants of Saibai Island (Torres Strait, off the north coast of Australia).

WAY OF LIFE

The original inhabitants of Australia (Aborigines) lived as nomadic hunters and gatherers in clans (hordes) of 20 to 30 individuals in a defined territory in relation to which, while it was not considered their property, a clan held exclusive rights of use; other clans entered this area only if invited. The men used long spears, spear-throwers (woomera), and throwing-sticks (boomerangs) as weapons for hunting and fighting, and the women used clubs for hunting small animals; they also gathered berries, tubers, and roots as well as insects and their protein-rich larvae. The Aborigines wore only minimal clothing and built simple huts or weather protection out of branches, leaves, and bark.

THE CLAN SYSTEM

The Aborigines did not see themselves as a uniform people, rather they gave their tribes and clans various self-designations. Since the Europeans found no state structures or traditional chief-led societies there, they saw the Aborigines as being quite simply "primitive" and only gradually came to understand their complex clan organization. The latter is based on the so-called Iroquois system, with the nuclear family being extended into the "skin

Background image: The rock paintings of the Aborigines in Nanguluwarr (Arhemland, northern Australia) show a male and a female figure as well as a fish.

group." Here, all the father's brothers are also called fathers, and all the mother's sisters are also called mothers; accordingly, their children are deemed to be brothers and sisters. Only the children of the mother's brothers and of the father's sisters are considered to be cousins, and only they are eligible as possible marriage partners (cross-cousin marriage), as they belong to a different skin group. The marriage rules are strictly exogamous: it is permissible to marry only persons outside one's own skin group or even moiety (section of the population).

DIVISIONS OF TRIBAL SOCIETY

Every clan views itself—right up to the present day—as a type of large family that is in each case divided into two halves (moieties); these are in turn divided into between two and four skin groups. This subdivision is always taken into account in marriages. Every tribe thus consists of four to eight skin groups that make up a social welfare system, with responsibility

for parenting, care, foraging for food, and even death ceremonies being primarily and undiscriminatingly toward all the members of one's own skin group. Further differentiations relate to age. Elderly, experienced clan members enjoy particular respect, and their advice is sought; they commonly form a council of elders, dominated by men, which makes decisions for the entire clan.

Three Aborigines playing traditional musical instruments; the player on the right is blowing on the didgeridoo, a wooden wind instrument that produces long drawn-out pulsating sounds (northern Australia).

"They have great Bottle Noses, pretty full Lips, and wide Mouths. The two Fore-teeth of their Upper jaw are wanting in all of them, Men and Women, Old and Young; whether they draw them out, I know not . . . . Their Hair is black, short and curl'd, like that of the Negroes . . . . The color of their Skins, both of their Faces and the rest of their Body, is coal black, like that of the Negroes of Guinea. They have no sort of Cloaths, but a piece of the Rind of a Tree ty'd like a Girdle about their Waists, and a handful of long Grass, or three or four small green Boughs full of Leaves, thrust under their Girdle, to cover their Nakedness."

William Dampier, *A New Voyage Round the World*, seventeenth/eighteenth century

THE WORLD VIEW OF THE ABORIGINES: DREAMTIME AND SONGLINES

The Aborigines' lack of any written culture and long adherence to their traditional way of life until the Europeans arrived and colonized the country caused the latter to see the original inhabitants as "peoples with no history." Only later did they discover the paintings on wood, pieces of bark, stones, and cave walls that principally serve ritual purposes, and the significance of sacred sites that—like the famous rock mountain Uluru (southwest of Alice Springs in the heart of the continent)—are overlaid with numerous taboos even today.

The myths of the dreamtime tell of a mythical early period in which the world was populated by dreamtime beings (usually a mixture of animal and human) and a close relationship existed between all living creatures. The dreamtime beings are considered to be ancestors and cultural heroes who brought humans culture (fire and hunting techniques, tribal organization, clan laws, rituals) and laid down rules for living; the Aborigines continue to see themselves today as their custodians on earth. A special role as a creator being is played by the rainbow snake (*Yurlunggur*), which emerged from the water and is often portrayed as bisexual, and which symbolizes fertility as

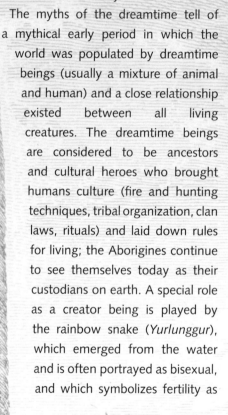

Below: A Maori war canoe from New Zealand (circa 1723); the Maoris were one of the more warlike peoples of the South Sea region and also used their longboats for raids and military expeditions across the sea.

Above: A Maori *heitiki* (eighteenth century); *heitikis* were believed to be charged with spiritual power (*mana*) and were worn by chieftains, but were sometimes also passed on as precious gifts.

well as creation and destruction. Early paintings on cave walls are believed to be the work of the cloud and rain spirits (*wondjina*), and numerous songlines across the land reveal the often labyrinthine pathways of the dreamtime beings and ancestors who left behind at sacred sites their "power-substances" for humans to experience; the term songlines is, however, also used to refer to the songs and singing of the Aborigines. Their ties with their ancestors are very close and are maintained in ritual dances and dance gatherings (*corroborees*).

NEW ZEALAND AND THE MAORIS

Probably between 800 and 1300, New Zealand was settled by Polynesian island inhabitants, arriving in several waves of migration, who were the ancestors of the indigenous inhabitants known as Maoris. These trace their origin back to the mythical land of Hawaiki: they came from there in canoes or outrigger craft (*waka*), whose names are still cited today when Maoris introduce themselves or their ancestral line. The Dutchman Abel Tasman discovered the land and its inhabitants in 1642, and New Zealand was colonized, chiefly by the British, from 1780. The Maoris lived initially by hunting large flightless birds—moas—and Haast's eagles, which were ultimately eradicated completely, and later cultivated kumara, a type of sweet potato. They were organized in tribes with chiefdoms, were believed to be warlike, and fought battles even among themselves after which the defeated tribe was enslaved. A particular characteristic feature was their elaborate tattooing of face and body, which demonstrated their social status.

The myths of the Maoris (like those of the Aborigines) relate to the origins of the land, the stars, the weather, and the people, and to the way in which death came to the world. A central myth is about Rangi and Papa, Sky Father and Earth Mother, respectively, from whose union all living things evolved.

A Maori with characteristic facial tattoo from Rotorua (North Island of New Zealand); ritual tongue baring and eyeball rolling, coupled with battle cries, showed the determination and fighting strength of warriors.

Polynesia, Melanesia, and Micronesia

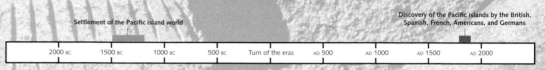

Settlement of the Pacific island world

Discovery of the Pacific islands by the British, Spanish, French, Americans, and Germans

2000 BC	1500 BC	1000 BC	500 BC	Turn of the eras	AD 500	AD 1000	AD 1500	AD 2000

The island world of Oceania in the Pacific Ocean, which comprises over 7,500 islands and island groups, is more accurately subdivided into the regions of Polynesia (in the east, includes New Zealand, Hawaii, and Samoa), Melanesia (northeast of Australia, includes New Guinea), and Micronesia (in the western Pacific, includes Nauru).

SETTLEMENT AND SOCIETY

The Pacific island world was settled by boat between 1500 and 1300 BC, probably from Taiwan and the Philippines, but in any case from the west. Due to the great nautical skills of Oceanians, it is sometimes suggested (though this is a controversial theory) that it may also have been settled from South America.

The social systems of Polynesia, in particular, can be viewed as prototypical for the entire island world, for despite regional differences, Oceanian culture taken as a whole exhibits many common features in terms of language, religion, and social structure. The original society of farmers (*manahune*) was overlaid in the course of subsequent waves of immigration by aristocrats (*ariki*) equipped with better boats,

Background image: A stone figure with a human countenance from Rarotonga (Cook Islands); the Cook Islands are an independent island group, but are associated with New Zealand.

Above: Tribal members at a traditional ceremonial dance in Port Vila (Vanuatu, Melanesia); dances and the ritual exchange of gifts or food continue to be a feature of meetings between tribes and clans.

who were also the landowners (*rangatira*) and priests, and who had their fields cultivated by the *manahune*.

The strictly hierarchical societies were ruled by chieftains or kings. The hereditary aristocracy could generally be traced back to the canoe occupants of the first *ariki* of an island; lineage therefore played an important role in subsequent generations. However, the aristocracy repeatedly topped up its ranks through adoption and allowed people with special skills (say in fighting or in boatbuilding) to ascend to its ranks. Tribal leaders or kings received a special share of the kill from hunting and of island resources, but they had to ensure that their tribal members were adequately provided for; their rule was underpinned by the priests and their knowledge. The status of ordinary free tribal members differed greatly and ranged from sharing in decision making in meetings to being at the beck and call of the rulers (as, for example, on Hawaii); there were also dependents with slave status (*teuteu*).

THE EXPERTS

Particularly in western Polynesia, societies showed a high degree of hierarchical organization and division of labor. Certain craftsmen, first and foremost boatbuilders and of course priests, who had proved themselves through their skills to be experts, advised the tribal leaders and aristocracy and were therefore accorded special respect. They passed on their skills and knowledge orally, usually within the family, but also often adopted gifted younger people. In many places the priesthood was also structured on the basis of its particular expertise—for example, in medicine, consulting the oracle, or in ceremonial matters; they looked after the temple or the spirit house and the ceremonial place that belonged to each village and community. Priests were considered particularly important because activities relating to food acquisition, handicrafts, and art carried ritual and cult significance, and the gods and ancestors were regularly consulted.

Wooden houses for storing yams—roots that not only have an important role as food, but also are the focal point of harvest festivals; such houses are found both on the islands of Polynesia and in Papua New Guinea (as in the picture here).

"The women are all handsome and some of them are extremely beautiful. Chastity does not seem to be considered as a virtue among them, for they not only readily and openly trafficked with our people for personal favors, but were brought down by their fathers and brothers for that purpose; they were, however, conscious of the value of beauty . . . ."

Samuel Wallis: *An Account of the Voyages Undertaken by the Order of His Present Majesty for Making Discoveries in the Southern Hemisphere*, Vol. 1, eighteenth century

and the women of many tribes were highly skilled in crafts such as basketwork and producing textiles. Monogamy was predominant, even if the men often lived polygamous lives; it was, however, expected that before marrying, young people of both sexes would gain sexual experience with a variety of partners. This aspect of their culture led the Europeans who landed on the islands in quick succession after 1767 to take the view that the island communities were on the whole promiscuous and displayed the "innocence of paradise." In Enlightenment Europe, tired of civilization, the island inhabitants of Oceania were therefore declared to be the "happy savages" of primitive times (e.g. by Jean-Jacques Rousseau, 1712–78). Infectious diseases brought in by Europeans wiped out entire tribes; later, the islanders became favored targets of slave-traders and Christian missionaries.

Traditional preparation of sago: the pulp of the sago palm is a basic food on the islands of Oceania and in Papua New Guinea. After being washed, it is ground into flour and then used for baking and cooking.

LIFE IN OCEANIA: FORMS OF SETTLEMENT AND ACQUISITION OF FOOD

The tribes of Oceania lived mainly in village communities consisting of permanent huts with a spirit house and ceremonial place as well as places for boats or boathouses and surrounding areas for agriculture. They cultivated taro (a starchy tuberlike rhizome), breadfruit, sweet potatoes, and bananas and kept as farm animals primarily chickens and in some areas pigs; another main source of food came from catching a wide variety of different kinds of fish and marine animals. Barter trade between villages and tribes played an important role. On larger islands, the territories of village communities were frequently surrounded by defensive palisade trenches because many tribes were constantly at war with their rivals and sometimes enslaved neighboring tribes (like the Maoris of New Zealand, see p. 285); some also practiced ritual cannibalism.

Right: A fisherman of the Ni-Vanuatu people in his traditional outrigger canoe with a wooden paddle; great experience was required in order to navigate such boats (Vanuatu, Melanesian island state in the south Pacific).

THE ROLE OF WOMEN AND THEIR IMAGE IN EUROPE

The societies were generally patriarchally dominated; however, there were also queens,

BOATBUILDING AND SEAFARING

Boatbuilding and navigation occupied a key place in the Oceanian identity, and experts in these disciplines enjoyed the utmost respect. They produced narrow slimline outrigger canoes and double-hulled canoes, the forerunners of the catamaran, the bow and stern of which were often decorated with richly carved wooden structures. They used movable square sails for navigating, while paddles at the stern or on the sides were used solely for steering. The boats, which were made of wood, were sealed with resin, and in double-hulled boats the two hulls were usually bridged by a wooden platform; all parts were lashed tightly together with coconut fibers.

Navigating between the sharp reefs of atolls without a compass, sextant, or map required a great deal of knowledge and skill, which was passed down orally. Besides fairly small fishing boats, they also built ocean-going war vessels measuring between 65 and 100 ft. (20 and 30 m) in length, which could carry up lo 200 people and were used for attacks and raids on other islands and for expeditions.

Reed-thatched Fijian huts; the traditional building methods of the islanders are still retained in many places today (Viti Levu, main island and seat of government of the Fijian islands, a republic since 1987).

RELIGION AND WORLD VIEW OF OCEANIANS: *MANA*

The myths of the Oceanic island inhabitants were not recorded in writing but were passed down orally in songs and chants. Like the Aborigines and Maoris, they maintained close ties with the world of the gods (who often resided in the still active volcanoes) and with spirits and ancestors, who were ever-present and were consulted before decisions were made; stories of their canoe-faring ancestors and heroes shaped their identity. For a long time, European theologians considered the Polynesian concept of *mana* to be the archetypal religious concept. *Mana* means a universal life force or spiritual force of extraordinary

Young islander performing traditional ancestral rites with two skulls of his forefathers in Marea Arahurahu, a shrine near Papeete (Tahiti); many Polynesians nowadays combine the Christian faith with traditional ceremonies.

power that permeates and interconnects all the layers of this world and the next (between which in the Oceanian belief system no clear distinction is made). Unusual natural events, incidents, objects, and people are believed to be charged with *mana*, and *mana* is the energy that enables certain people to perform outstanding deeds or achievements. This spiritual force is understood to be individual, that is, every person, thing, or event has its own *mana*. Even expertise and social ranking are considered to be sustained by *mana*; the *ariki* therefore possess particularly great or powerful *mana*. However, adoptions make it possible to share a person's own *mana* with adopted people and to let them enter someone's own line of force, as *mana* can be passed on.

RULES OF TABOO

Places, objects, food, animals, people, and names that possess *mana* carry taboo, a ban (Polynesian *tapu*: sacrosanct, untouchable, prohibited)—though usually only for a certain period. Nobody may go close to them or touch them, or only certain persons may come into contact with them. Rules of taboo are seen in Oceanic societies as the establishment of a strict religious order of purity that makes it possible for certain phenomena perceived to be threatening to the everyday order of things (such

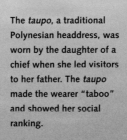

The *taupo*, a traditional Polynesian headdress, was worn by the daughter of a chief when she led visitors to her father. The *taupo* made the wearer "taboo" and showed her social ranking.

▶ **THE ROLE OF MAGIC**

The simple observance of taboos and adherence to the rules of taboo provide protective and defensive magic. Since the force of *mana* connects the various worlds with one another, it is important to consult the ever-present ancestral and protective spirits (*aitu*) through magic ceremonies and rituals, and to propitiate them before undertaking ventures. Practices of warding off harm and of seeking the favor of the ancestors therefore go together.

as death and corpses, or female menstruation) to be demarcated and kept at a distance. As a violation of a rule, a breach of taboo is punished severely; taboos create reverence and awe and serve to uphold the social order—particularly in societies with no codified law—in that many taboos apply to ordinary members of the tribe but not to those of elevated status. Taboos generally also regulate dealings between the social groups within the hierarchy and between the sexes.

View of the Yasawa islands, which politically belong to the Republic of Fiji; the twenty or so islands are of volcanic origin. Their mountain peaks rise to heights of between 820 and 1,968 ft. (250 and 600 m).

Rapa Nui: Easter Island

Petroglyphs of the birdman on a stone in Orongo (Easter Island), center of the birdman cult, which probably superseded earlier Rapa Nui cults.

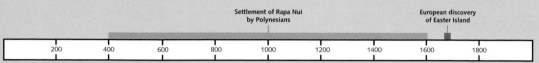

			Settlement of Rapa Nui by Polynesians			European discovery of Easter Island	
200	400	600	800	1000	1200	1400	1600	1800

This southeast Pacific island, which politically is part of Chile, aroused the interest of researchers at an early date due to its unique cultural artifacts. Settled by Polynesians in several waves, from 400 to 1600 or later, it was discovered by Europeans in 1687 and explored from 1722 onward. The reasons for the demise of the Rapa Nui culture, which had by then already taken place, whether as a result of civil wars or through overexploitation of natural resources, are a subject of controversy.

existed originally, only 638 remain today, some having been violently overturned. They probably represent ancestral chiefs or important nobles and do not stand singly but in groups on *ahu*, rectangular stone ceremonial platforms that are all located near to the coast. Each village or clan probably had such a site for worshiping its ancestors; in some, burial chambers are found. Around the volcanic crater Rano Raraku there are approximately 300 moai that have been buried in the ground up to the chest or the neck.

A row of stone *moai* at Ahu Tongariki (Easter Island); the *moai* stand on stone platforms and were probably representations of ancestors who were revered by the individual clans or settlements.

THE *MOAI*

The colossal stone figures of individually designed male torsos with oversized heads (which probably originally also had headdresses) are considered a characteristic feature of the island. Of the more than 1,000 *moai* that

THE RONGORONGO SCRIPT

The tribes on Rapa Nui were alone among the Pacific island peoples in possessing their own pictographic script interspersed with phonograms (Rongorongo), which survives engraved on pieces of wood and is read from left to right and from bottom to top; each line continues upside-down immediately above the previous line. Since the characters of the script, which has not yet been deciphered, although attempts have been made at interpreting it, are not pictographs that represent objects in a real way, some researchers assume that only core concepts or names were recorded as characters as aide-memoires, while the associated sentences or contexts were supplemented from memory. The texts probably relate to the genealogies of ancestors and to ritual chants.

PETROGLYPHS AND THE BIRDMAN CULT

Petroglyphs—carvings on stones and rocks—that are associated with the cult center of Orongo, a site that also features stone huts, are to be found principally on the cliff that slopes steeply down approximately 1,000 ft. (300 m) to the sea from the volcano Rano Kau. Their main motif, besides the creator-god Make-Make with his over-large eyes, is the birdman (Polynesian: *tangata manu*):

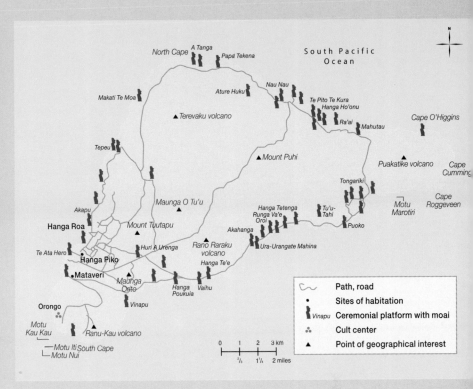

RAPA NUI—EASTER ISLAND The map shows the distribution of the stone moai predominantly in the coastal regions of the island; Orongo, the center of the birdman cult, with the rocky islet of Motu Nui offshore on the southwest point of the island, can be seen at bottom left.

a being combining characteristics of human and frigate bird. The birdman cult, which probably did not become important until the island's later history (after about 1500) and possibly ousted more ancient ancestor cults, culminated in a competition between the younger men, who at breakneck speed plunged from the cliffs and swam to the offshore rocky island of Motu Nui in order to fetch a sooty tern's egg. The one who returned to the main island first with an intact egg was the birdman for a year and enjoyed cult privileges.

CHRONOLOGY OF THE LOST CIVILIZATIONS

Timeline axis: 4000 BC — 3000 BC — 2000 BC — 1000 BC — Turn of the eras — AD 1000 — AD 2000

Asia Minor

Early peoples in Anatolia
9500–900 BC: Göbekli Tepe, Çatal Hüyük, Tell cultures in Anatolia

Sumerians and Akkadians
3900–1200 BC: Sumerian city-states, Uruk, Jemdet Nasr, Ur, Lagash, Akkadian Empire, Sumerian renaissance

Elamites, Medes, and Persians
3500 BC–AD 640: Elamite city-states, Kingdom of Elam, Median Kingdom, Persian empires of the Achaemenids, Parthians, and Sassanids, conquest by Islamic Arab troops

Peoples of Syria
2500–1194 BC: City-states of Ebla, Mari, Ugarit, decline following invasion by the Sea Peoples

Hurrians
2000–1200 BC: City-states, Kingdom of Mitanni

Babylonians
1894–539 BC: First Babylonian Dynasty, Sealand and Kassite rule, Second Dynasty of Isin, Assyrian rule, Neo-Babylonian Empire of the Chaldeans, decline following Persian conquest of Babylon

Assyrians
1830–609 BC: Old Assyrian Kingdom, Middle Assyrian Kingdom, and Neo-Assyrian Empire, decline following invasion of Scythians, Babylonians, and Medes

Hittites
1700–1190 BC: Old Hittite Kingdom, Middle Hittite Kingdom, Hittite Empire, occupation by the Sea Peoples

Peoples of Ancient Arabia
1000 BC–AD 597: Kingdoms of Saba, Qataban, Hadramaut, Ma'in, Kingdom of Himyar, AD 597 occupation by Sassanids

Nabataeans
550 BC–AD 106: Nabataean settlement of Petra, economic power, and Kingdom of the Nabataeans, AD 106 conquest by Rome

Mesopotamia

Egyptians
4500–30 BC: Pre-Dynastic Period–Naqada culture and Early Dynastic Period, Old Kingdom, First Intermediate Period, Middle Kingdom, Second Intermediate Period–Hyksos, New Kingdom, Third Intermediate Period, Late Period, Alexander and Ptolemies, occupation by Rome

Greeks
3000–150 BC: Minoan culture of Crete, Mycenaean culture of the mainland, Doric migrations, polis culture, Sparta, Athens, rule of the tyrants, Persian Wars, Peloponnesian War, end of independence with supremacy of Rome

Phoenicians
2500–332 BC: Settlement of the coast of Lebanon, city-states of Tyros, Byblos, Ugarit, Tripolis, Sidon, vassal status under Assyrians, Babylonians, and Persians, conquest by Alexander the Great

Israelites
1250 BC–AD 70: Settlement in Canaan, Time of the Judges, biblical kings, Kingdoms of Israel in the north and Judah in the south, Babylonian exile, sovereignty of Assyrians, Babylonians, Persians, and Diadochi, Maccabean revolt, Hasmonaeans, Kingdom of Herod and the Herodians, occupation by Rome

Mediterranean region

Sicilians—Western Greeks
1000–212 BC: Original inhabitants, settlers from Phoenicia, Carthage, Greece, tyrants of Syracuse, occupation by Rome

Carthaginians
814–146 BC: Foundation and rise to great power of Carthage, destruction following three (Punic) wars by Rome

Macedonians
805–168 BC: Macedonian Kingdom, occupation by Rome

Etruscans
800–200 BC: Culture of the Etruscans, end following Roman occupation and absorption into the culture of Rome

Romans
753 BC (myth.)–650 BC–AD 1453: Monarchy and Republic, civil wars and triumvirates, empire: Augustus and Julio-Claudian Dynasty, Flavians, Five Good Emperors, Antonines, Severans; barracks emperors; tetrarchy; Constantinian, Valentinian, and Theodosian Dynasties, Division of the Empire: Western Roman Empire (until 476) and Eastern Roman Empire–Byzantium (until 1453)

Diadoch Empires
323–30 BC: Kingdoms of Alexander the Great's Diadochi and their heirs in the eastern Mediterranean region, Asia Minor, Middle East as far as India

Seleucids
320–63 BC: Seleucid rule in Greater Syria and Persia, occupation by Rome

Pergamonians
221–133 BC: Kingdom of the Attalids of Pergamon, Roman province

Europe

Scythians and Cimmerians
Seventh millennium BC–575: Rule of Scythians in southern Russia and on the Black Sea, rule of Cimmerians in Asia Minor, ended by Lydia

Slavs
Since 2000 BC: Slavs in eastern and central Europe, division into western, eastern, and southern Slavs

Celts and Galatians
1300–51 BC: Development of Celtic culture, Hallstatt and La Tène cultures, Celtic migrations; decline following Caesar's subjugation of Gaul, Gallo-Roman culture, Galatians in Asia Minor, Gallo-Greek culture

Germanic peoples
100 BC–AD 774: Merger of Germanic tribes, Italian migrations of Cimbri and Teutons, military service in the Roman Empire, Kingdoms of Visigoths, Vandals, Ostrogoths, and Lombards

Franks
AD 200–911–987: Merger of Frankish tribes, Merovingian and Carolingian Kingdom, divisions of the empire, Carolingians in eastern kingdom (Germany), in western kingdom (France)

Vikings and Normans
Circa AD 500–1200: Vikings in Scandinavia (Kingdoms of Denmark, Norway, Sweden), Viking rule in England; Norman rule in Normandy and in England (merger with Anglo-Saxons), Normans in southern Italy and Sicily, end in south by Hohenstaufen Dynasty

Avars, proto-Bulgarians, and Khazars
AD 567–1018: Avar Kingdom in Pannonia, Empire of (proto-)Bulgarians in eastern Europe, Khazar Kingdom in southern Russia

Hsiung-nu
300 BC–AD 352: Spread of Hsiung-nu in central Asia and in the Chinese region; Zhao Kingdom in northern China

Hephthalites

Central Asia

South and East Asia

Huns
AD 374–454: Hun migrations from central Asia as far as western Europe

Mongols
AD 1130–1502: Mongol rule in central Asia, Genghis Khan and successors (Karakorum), Persia (Il-Khans), China (Yuan), Golden and Blue Hordes, and Crimean Khanate in Russia

Japanese
Since 10,000 BC: Jomon culture, Yayoi period, Kofun period, Asuka period, Nara period, Heian period, Kamakura shogunate, Kemmu Restoration, Ashikaga shogunate

Chinese
5000 BC–AD 1368: Yang-shao and Lung-shan cultures, ruling dynasties: Xia, Shang, Western and Eastern Zhou, Warring States; Empire: Qin, Han, Three Kingdoms, Jin, southern and northern dynasties; Sui, Tang, Five Kingdoms, Northern and Southern Song, Yuan (Mongols)

Indians and Aryans—Indo-Europeans
2600 BC–AD 1279: Indus culture, Aryan migration, Vedic periods; Kingdoms: Magadha, Nanda, Maurya, Kushan, Gupta, Hephthalite states, Harsha, Pratihara (northern India), Pala (Bengal), Rashtrakuta (central India), Chola Kingdoms (south); northern India largely Islamic

Koreans
2333 BC–AD 1392: Kingdom of Gojoseon, Kingdoms of Goguryeo, Silla, Baekje, Kaya, Kingdom of Great Silla, Kingdom of Goryeo, Kingdom of Choson

Burmans
AD 240–1287: Kingdoms of Pyu and Pagan in Burma

Cham
AD 350–1312: Champa Kingdom in Vietnam

Mon
AD 500–1283: Mon Kingdoms in Thailand, Mangrai Dynasty of Lanna

Khmer
AD 707–1431: Khmer Kingdom in Cambodia

Dai Viet
AD 1009–1400: Dai Viet Kingdom of Ly and Tran in Vietnam

North and South America

Indian peoples of North America
Up to AD 500: Clovis culture, Folsom culture, Hopewell culture; various tribal and cultural groups to present day

Maya
3000 BC–AD 1544: Preclassic, Classic, and Postclassic periods of the Maya culture, decline following Spanish conquest

Olmecs
Circa 1700–200 BC: Olmec culture

Paracas
Circa 1000–200 BC: Paracas culture

Huastecs and Zapotecs
1000 BC–AD 1500: Huastec and Zapotec cultures

Moche
Circa 100 BC–AD 700: Moche culture

Mixtecs
Circa AD 700–1500: Mixtec culture

Toltecs
Circa AD 720–1150: Toltec culture

Aztecs
AD 1200–1521/35: Foundation and center of rule in Tenochtitlan, decline following Spanish conquest

Inca
AD 1200–1536: Rule of Sapa Inca in Cuzco, civil war, decline following Spanish conquest

Africa

Ethiopians
975 BC–AD 1500: Kingdom of Ethiopia, Kingdom of Aksum, empire of Ethiopia under Zagwe and Solomonic Dynasties

Kushites
750 BC–AD 350: Black Pharaohs in Egypt, Kushite Kingdom of Napata and Meroë

Soninké
AD 750–1076: Kingdom of Ghana

Berbers
AD 1042–1147: Berber Dynasty of the Almoravids in West Africa and southern Spain

Mandinka
AD 1076–1375: Mali Empire

Shona
Eleventh–fourteenth centuries AD: Great Zimbabwe, Munhumutapa Kingdom, Mutapa (Karanga), Changamire (Rosvi)

Banza and Hausa
Since twelfth century AD: Banza and Hausa states

Songhai
AD 1375–1591: Kingdom of the Songhai

Bantu
AD 1390–1665: Kongo Kingdom

Australia and Oceania

Polynesians
1500–1300 BC: Oceanic tribes in Polynesia, Melanesia; from AD 400: and Micronesia, Polynesian settlement of New Zealand (Maori) and of Easter Island (Rapa Nui culture)

Aborigines
From 60,000–32,000 BC: Settlement of Australia by Aborigines

BIBLIOGRAPHY

Ackroyd, P.R. and Evans, C.F. *The Cambridge History of the Bible*. Cambridge, England, 1975

Bengtson, H. *Griechische Geschichte*. Munich, Germany, 1960

Boardman, J., Edwards, I.E.S., Sollberger, E. and Hammond, N.G.L. *The Cambridge Ancient History*. Cambridge, England, 1992

Brandau, B. and Schickert, H. *Hethiter. Die unbekannte Weltmacht*. Munich, Germany, 2001

Breasted, J.H. *A History of Egypt*. Phoenix, AZ, 1937

Burckhardt, J. *History of Greek Culture* Mineola, NY, 2002

Carrasco, D. *Daily Life of the Aztecs: People of the Sun and Earth*. Santa Barbara, CA, 1998

Chavalas, C. *The Ancient Near East*. London, England, 2006

Church, P. *A Short History of South-East Asia*. Oxford, England, 2005

Coulborn, R. *The Origin of Civilized Societies*. Princeton, NJ, 1959

Droysen, J.G. *Geschichte des Hellenismus*. 3 vols, new ed, Darmstadt, Germany, 1998

Fage, J.D. *A History of West Africa*. Farnham, England, 1993

Frye, R. *Heritage of Persia*. Costa Mesa, CA, 1993

Gardiner, A. *Egypt of the Pharaohs: An Introduction*. Oxford, England, 1966

Grant, M. *The Twelve Caesars*. New York, NY, 1996

——— *The History of Rome*. London, England, 2002

Härtel, H. and Schönfeld R. *Bulgarien. Vom Mittelalter bis zur Gegenwart*. Ratisbon, Germany, 1998

Herm, G. *The Phoenicians: The Purple Empire of the Ancient World*. New York, NY, 1975

Hinz, W. *Das Reich Elam*. Stuttgart, 1964

James, E. *The Franks*. London, England, 1991

Julien, C. *Reading Inca History*. Iowa City, IA, 2002

Jursa, M. *Die Babylonier*. Munich, Germany, 2004

Kaeppler, A.L., Kaufmann C., and Newton D. *Ozeanien. Kunst und Kultur*. Freiburg, 1974

Liverani, M. *Israel's History and the History of Israel*. London, England, 2007

Macqueen, J.G. *The Hittites*. London, England, 1996

Maenchen-Helfen, O.J. *The World of the Huns: Studies in Their History and Culture*. Los Angeles, CA, 1983

Mommsen, T. *A History of Rome under the Emperors*. New York, NY, 1999

Mühlenberg, E. *Die Konstantinische Wende*. Munich, Germany, 1998

Parzinger, H. *Die Skythen*. Munich, Germany, 2004

Prentis, M. *A Concise Companion to Aboriginal History*. Kenthurst, Australia, 2008

Riese, B. *Die Maya*. Munich, Germany, 2004

Roth, A. *Chasaren. Das vergessene Grossreich der Juden*. Neu-Isenburg, Germany, 2006

Schmökel, H. *Kulturgeschichte des Alten Orients*. Stuttgart, Germany, 1995

Selz, G.J. *Sumerer und Akkader*. Munich, Germany, 2005

Soden, W. von. *Herrscher im Alten Orient*. Berlin-Göttingen-Heidelberg, Germany, 1954

Stöver, H.D. *Die Römer*. Düsseldorf-Vienna, Germany, 1976

Swain, S. *Hellenism and Empire*. Oxford, England, 1998

Voigt, J.H. *Geschichte Australiens*. Stuttgart, Germany, 1988

Weiers, M. *Geschichte der Mongolen*. Stuttgart, Germany, 2004

Wiesehöfer, J. *Das frühe Persien. Geschichte eines antiken Weltreiches*. Munich, Germany, 1999

Worlfram, E. *A History of China*. Charleston, SC, 2008

SOURCES

p. 23 Schmökel, H. "Sargon von Akkad." In *Exempla historica*. Frankfurt, Germany, 1985

p. 25 Soden, W. von. *Herrscher im Alten Orient*. Berlin-Göttingen-Heidelberg, Germany, 1954

p. 27 Bermant, C. and Weitzman M. *Ebla. Neu entdeckte Zivilisation im Alten Orient*. Frankfurt, Germany, 1979

p. 29 Herm, G. *The Phoenicians: The Purple Empire of the Ancient World*. New York, NY, 1975

p. 31 Marzahn, J. *Babylon und das Neujahrsfest*. Berlin, Germany, 1981

p. 32 Soden, W. von. *Herrscher im Alten Orient*. Berlin-Göttingen-Heidelberg, Germany, 1954

p. 37 Schmökel, H. *Ur, Assur und Babylon*. Stuttgart, Germany, 1955

p. 43 Riemschneider, M. *Die Hethiter*. Essen, Germany

p. 45 Lehmann, J. *Hittites: People of a Thousand Gods*. New York, NY, 1977

p. 55 Hinz, W. *Das Reich Elam*. Stuttgart, Germany, 1964

p. 57 Frye, R. *Heritage of Persia*. Costa Mesa, CA, 1993

p. 69 Assmann, J. *Ägyptische Hymnen und Gebete*. Zurich, Germany, 1975

p. 73 *The Egyptian Book of the Dead*. Quoted in Hornung, E. *Gesänge vom Nil*. Zurich, Germany, 1990

p. 77 Schott, S. *Die Schrift der verborgenen Kammer in Königsgräbern der 18. Dynastie*. Göttingen, Germany, 1958

p. 81 Plutarch. *Lives*. New York, NY, 2006

p. 83 *New Jerusalem Bible*. New York, NY, 1990

p. 85 *Ibid*.

p. 91 Herm, G. *The Phoenicians: The Purple Empire of the Ancient World*. New York, NY, 1975

p. 95 Livy. *History of Rome* (excerpt from *Ab urbe condita*). New York, NY, 1976

p. 97 Homer. *The Iliad*. New York, NY, 2008

p. 100 Plutarch. *Lives*. New York, NY, 2006

p. 103 Hoenn, K. (ed) *Griechische Lyriker*. Zurich-Stuttgart, Austria, Germany, 1968

p. 104 Aristotle. *Politics*. New York, NY, 2005

p. 111 Rufus, Q.C. *The History of Alexander*. New York, NY, 1984

p. 113 Plutarch. *Lives*. New York, NY, 2006

p. 119 *Ibid*.

p. 121 Cicero. *On the Republic*. New York, NY 1998.

p. 125 Suetonius. *Lives of the Caesars*. New York, NY, 2004

p. 126 Marcus Aurelius. *Epigrams*. New York, NY, 2002

p. 129 Marcus Aurelius. *Thoughts*. Whitefish, MT, 2005

p. 131 Cassius Dio. *History of Rome*. Cambridge, MA, 1917

p. 133 Eusabius of Caesarea. *History of the Church*. Grand Rapids, MI, 2007

p. 145 Julius Caesar. *The Gallic Wars*. Mineola, NY, 2006

p. 151 Tacitus. *Germania*. Oxford, England, 1999

p. 155 Paul the Deacon. *History of the Lombards*. Philadelphia, PA, 2003

p. 158 Gregory of Tours. *A History of the Franks*. New York, NY, 1976

p. 163 Einhard. *Life of Charlemagne*. Ann Arbor, MI, 1960

p. 167 Logan, F.D. *Vikings in History*. Philadelphia, PA, 2005

p. 175 Theophanes. *Chronicles*. Philadelphia, PA, 2006

p. 184 Schreiber, H. *Die Hunnen*. Vienna-Düsseldorf, Austria, Germany, 1976

p. 198 Glasenapp, H. von. *Indische Geisteswelt*. Hanau, Germany, 1986

p. 201 Nikam, A.N and McKeon, R. (eds) *Edicts of Asoka*. Chicago, IL, 1978

p. 204 Meyer J.J. *Das Altindische Buch vom Welt- und Staatsleben—Das Arthashastra des Kautilya*. Leipzig, Germany, 1926

p. 209 Lao Tzu. *Tao Te Ching*. New York, NY, 2005

p. 212 Confucius. *The Analect—Lun Yu*. New York, NY 2001

p. 218 Martin, R. (transl) *Jou P'u T'uan (The Prayer Mat of Flesh)*. New York, NY, 1963

p. 227 Benl, O. and Hammitzsch, H. *Japanische Geisteswelt*. Baden-Baden, Germany, 1956

p. 233 Mazzeo, D. and Antonini, C.S. *Angkor*. Luxembourg, 1974

p. 236 "Korea—Die alten Königreiche." The Ruhr Arts Trust, Villa Hügel. Munich, Germany, 1999

p. 242 Tedlock, D. and B. (eds) *Teachings from the American Earth: Indian Religion and Philosophy*. New York, NY, 1992

p. 251 Tedlock, D. (ed) *Popol Vuh*. New York, NY, 1996

p. 258 Davis, N. *The Aztecs, a History*. London, 1973

p. 263 Razzeto, M. (ed) *Ketschua-Lyrik*. Leipzig, Germany, 1976

p. 271 Schneider, T. *Lexikon der Pharaonen*. Munich Germany, 1996

p. 274 Ki-Zerbo, J. *Die Geschichte Schwarzafrikas*. Frankfurt, Germany, 1981

p. 278 Hertel, P. *Zu den Ruinen von Simbabwe*. Gotha, Germany, 2000

p. 283 Dampier, W. *A New Voyage round the World*. Warwick, NY, 2007

p. 287 Ritz, H. *Die Sehnsucht nach der Südsee*. Göttingen, Germany, 1983

INDEX

PICTURE CREDITS

(b. = bottom, t. = top, l. = left, r. = right)

Corbis: 2 Richard A. Cooke, 4–5 Bo Zaunders, 4 Steven Vidler (l.), 5 Macduff Everton (t.), Paul Almasy (b.), Bettmann (r.), 6 Steve Allen–Brand X, 8–9 Chris Hellier, 8 Asian Art & Archaeology, 9 Skyscan, 10 Philip Spruyt, 12–13 Yann Arthus-Bertrand, 14 Gianni Dagli Orti, 17 (from l. to r.) Nico Tondini, Paul Almasy, Gianni Dagli Orti, Gianni Dagli Orti, Sergio Pitamitz, 18 Alfredo Dagli Orti, 19–20 Nik Wheeler, 21 Werner Forman, 23 Gianni Dagli Orti (t.), Nik Wheeler (b.), 24 Macduff Everton, 25 Adam Woolfitt, 26 Ali Jarekji (l.), Gianni Dagli Orti (r.), 27–28 Charles Lenars, 29 Gianni Dagli Orti (t.), Charles Lenars (b.), 30 Adam Woolfitt, Bettmann, 31 Nico Tondini, 32 Gianni Dagli Orti, 33 Stefano Bianchetti, 34 Francis G. Mayer, 35 Nico Tondini (t.), Bettmann (b.), 36 Gianni Dagli Orti (l.), Werner Forman (b.), 37 Krause–Johansen, 38–39 Stapleton Collection, Bettmann (b.), 40 Nik Wheeler, 41 Bettmann, 42 David Forman (l.), Oriol Alamany (r.), 43 Chris Hellier, 45 Chris Hellier, 46–47 George Steinmetz, 47 Hans Reinhard (t.), Kazuyoshi Nomachi (b.), 48 Michele Falzone, 49 Aldo Pavan, 50 Jose Fuste Raga (l.), Sergio Pitamitz (r.), 51 Jon Arnold, 52 Sergio Pitamitz, 53 Jon Arnold, 54 Roger Wood, 55 Bettmann (t.), Gianni Dagli Orti (b.), 56 Robert Harding, 57 Paul Almasy (t.), Diego Lezama Orezzoli (b.), 58–59 Roger Wood, 60 Chris Hellier, 61 Werner Forman (t.), Hulton-Deutsch Collection (b.), 62 Roger Wood, 63 Gianni Dagli Orti, 65 (from l. to r.) Dave Bartruff, Bettmann, Gianni Dagli Orti, Mimmo Jodice, Richard T. Nowitz, 66 Jose Fuste Raga (l.), Bernard Annebicque (r.), 68 Werner Forman (t.), 68–69 Gianni Dagli Orti (b.), 70–71 Jon Arnold, 70 Sandro Vannini, 71 Gianni Dagli Orti (t.), 72 Jose Fuste Raga, 73 Richard T. Nowitz (t.), Philip de Bay (b.), 74–75 Kelly-Mooney Photography, 75 Sandro Vannini (t.), 76 Ruggero Vanni (t.), Jon Arnold (large), 77 Claudius, 78 Design Pics, 79 Mark Karrass, 80 Sandro Vannini (l.), 80–81 Philip de Bay, 81 Bettmann (r.), 82 Philip de Bay (l.), Alfredo Dagli Orti (r.), 83 Chris Hellier, 84 Bojan Brecelj, 85 Hanan Isachar, 86 Bettmann, 87 Bettmann (t.), Massimo Borchi (b.), 88 Paul Almasy (l.), Mimmo Jodice (r.), 89 Bettmann, 90 Dave Bartruff, 91 Carmen Redondo (t.), Hulton-Deutsch Collection (b.), 92 Guenter Rossenbach, 93 The Gallery Collection, 94 Gianni Dagli Orti, 95 Bettmann, 96 Chris Hellier (l.), Gianni Dagli Orti (r.), 97 Gail Mooney, 98 Araldo de Luca, 99 Wolfgang Kaehler (r.), Bettmann (small), 100–101 Richard T. Nowitz, 100 Wolfgang Kaehler (b.), 102 Richard T. Nowitz, 103 Gianni Dagli Orti (t.), Bettmann (b.), 104 Mimmo Jodice, 105 Bettmann (t.), Jose Fuste Raga, 106 Massimo Borchi, 107 Massimo Borchi (t.), Jose Fuste Raga (b.), 108 Jon Arnold–JAI (l.), John Heseltine (r.), 109 Bettmann, 110 Reza–Webistan, 111 Araldo de Luca, 112 Gian Berto Vanni (l.), Araldo de Luca (r.), 113 Adam Woolfitt, 114 Ruggero Vanni, 115 Araldo de Luca (t.), Hulton-Deutsch Collection (b.), 116–117 Alfredo Dagli Orti, 116 Massimo Listri (b.), 117 Franz-Marc Frei (b.), 118 Steven Vidler (l.), Francis G. Mayer (r.), 119 Ron Chapple Stock, 120 Carmen Redondo, 121 Gianni Dagli Orti, 122–125 (t.) Bettmann, 125 Ron Chapple Stock (b.), 126 David Ball, 127 Massimo Listri, 128 Guido Cozzi (t.), John and Lisa Merrill (l.), 129 Jim Zuckerman, 130 Bettmann (l.), Tibor Bognar (r.), 131 Alfredo Dagli Orti, 132 Hubert Stadler (t.), Araldo de Luca (b.), 133 Araldo de Luca, 134 Werner Forman, 135 Bettmann (t.), Philip Spruyt (b.), 136 Ruggero Vanni, 137 Adam Woolfitt (t.), Bettmann (b.), 139 (from l. to r.) Gianni Dagli Orti, Nik Wheeler, The Irish Image Collection, Bettmann, Macduff Everton, 140 Werner Forman, 141 Philip de Bay, 142–143 The Irish Image Collection, 142–143 (small) Werner Forman, 144 The Irish Image Collection, 145 Goodshoot (l.), Robert Harding World Imagery (r.), 148 Macduff Everton (t.), Ruggero Vanni (b.), 149 Bettmann, 150 Bettmann (t.), Steven Vidler (b.), 151 Ruggero Vanni, 152 Bettmann, 153 Bettmann (small), Guido Baviera (large), 154 Alfredo Dagli Orti, 155 Elio Ciol (l.), Bettmann (b.), 156–157 Adam Woolfitt, 157 Stapleton Collection, 158 Gianni Dagli Orti, 159 Bettmann, 160 Ali Meyer, 161 Ruggero Vanni (t.), Philip Spruyt (b.), 162 Nik Wheeler, 163 Dean Conger, 164–165 Frank Lukasseck, 165 Stefano Bianchetti (t.), 166 Michael Nicholson (t.), Nik Wheeler (b.), 167 Colin Dixon, 168 Massimo Listri (t.), Jean-Pierre Lescourret (b.), 169 Rachel Royse, 170 NASA (l.), Josè F. Poblete (r.), 171 Massimo Listri, 172 Gianni Dagli Orti, 173 Gianni Dagli Orti (t.), Charles O'Rear (b.), 174 Sandro Vannini, 176–177 Roger Ressmeyer, 176 Philip Spruyt (small), 177 Pat O'Hara (b.), 179 (from l. to r.) Nik Wheeler, Bettmann, James L. Stanfield, Liu Liqun, Hulton-Deutsch Collection, 180–181 Xiaoyang Liu, 182–183 Bettmann, 184 Bettmann (t.), 185 Hulton-Deutsch Collection (t.), 186–187 Liu Liqun, 186 Nik Wheeler (t.), 187 Liu Liqun (t.), 188 Barry Lewis, 189 Barry Lewis (b.), 190–191 Michel Setboun, 193 Ed Kashi (t.), 195 (from l. to r.) Sakamoto Photo Research Laboratory, Macduff Everton, Asian Art & Archaeology Inc., Luca I. Tettoni, Keren Su, 196 John A. Giordano (l.), 196, 197, 198 Philip de Bay (l.), David Paterson (r.), 199 Sheldan Collins, 200 Macduff Everton (t.), Burstein Collection (b.), 201 Adam Woolfitt, 202–203 Michael Freeman, 203 Massimo Borchi, 204 Gian Berto Vanni (t.), Barney Burstein (b.), 205 Keren Su, 206–207 Bernard Bisson–Sygma, 206–207 Asian Art & Archaeology Inc.(small), 208 Liu Liqun, 209 Frank Lukasseck (b.), 210 Asian Art & Archaeology Inc., 211 Danny Lehman, 212 Barney Burstein, 213 Keren Su (t.), Burstein Collection (b.), 214 Pierre Colombel (t.), Philip Spruyt (b.), 215 Frank Lukasseck, 216 Frank Lukasseck (l.), Royal Ontario Museum (r.), 217 Pierre Colombel, 218 Bettmann (t.), Brian A. Vikander (b.), 219 Asian Art & Archaeology Inc., 220 Asian Art & Archaeology Inc. (l.), Kimimasa Mayama (r.), 221 Sakamoto Photo Research Laboratory, 222 McIntyre Photography Inc., 223 Angelo Hornak (t.), Sakamoto Photo Research Laboratory (b.), 224 Sakamoto Photo Research Laboratory (t.), Robert Harding World Imagery (b.), 225 Travel Pix Collection, 226 Asian Art & Archaeology Inc., 227 Burstein Collection, 228 Richard Bickel (l.), Luca I. Tettoni (r.), 229 Gavin Hellier, 230 Macduff Everton (t.), Steve Raymer (b.), 231 Nik Wheeler, 232 Carson Ganci–Design Pics, 233 Luca I. Tettoni, 234 Sam Diephuis, 235 Luca I. Tettoni, 237 Kevin R. Morris (t.), Massimo Borchi (b.), 239 (from l. to r.) Angelo Hornak, JJamArt (center), Marilyn Angel Wynn, Gavin Hellier, 240 David Muench, 241 William S. Soule, 242 Philip de Bay, 243 Edward S. Curtis (t.), Bettmann (b.), 244 Marilyn Angel Wynn, 245 Robert Harding (t.), 245 (b.), 246 Angelo Hornak (l.), Richard Melloul (r.), 248 Kevin Schafer, 249 Werner Forman (t.), Roman Soumar (b.), 250 Massimo Borchi (l.), Charles Lenars (r.), 251 Massimo Borchi, 252–253 Massimo Borchi, 253 Upperhall Ltd.—Robert Harding World Imagery (t.), 254 Bettmann (t.), Geoffrey Clements (b.), 255 Gianni Dagli Orti, 256–257 Danny Lehman, 256 JJamArt, 257 Jonathan Blair, 258 Alfredo Dagli Orti, 259 Gianni Dagli Orti, 260 Wolfgang Kaehler (t.), 261 PoodlesRock, 262 Dana Hoff (l.), Gianni Dagli Orti (r.), 263 Werner Forman, 264 Gavin Hellier, 265 Christie's Images, 266 Bettmann (t.), Pablo Corral Vega (b.), 267 Danny Lehman, 269 (from l. to r.) Paul Almasy, Jonathan Blair, Sebastien Cailleux (2nd from r.), Peter Harholdt, 270 Michael Freeman (l.), Jonathan Blair (r.), 272 Jane Sweeney (l.), 273 Gavin Hellier, 274 Sebastien Cailleux, 275 Sandro Vannini, 276 Ivan Vdovin (t.), Peter Harholdt (b.), 277 Christine Osborne, 278 David Reed, 279 Paul Almasy (t.), 281 (from l. to r.) Werner Forman, Anders Ryman, Werner Forman, Penny Tweedie, Guido Cozzi, 282 Penny Tweedie (l.), Oliver Strewe (r.), 283 Claire Leimbach, 284–285 Philip de Bay, 284 Werner Forman (small), 285 Neil Farrin (small), 286 Neil Farrin, 287 Ludo Kuipers, 288 Rob Howard, 288–289 Neil Farrin, 289 Anders Ryman (t.), 290–291 Louise Murray, 290 Peter Guttman (t.), 291 Werner Forman (t.), 292–293 Guido Cozzi, 292 James L. Amos (t.).

Bridgeman Art Library: 11 Klaus Obermeier (large), 11 (small), 13 (small), 15, 146, 147, 190 (t.), 192, 193 (b.).

Getty Images: 184–185 Time Life Pictures, 189 James L. Stanfield (t.), 209 Dorling Kindersley (t.), 239 The Bridgeman Art Library (2.l), 260 The Bridgeman Art Library (b.), 269 Gavin Hellier (center), 271 The Bridgeman Art Library, 272–273 Gavin Hellier.

This edition published in 2009

Parragon Books Ltd
Queen Street House
4 Queen Street
Bath BA1 1HE, UK

Production: ditter.projektagentur GmbH
Project editor: Kirsten E. Lehmann
Design and layout: Claudio Martinez
Picture research: Claudia Bettray
Cartography and illustration: Burga Fillery, MILCH
Source mapping: M. Sc. Nadja Lemcke
Lithography: Klaussner Medien Service GmbH

**English-language edition produced by
Cambridge Publishing Management Ltd**
Project editor: Diane Teillol
Translator: David Darrah-Morgan
Copy editor: Nina Hnatov
Typesetter: Donna Pedley
Proofreader: Karolin Thomas
Indexer: Marie Lorimer

ISBN: 978-1-4075-6403-6

Printed in Malaysia

Frontispiece (p. 2): This bizarre-looking ornament
in the form of a bird's claw is a testimony to the
North American Hopewell Indians, whose culture
continues to pose a number of puzzles to this day
(made between 100 BC and AD 350).